PAPER



# CHRISTMAS CAROLS

**MELODY LINE, CHORDS AND LYRICS**
**FOR KEYBOARD • GUITAR • VOCAL**

HAL•LEONARD®

ISBN 0-634-00704-1

HAL•LEONARD®
CORPORATION

7777 W. Bluemound Rd. P.O. Box 13819 Milwaukee, WI 53213

Visit Hal Leonard Online at
**www.halleonard.com**

Welcome to the PAPERBACK SONGS SERIES.

Do you play piano, guitar, electronic keyboard, sing or play any instrument for that matter? If so, this handy "pocket tune" book is for you.

The concise, one-line music notation consists of:

## MELODY, LYRICS & CHORD SYMBOLS

Whether strumming the chords on guitar, "faking" an arrangement on piano/keyboard or singing the lyrics, these fake book style arrangements can be enjoyed at any experience level – hobbyist to professional.

The musical skills necessary to successfully use this book are minimal. If you play guitar and need some help with chords, a basic chord chart is included at the back of the book.

While playing and singing is the first thing that comes to mind when using this book, it can also serve as a compact, comprehensive reference guide.

However you choose to use this PAPERBACK SONGS SERIES book, by all means have fun!

# CONTENTS


8 A la nanita nana (Hear Lullabies and Sleep Now)

9 All My Heart This Night Rejoices

10 Angels from the Realms of Glory

12 Angels We Have Heard on High

11 As Each Happy Christmas

14 As Lately We Watched

15 As with Gladness Men of Old

16 At the Gates of Heaven Above

17 Away in a Manger (*Murray*)

18 Away in a Manger (*Kirkpatrick*)

19 The Babe

20 A Babe Is Born in Bethlehem

22 A Baby in the Cradle

24 Baloo, Lammy

26 Bells Over Bethlehem

21 Beside Thy Cradle Here I Stand

28 The Birthday of a King

29 The Boar's Head Carol

30 A Boy Is Born in Bethlehem

31 Break Forth, O Beauteous, Heavenly Light

32 Bring a Torch, Jeannette, Isabella

34 Carol of the Bagpipers

36 Carol of the Birds

35 The Cherry Tree Carol

38 A Child Is Born in Bethlehem

40 Child Jesus

39 Christ Is Born This Evening

42 Christ Was Born on Christmas Day

44 Christians, Awake! Salute the Happy Morn

43 Come, All Ye Children

46 Come, All Ye Shepherds

48 Come Running, You Shepherds

50 Come, Thou Long Expected Jesus

52 Companions, All Sing Loudly

47 Coventry Carol

54 A Day, Bright Day of Glory
55 Deck the Hall
56 Ding Dong! Merrily on High!
57 Everywhere, Everywhere, Christmas Tonight
58 A Fire Is Started in Bethlehem
60 The First Noel
62 The Friendly Beasts
64 From Out the Deep Woods a Cuckoo Flew
66 From Starry Skies Thou Comest
68 From the Eastern Mountains
70 Fum, Fum, Fum
72 Gather Around the Christmas Tree
71 Glad Christmas Bells
74 Gloria
75 Go Tell It on the Mountain
76 God Rest Ye Merry, Gentlemen
78 Going to Bethlehem
80 The Golden Carol
82 Good Christian Men, Rejoice
84 Good King Wenceslas
86 The Happy Christmas Comes Once More
88 Hark! The Herald Angels Sing
90 Hark! Ye Shepherds
92 He Is Born
94 Hear Them Bells
95 Hear, O Shepherds
96 The Holly and the Ivy
98 How Brightly Beams the Morning Star
100 The Huron Carol
102 I Am So Glad on Christmas Eve
103 I Go to Bethlehem
104 I Heard the Bells on Christmas Day
105 I Saw Three Ships
106 The Icy December
108 In Bethlehem, the Lowly
110 In Bethlehem's Cradle
112 In the Bleak Midwinter
109 Infant Holy, Infant Lowly
114 Infant So Gentle
116 Irish Carol

*(contents continued)*

120 It Came Upon the Midnight Clear (*Willis*)

122 It Came Upon the Midnight Clear (*Sullivan*)

124 Jesus, the Newborn Baby

126 Jingle Bells

128 Jolly Old St. Nicholas

130 Joseph Dearest, Joseph Mine

132 Joy to the World

134 King Herod

136 Let Our Gladness Know No End

138 Lo, How a Rose E'er Blooming

119 Love Came Down at Christmas

140 Lovely Is the Dark Blue Sky

142 Lullaby, Jesus

144 March of the Three Kings

143 Mary Had a Baby

146 Mary, Dear Mother of Jesus

148 Masters in This Hall

147 Noël Nouvelet

150 O Bethlehem

152 O Christmas Tree

153 O Christmas, You Season of Childlike Delights

154 O Come, All Ye Faithful

156 O Come, Little Children

157 O Come, O Come Immanuel

158 O Holy Night

160 O Leave Your Sheep

162 O Little Town of Bethlehem

161 O Sanctissima

164 O Thou Joyful

165 Oh! Dear Jesus

166 Oh! Infant Jesus

167 Oh! Night Among the Thousands

168 Once in Royal David's City

170 Pastores a Belén

172 Pat-a-Pan

174 Pray, Give Us Lodging

176 Quickly Now, O Shepherds

177 Rejoice and Be Merry

178 Ring Out, Ye Wild and Merry Bells

180 Ring, Little Bells

182 Rise Up, Shepherd, and Follow

181 Rocking

184 Shepherd! Shake Off Your Drowsy Sleep

**186** Silent Night

**188** The Simple Birth

**187** Sing We Now of Christmas

**190** Sleep, O Sleep, My Precious Child

**192** The Sleep of the Infant Jesus

**194** The Snow Lay on the Ground

**196** The Son of Mary

**198** Song of the Wise Men

**200** Star of the East

**193** Still, Still, Still

**202** Susani

**204** Sussex Carol

**206** There's a Song in the Air

**208** To Us Is Born a Little Child

**210** Today We Welcome a Tiny Child

**214** Touro-Louro-Louro

**216** 'Twas the Night Before Christmas

**211** The Twelve Days of Christmas

**218** Up on the Housetop

**220** A Virgin Unspotted

**222** Wassail Song

**219** Wassail, Wassail

**224** Watchman, Tell Us of the Night

**226** We Are Singing

**228** We Three Kings of Orient Are

**230** We Wish You a Merry Christmas

**232** Welsh Carol

**234** Wexford Carol

**236** What Child Is This?

**238** What Is This Fragrance So Appealing?

**240** When Christ Was Born of Mary Free

**231** Whence Art Thou, My Maiden?

**242** Whence Comes This Rush of Wings

**244** While By My Sheep

**246** While Shepherds Watched Their Flocks

**243** Winds Through the Olive Trees

**248** Ya viene la vieja

**250** You Green and Glittering Tree

**249** Yuletide Is Here Again

**252** **Guitar Chord Guide**

# A LA NANITA NANA

## (Hear Lullabies and Sleep Now)

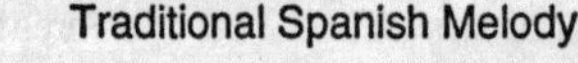
Traditional Spanish Melody

Dm
A la na - ni - ta na - na na - ni - ta,

C7 F
e - a na - ni - ta e - a,

C Dm
Sleep, sleep my dear - est Je - sus, May peace at -

A7 Dm A7 Dm
tend ___ Thee, may peace at - tend ___ Thee.

D A7 D
To the world lit - tle Sav - ior, New hope Thou art bring - ing

A7 D
All the world, lit - tle Sav - ior, Thy prais - es sing - ing,

C#dim7 D C#dim7 D
God's an - gels float - ing o'er Thee chant al - le - lu - ia.

C#dim7 D C#dim7 D
A la na - ni - ta na - na, na - ni - ta e - a.

# ALL MY HEART THIS NIGHT REJOICES

Words and Music by JOHANN EBELING
and CATHERINE WINKWORTH

Bb Bb+ Eb Bbsus Bb
All my heart this night re - joic - es,
Hark! a voice from yon - der man - ger,
Come, then, let us has - ten yon - der;
Cm7 F7 Bb F
As I hear, far and near, Sweet - est an - gel
Soft and sweet doth en - treat, "Flee from woe and
Here let all, great and small, Kneel in awe and
C7sus C7 F Cm Cm7
voic - es; "Christ is born," their
dan - ger. Breth - ren, come; from
won - der. Love Him who with
F7 Bb Bb6 F7
choirs are sing - ing, Till the air,
all that grieves you, You are freed,
love is yearn - ing, Hail the star
Bb Bb7 Cm7 F7 Bb
Ev - 'ry - where, Now with joy is ring - ing.
All you need I will sure - ly give you."
That from far Bright with hope is burn - ing!

# ANGELS FROM THE REALMS OF GLORY

Words by JAMES MONTGOMERY
Music by HENRY SMART

C
F
C
Am

1. An - gels from the realms of glo - ry, Wing your flight o'er
2. Shep - herds, in the field a - bid - ing, Watch - ing o'er your
3.,4. *(See additional verses)*

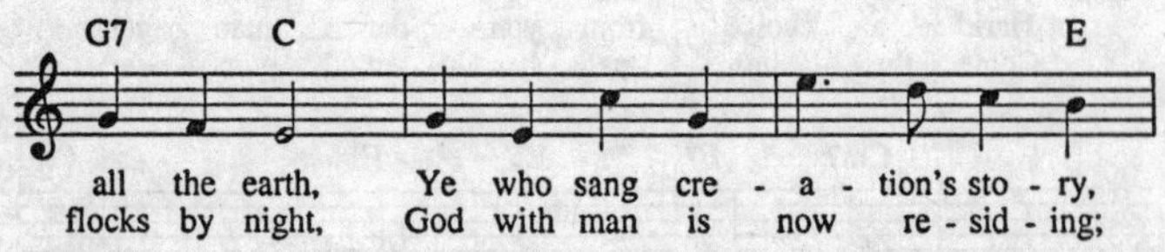
G7
C
E
all the earth, Ye who sang cre - a - tion's sto - ry,
flocks by night, God with man is now re - sid - ing;

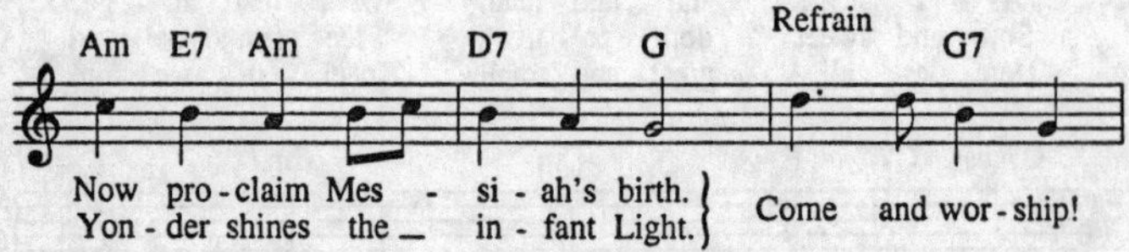
Am
E7
Am
D7
G
Refrain
G7
Now pro - claim Mes - si - ah's birth.
Yon - der shines the in - fant Light.
Come and wor - ship!

C7
F
Dm
F
Am
G7
C
Come and wor - ship! Wor - ship Christ the new - born King!

*Additional Verses*

3. Sages, leave your contemplations,
Brighter visions beam afar;
Seek the great Desire of Nations;
Ye have seen His natal star.
*(Refrain)*

4. Saints,before the altar bending,
Watching long in hope and fear,
Suddenly the Lord, descending,
In His temple shall appear.
*(Refrain)*

# AS EACH HAPPY CHRISTMAS

Traditional

G
Am7
D7
As each hap - py Christ - mas

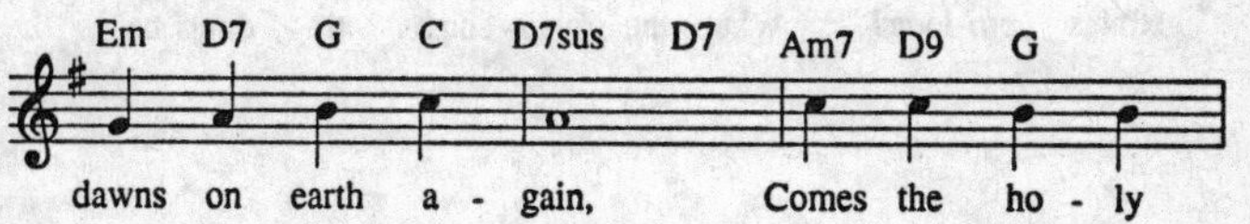
Em
D7
G
C
D7sus
D7
Am7
D9
G
dawns on earth a - gain, Comes the ho - ly

C
G
D7
G
Christ - child to the hearts of men.

# ANGELS WE HAVE HEARD ON HIGH

19th Century French Carol

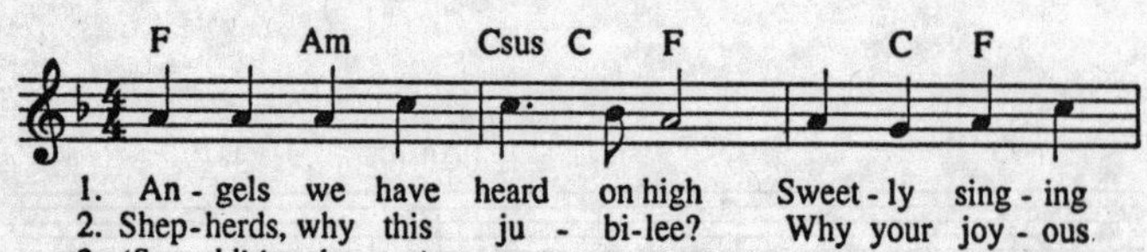
F Am Csus C F C F
1. An - gels we have heard on high Sweet - ly sing - ing
2. Shep - herds, why this ju - bi - lee? Why your joy - ous

3. *(See additional verses)*

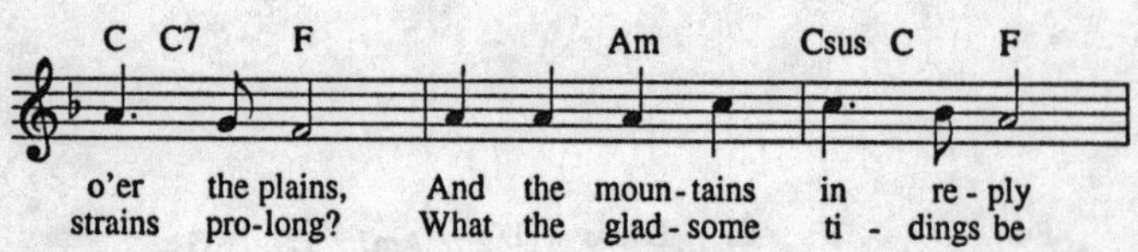
C C7 F Am Csus C F
o'er the plains, And the moun - tains in re - ply
strains pro - long? What the glad - some ti - dings be

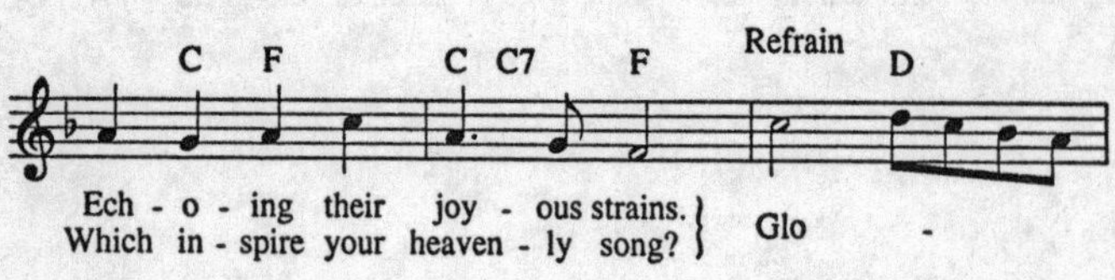
Refrain
C F C C7 F D
Ech - o - ing their joy - ous strains.
Which in - spire your heaven - ly song?
Glo -

Gm C F B♭

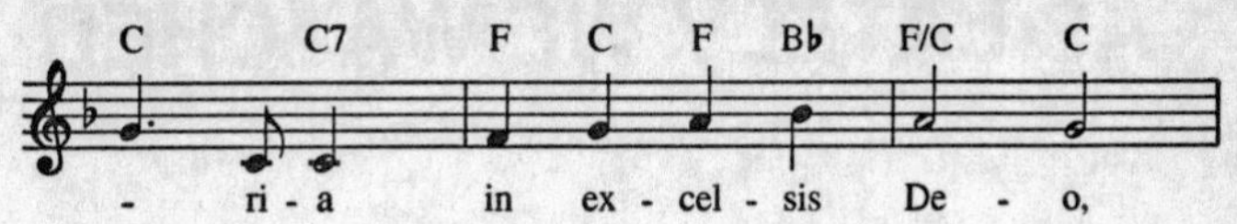
C
C7
F
C
F
B♭
F/C
C
- ri - a in ex - cel - sis De - o,

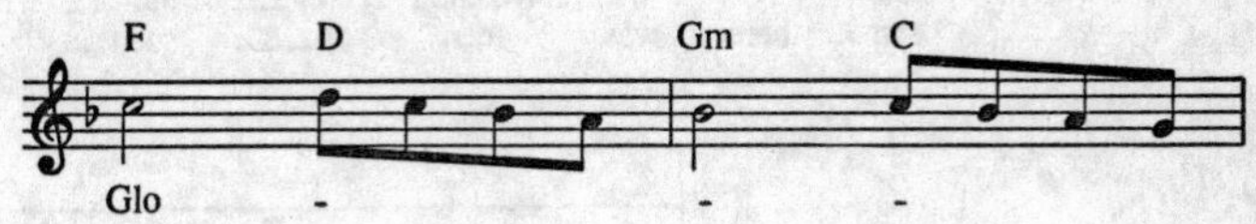
F
D
Gm
C
Glo - - -

F
B♭
C
C7
- - - ri - a

F
C
F
B♭
F/C
C7
F
in ex - cel - sis De - o.

*Additional Verses*

3. Come to Bethlehem and see
Him whose birth the angels sing;
Come, adore on bended knee
Christ the Lord, the newborn King.
*(Refrain)*

4. See within a manger laid
Jesus, Lord of heaven and earth!
Mary, Joseph, lend your aid,
With us sing our Savior's birth.
*(Refrain)*

# AS LATELY WE WATCHED

19th Century Austrian Carol

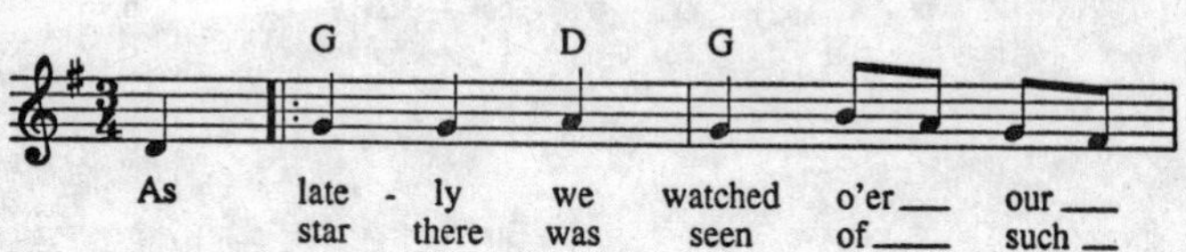
G D G
As late - ly we watched o'er our
star there was seen of such

C D7 1 G 2 G
fields thro' the night, A
glo - ri - ous light.

C
All thro' the night,

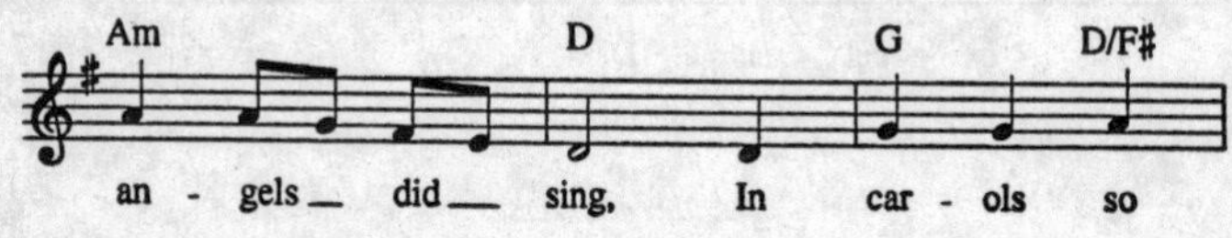
Am D G D/F#
an - gels did sing, In car - ols so

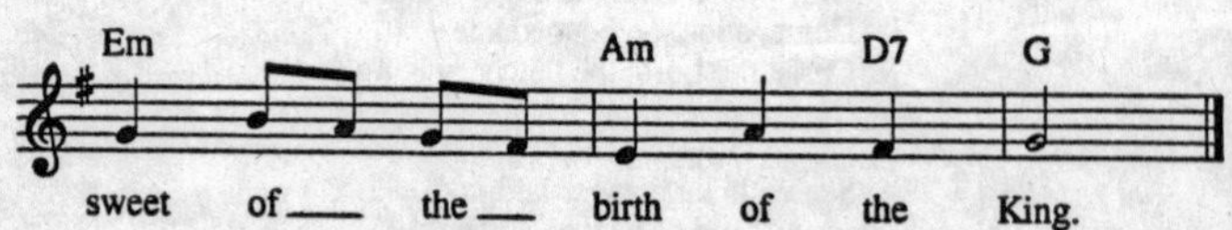
Em Am D7 G
sweet of the birth of the King.

# AS WITH GLADNESS MEN OF OLD

Words by WILLIAM CHATTERTON DIX
Music by CONRAD KOCHER

G D G C D7 G C G C
1. As with_ glad- ness men of old Did the guid- ing
2. As with_ joy - ful steps they sped To that low - ly
3.,4. (See additional verses)
Dsus D G D G C D7 G
star be - hold; As with_ joy they hailed its light,
man - ger bed, There to___ bend the knee be - fore
C G C Dsus D G
Lead - ing on - ward, beam - ing bright; So, most gra - cious
Him whom heaven and earth a - dore; So may we with
D G C G/B C G/D D G
Lord, may we Ev - er - more be led to Thee.
will - ing feet Ev - er seek Thy mer - cy seat.

*Additional Verses*

3. As they offered gifts most rare
At that manger rude and bare,
So may we with holy joy,
Pure and free from sin's alloy,
All our costliest treasures bring,
Christ, to Thee, our heavenly King.

4. Holy Jesus, every day
Keep us in the narrow way;
And, when earthly things are past,
Bring our ransomed souls at last
Where they need no star to guide,
Where no clouds Thy glory hide.

# AT THE GATES OF HEAVEN ABOVE

Traditional Romanian Carol

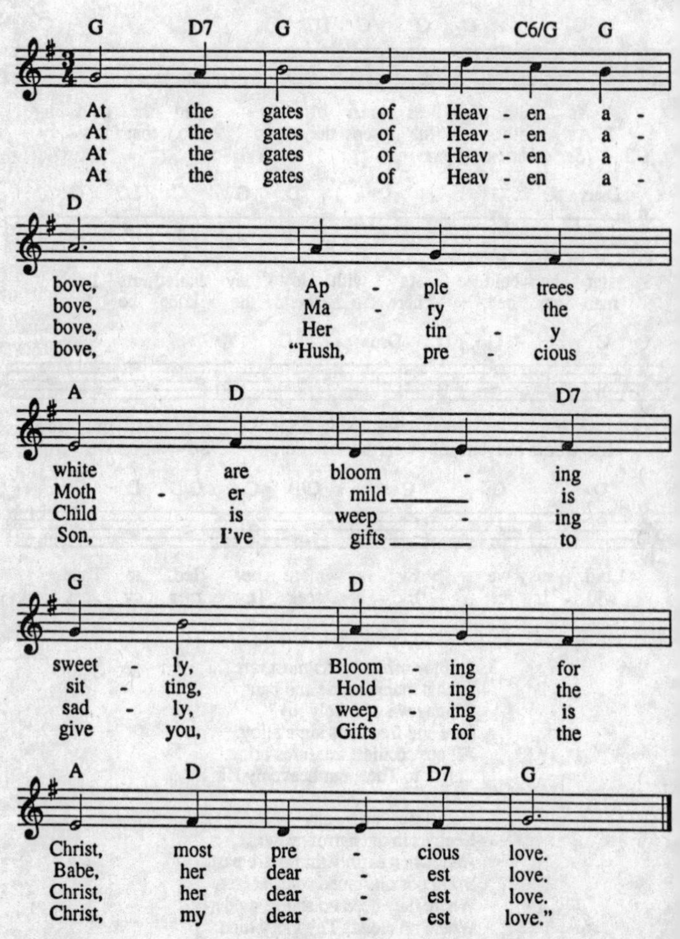
G D7 G C6/G G
At the gates of Heav - en a -
At the gates of Heav - en a -
At the gates of Heav - en a -
At the gates of Heav - en a -
D
bove, Ap - ple trees
bove, Ma - ry the
bove, Her tin - y
bove, "Hush, pre - cious
A D D7
white are bloom - ing
Moth - er mild ______ is
Child is weep - ing
Son, I've gifts ______ to
G D
sweet - ly, Bloom - ing for
sit - ting, Hold - ing the
sad - ly, weep - ing is
give you, Gifts for the
A D D7 G
Christ, most pre - cious love.
Babe, her dear - est love.
Christ, her dear - est love.
Christ, my dear - est love."

# AWAY IN A MANGER

Anonymous (vv.1,2)
Text by JOHN T. McFARLAND (v.3)
Music by JAMES R. MURRAY

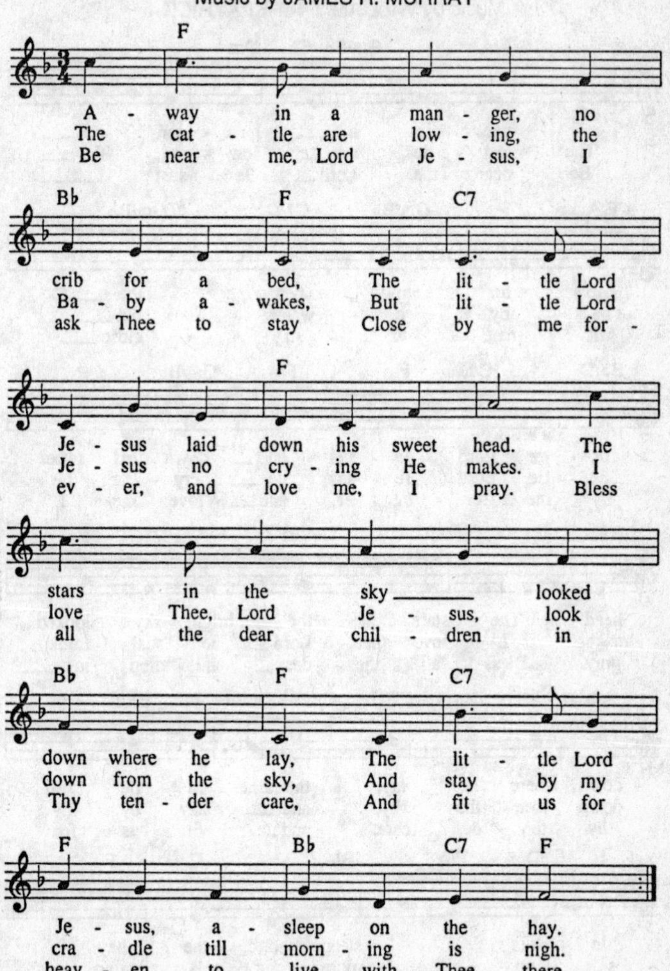
F
A - way in a man - ger, no
The cat - tle are low - ing, the
Be near me, Lord Je - sus, I
B♭ F C7
crib for a bed, The lit - tle Lord
Ba - by a - wakes, But lit - tle Lord
ask Thee to stay Close by me for -
F
Je - sus laid down his sweet head. The
Je - sus no cry - ing He makes. I
ev - er, and love me, I pray. Bless
stars in the sky looked
love Thee, Lord Je - sus, look
all the dear chil - dren in
B♭ F C7
down where he lay, The lit - tle Lord
down from the sky, And stay by my
Thy ten - der care, And fit us for
F B♭ C7 F
Je - sus, a - sleep on the hay.
cra - dle till morn - ing is nigh.
heav - en to live with Thee there.

# AWAY IN A MANGER

Anonymous Text (vv. 1,2)
Text by JOHN T. McFARLAND (v.3)
Music by WILLIAM J. KIRKPATRICK

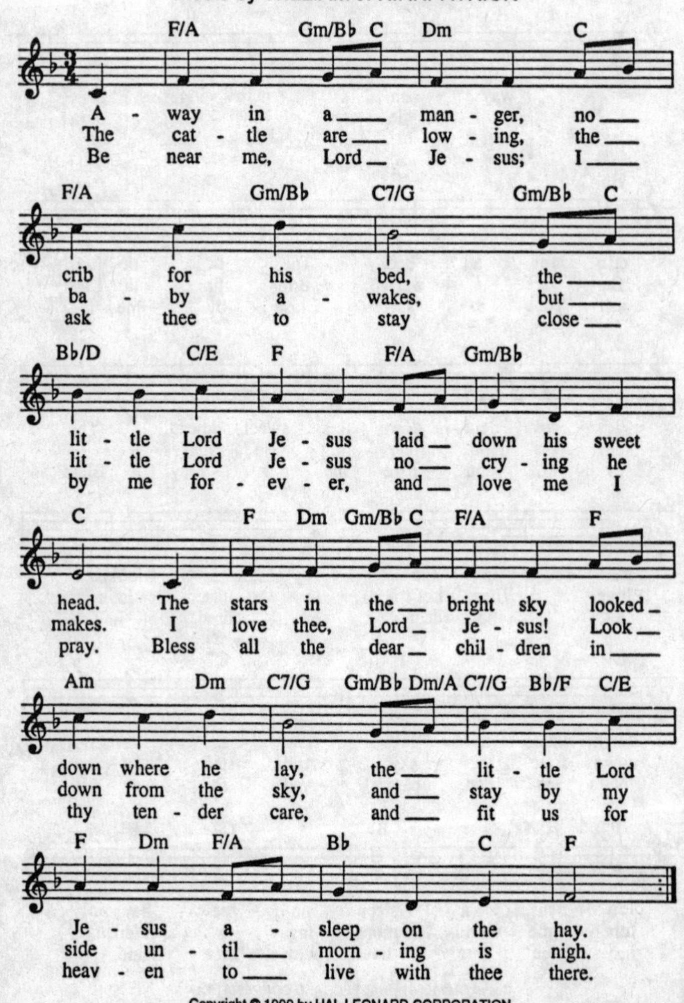
F/A Gm/B♭ C Dm C
A - way in a man - ger, no
The cat - tle are low - ing, the
Be near me, Lord Je - sus; I
F/A Gm/B♭ C7/G Gm/B♭ C
crib for his bed, the
ba - by a - wakes, but
ask thee to stay close
B♭/D C/E F F/A Gm/B♭
lit - tle Lord Je - sus laid down his sweet
lit - tle Lord Je - sus no cry - ing he
by me for - ev - er, and love me I
C F Dm Gm/B♭ C F/A F
head. The stars in the bright sky looked
makes. I love thee, Lord Je - sus! Look
pray. Bless all the dear chil - dren in
Am Dm C7/G Gm/B♭ Dm/A C7/G B♭/F C/E
down where he lay, the lit - tle Lord
down from the sky, and stay by my
thy ten - der care, and fit us for
F Dm F/A B♭ C F
Je - sus a - sleep on the hay.
side un - til morn - ing is nigh.
heav - en to live with thee there.

# THE BABE

Traditional Mexican Lullaby Carol

G D7

A la ru - ru - ru, My love - ly

G D7

Je - sus, In sweet - est slum - ber now rest, my

G Fine G D7/G

dear - est. ______

You el - e -
O night of
Such heav'n - ly

C G

phant so huge, you small mos - qui - to, Be ver - y
glo - ry, night of ce - le - bra - tion, So rich - ly
voi - ces in sweet ac - cents sing - ing, The glo - rious

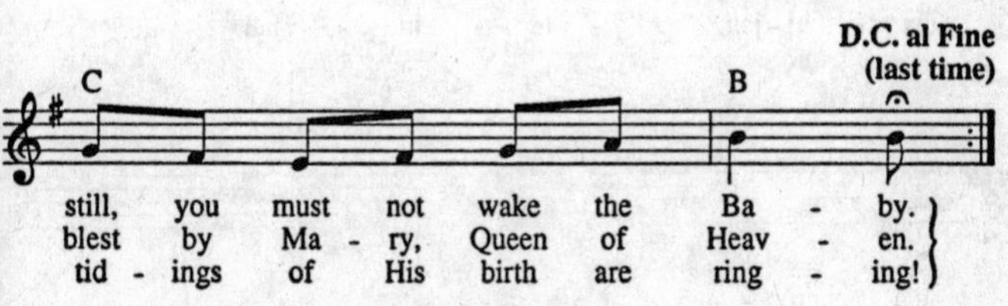
D.C. al Fine
(last time)
C B
still, you must not wake the Ba - by.
blest by Ma - ry, Queen of Heav - en.
tid - ings of His birth are ring - ing!

# A BABE IS BORN IN BETHLEHEM

Translated by PHILIP SCHAFF
Music by LUDVIG LINDEMAN

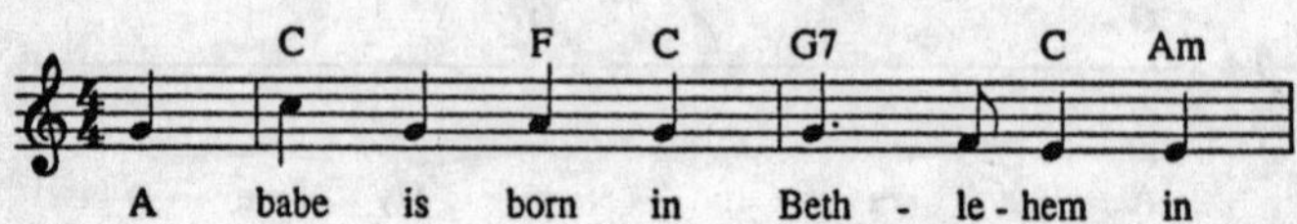
C F C G7 C Am
A babe is born in Beth - le - hem in

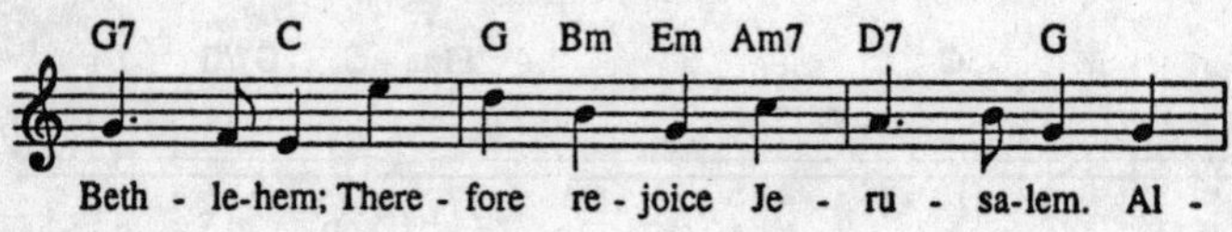
G7 C G Bm Em Am7 D7 G
Beth - le-hem; There - fore re - joice Je - ru - sa-lem. Al -

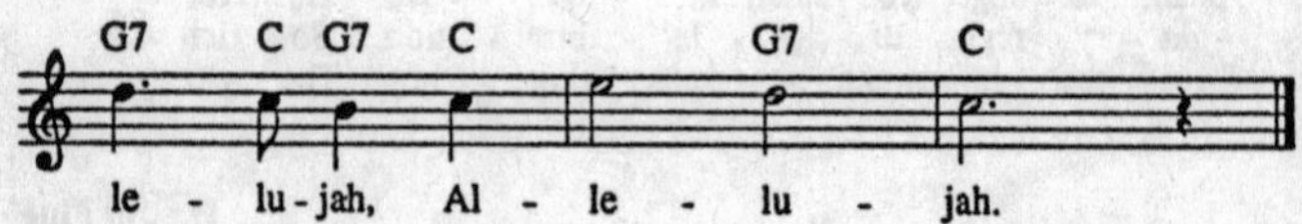
G7 C G7 C G7 C
le - lu - jah, Al - le - lu - jah.

# BESIDE THY CRADLE HERE I STAND

Words by PAUL GERHARDT
Translated by JOHN TROUTBECK
Music from the GEISTLICHE GESANGBUCH
Harmonized by J.S. BACH

Em C Am7 D G C
Be - side Thy cra - dle here I stand, O
And bring Thee with a will - ing hand The
G C/E Bm G Dsus D7 G
Thou that ev - er liv - est,
ver - y gifts Thou giv - est. Ac -
D7 G B Em G D D7
cept me, 'tis my mind and heart, My
G D7 G Em C B Em
soul, my strength, my ev - 'ry part That
C Bm G D D7 G
Thou from me de - sir - est.

# A BABY IN THE CRADLE

By D.G. CORNER

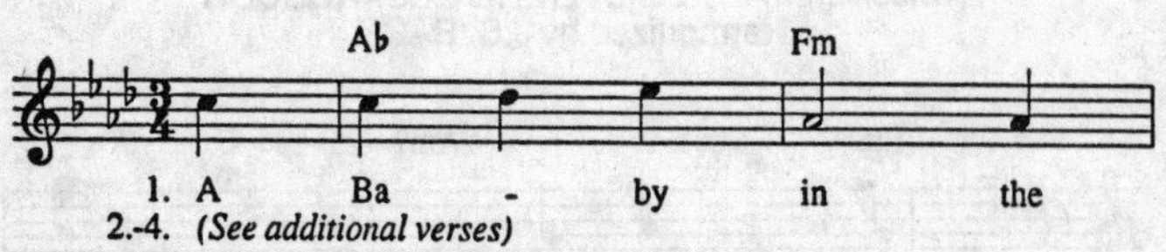
Ab
Fm
1. A Ba - by in the
2.-4. (See additional verses)

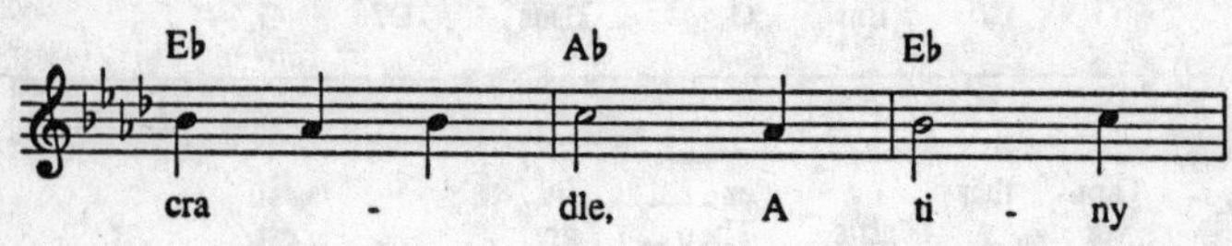
Eb
Ab
Eb
cra - dle, A ti - ny

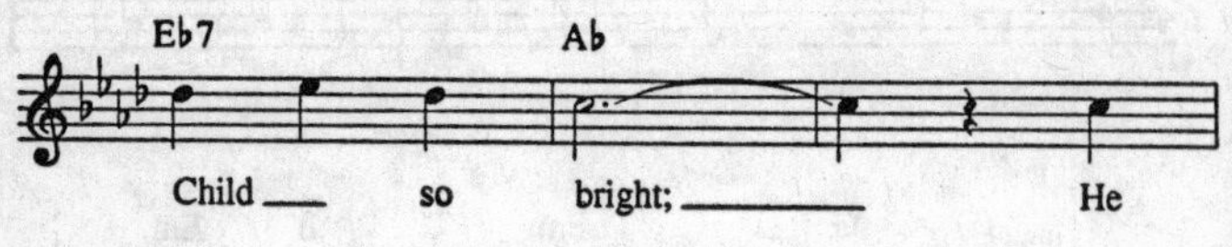
Eb7
Ab
Child so bright; He

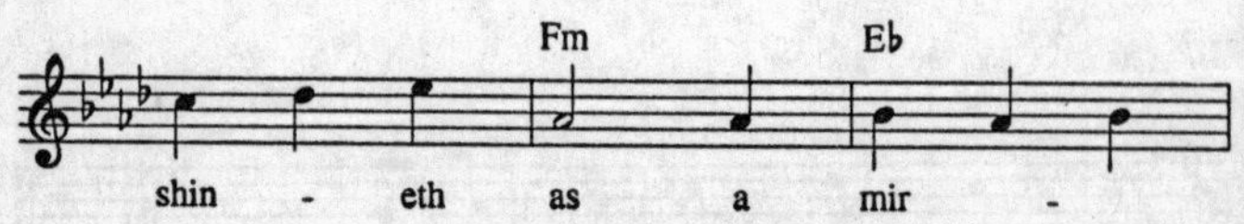
Fm
Eb
shin - eth as a mir -

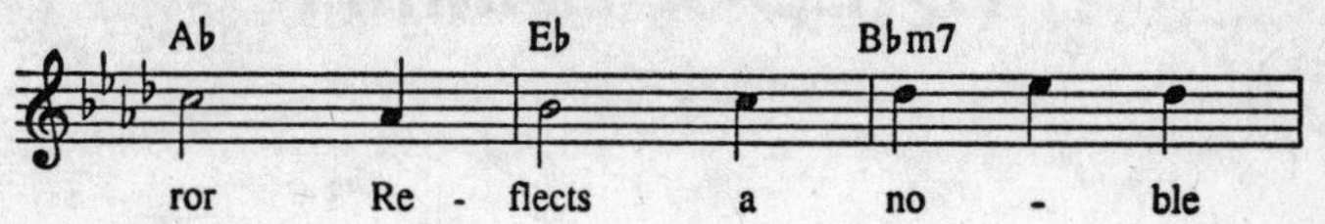
Ab
Eb
Bbm7
ror Re - flects a no - ble

C
F7
Bb7
light, This ti - ny

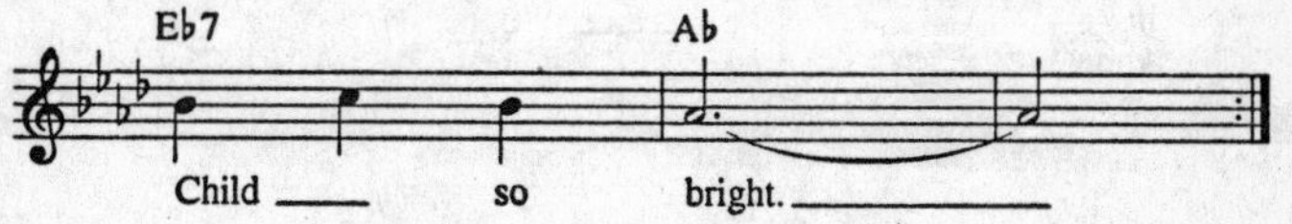
Eb7
Ab
Child so bright.

*Additional Verses*

2. The Child of whom we're speaking
 Is Jesus Christ, the Lord;
 He brings us peace and brotherhood
 If we but heed his word,
 Doth Jesus Christ, the Lord.

3. And he who rocks the cradle
 Of this sweet Child so fine
 Must serve with joy and heartiness,
 Be humble and be kind,
 For Mary's Child so fine.

4. O Jesus, dearest Savior,
 Although Thou art so small,
 With Thy great love o'erflowing
 Come flooding through my soul,
 Thou lovely Babe so small.

# BALOO, LAMMY

17th Century Scottish Melody

Gm/F F B♭/F Gm/F F
This day to you is
And now shall Ma - ry's
Sleep sound - ly, King Je - sus, and

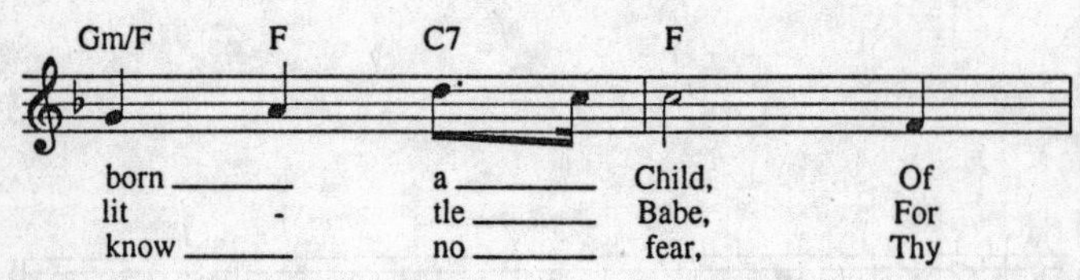
Gm/F F C7 F
born a Child, Of
lit - tle Babe, For
know no fear, Thy

Gm/F F B♭/F Gm/F F C7
Ma - ry meek, the
ev - er be our
sub - jects a - dor - ing, watch

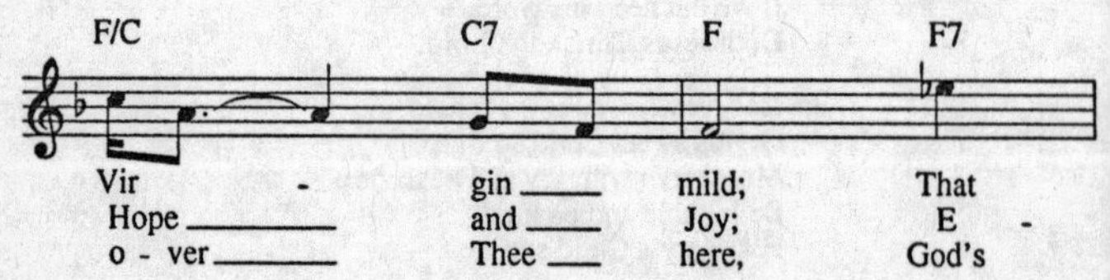
F/C C7 F F7
Vir - gin mild; That
Hope and Joy; E -
o - ver Thee here, God's

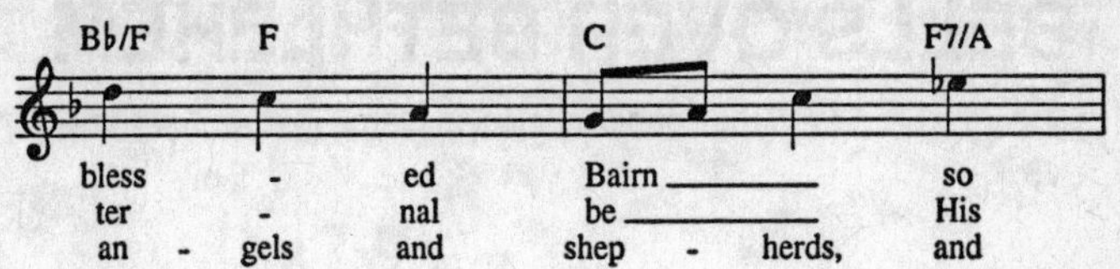
Bb/F F C F7/A
bless - ed Bairn so
ter - nal be His
an - gels and shep - herds, and

Bb/F F C F7/A
lov - ing and kind, Shall
reign on earth, Re -
kine in their stall, And

Bb/F F C Bb/F
now sing prais - es both
joice, then all peo - ple, for
wise men and Vir - gin Thy

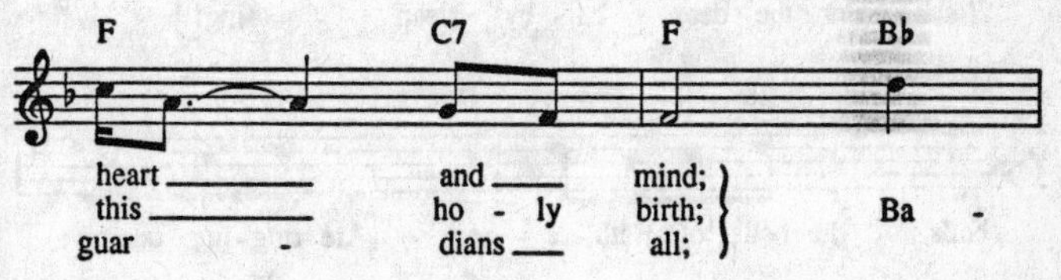
F C7 F Bb
heart and mind;
this ho - ly birth; Ba -
guar - dians all;

F C7 F
loo, Lam - my.

# BELLS OVER BETHLEHEM

Traditional Andalucian Carol

F C7/G F C
Bells o - ver Beth - le - hem peal - ing,
Shep - herds if you but will has - ten,
C7 F C7 F
God's sa - cred pres - ence re - veal - ing!
Ma - ry, the most Bless - ed Vir - gin,
C7/G F C
There in the man - ger is rest - ing
May grant that you may be keep - ing
C7 F C7 F
Je - sus, the earth's rich - est bless - ing!
Watch o'er the dear ba - by sleep - ing!
The
Bb F Bb
bells, the bells of Beth - le - hem Are ring - ing out the
F/A Dm C7 F
ti - dings, "Good will ___ to all men!"

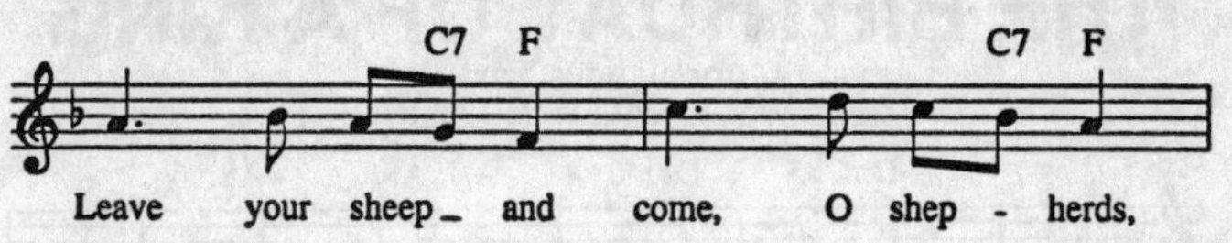
C7
F
C7
F
Leave your sheep _ and come, O shep - herds,

G
C7
pres - ents bring the Child so low - ly, ___

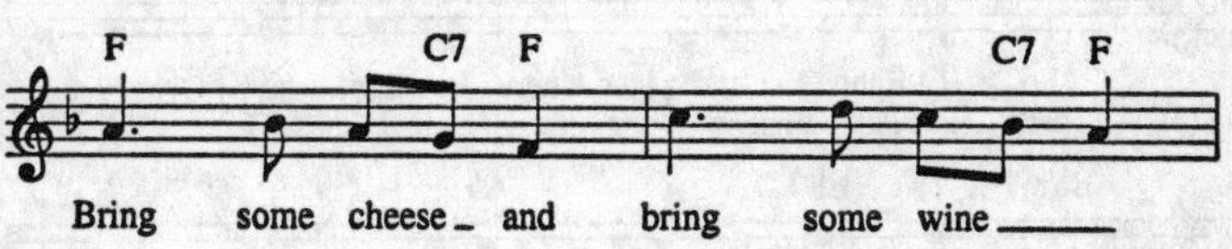
F
C7
F
C7
F
Bring some cheese _ and bring some wine ______

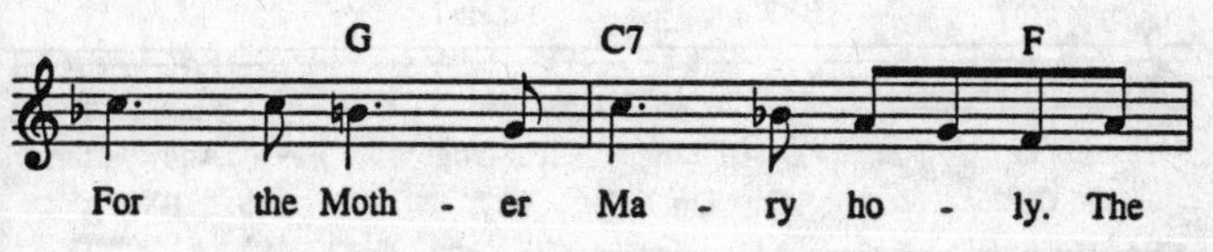
G
C7
F
For the Moth - er Ma - ry ho - ly. The

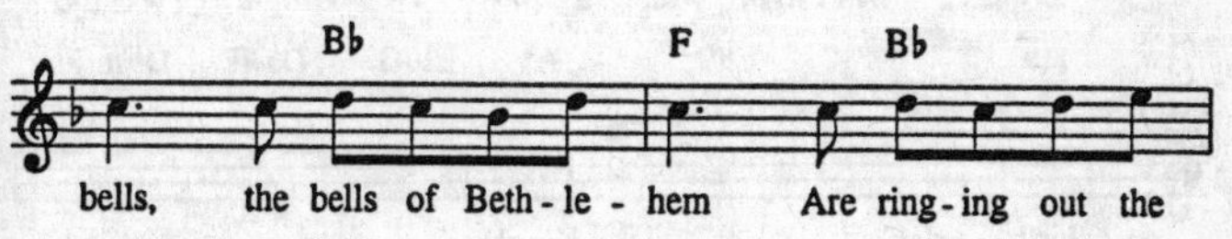
B♭
F
B♭
bells, the bells of Beth - le - hem Are ring - ing out the

F/A
Dm
C7
F
tid - ings, "Good will ___ to all men!"

# THE BIRTHDAY OF A KING

Anonymous Text
Music by WILLIAM H. NEIDLINGER

Dm7♭5 D♭m6 A♭/C A♭m6/C♭
In the lit - tle vil - lage of Beth - le - hem There
hum - ble birth-place, but O how much God
B♭m7 E♭7 A♭ E♭/G B♭7/F Fm7/E♭
lay a Child one day. And the sky was bright with a
gave to us that day! From the man - ger bed what a
B♭7 E♭ A♭6 B♭7 E♭7
ho - ly light O'er the place where Je - sus lay.
path has led, What a per - fect ho - ly way.
Al - le -
B♭m7 E♭7 A♭
lu - ia, O how the an - gels sang! Al - le -
Fm7 B♭7 E♭7
lu - ia, how it rang! And the
C7 Fm Dm7♭5 E♭7 A♭ B♭9
sky was bright with a ho - ly light; 'Twas the
A♭ E♭9 A♭ E♭/G D♭/F D♭m/F♭
birth - day of a King!
1
E♭7sus E♭7
'Twas a
2
E♭7sus E♭7 A♭

# THE BOAR'S HEAD CAROL

Traditional English

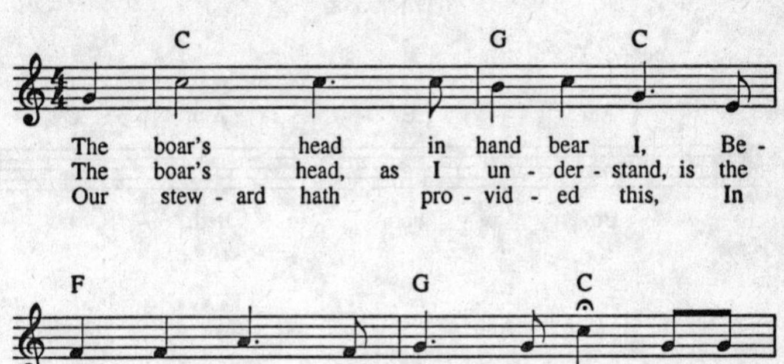
The boar's head in hand bear I, Be -
The boar's head, as I un - der - stand, is the
Our stew - ard hath pro - vid - ed this, In

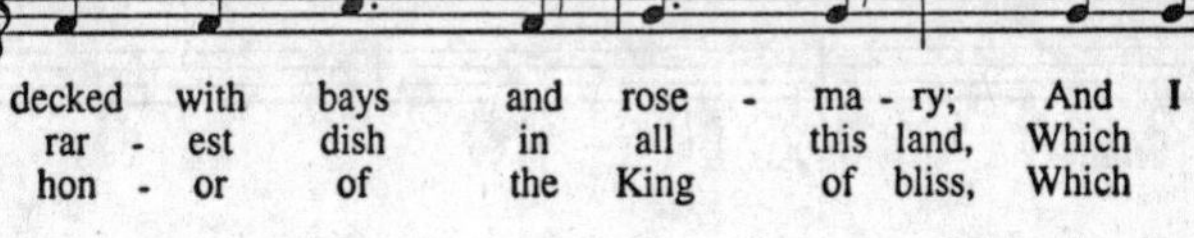
decked with bays and rose - ma - ry; And I
rar - est dish in all this land, Which
hon - or of the King of bliss, Which

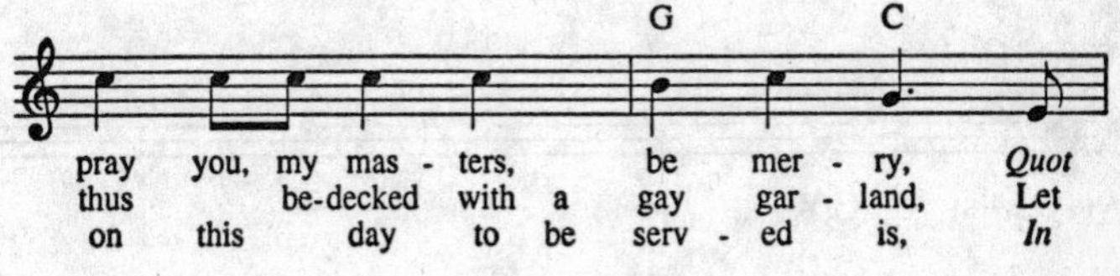
pray you, my mas - ters, be mer - ry, Quot
thus be-decked with a gay gar - land, Let
on this day to be serv - ed is, In

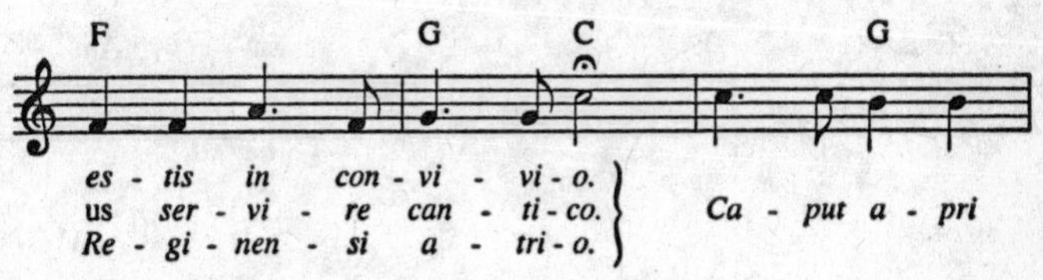
es - tis in con - vi - vi - o.
us ser - vi - re can - ti - co.
Re - gi - nen - si a - tri - o.
Ca - put a - pri

de - fe - ro, Red - dens lau - des Do - mi - no.

# A BOY IS BORN IN BETHLEHEM

Traditional

Am E7 Am G9
A Boy is born in Beth - le -
C Am Dm Gsus G
hem, Al - le - lu -
C E7 Am
ja! And joy is in Je -
Esus E Am Em Am
ru - sa - lem, Al - le - lu -
E7 Bdim Am Bdim Am E Am
ja, Al - le - lu - jah!

# BREAK FORTH, O BEAUTEOUS HEAVENLY LIGHT

Words by JOHANN RIST
Translated by JOHN TROUTBECK
Melody by JOHANN SCHOP

Cm Bb Eb Bb/D Fsus F7 Bb G/B
Break forth, O beau - teous heaven - ly light, and
Ab/C Eb Ab Bb Eb Bbsus Bb Eb Cm Bb Eb Bb/D
ush - er in the morn - ing, You shep-herds, shud-der not
Fsus F7 Bb G/B Ab/C Eb Bb Eb Bbsus Bb Eb Bb
with a - fright, but hear the an - gel's warn - ing. This
Gm Fm Bdim7 Csus C7 Fm Cm
child, now weak in in - fan - cy, our
C7/E Fm F#dim7 Gsus G7 Cm Bb Eb Ab/C Eb
con - fi - dence and joy shall be, the power of Sa - tan
F7 Bb Eb/G Ab Bb7 Ab/C Bb/D Eb Ab6 Bb Eb
break - ing, our peace e - ter - nal mak - ing.

# BRING A TORCH, JEANNETTE, ISABELLA

17th Century French Provençal Carol

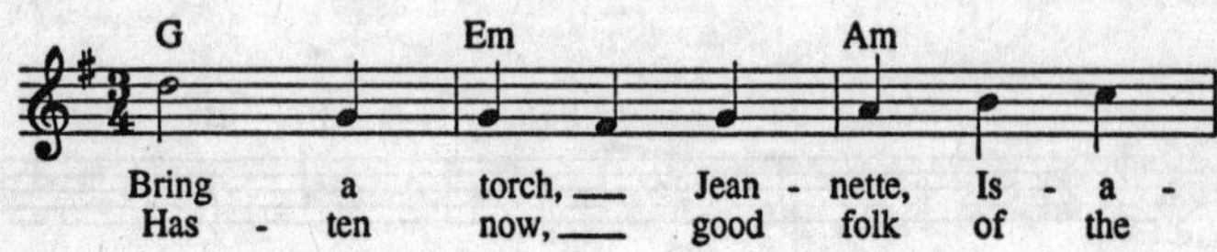
G
Em
Am
Bring a torch, ___ Jean - nette, Is - a -
Has - ten now, ___ good folk of the

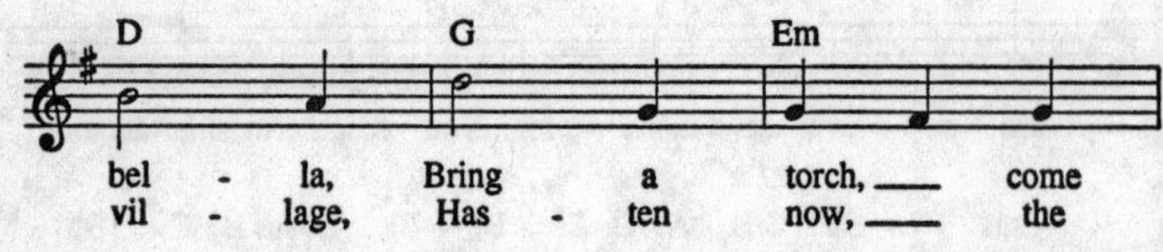
D
G
Em
bel - la, Bring a torch, ___ come
vil - lage, Has - ten now, ___ the

C
D
G
swift - ly and run. Christ is
Christ Child to see. You will

D
born, tell the folk of the vil - lage,
find him a - sleep in a man - ger,

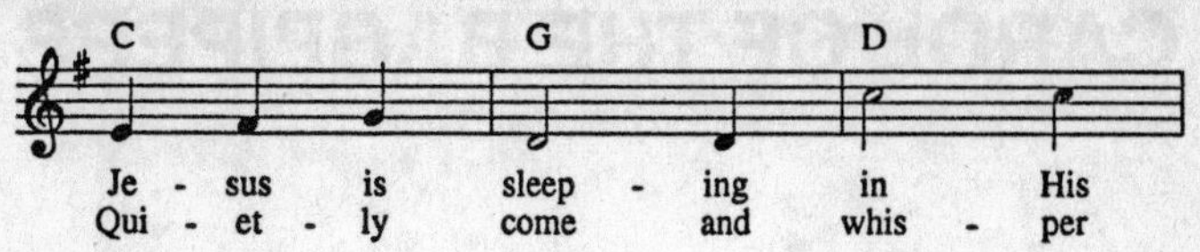
C
G
D
Je - sus is sleep - ing in His
Qui - et - ly come and whis - per

Em
D
cra - dle, Ah, ah,
soft - ly, Hush, hush,

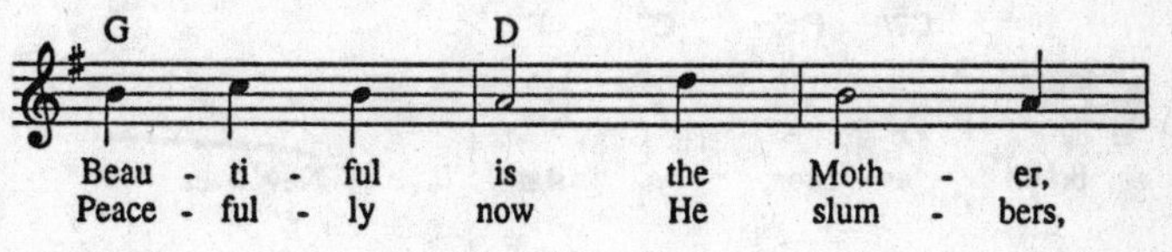
G
D
Beau - ti - ful is the Moth - er,
Peace - ful - ly now He slum - bers,

Em
D
G
Ah, ah, Beau - ti - ful
Hush, hush, Peace - ful - ly

D7
G
is her Son.
now He sleeps.

# CAROL OF THE BAGPIPERS

Traditional Sicilian Carol

F C7/F F C7/F F C7/F
When Christ our Lord was born at
F C7/F F C F/C
Beth - le - hem a - far, Al -
C C7
though 'twas night, there shone as
F C7/F F/C C7 F
bright as noon, a star. Nev - er so
C7 F
bright - ly nev - er so white - ly, Shone the
C7 F C F C7/F F
stars, as on that night! The bright - est star
C F/C C F/C C F/C C7
went A - way to call the Wise Men
F C7/F F C7 F
from the O - ri - ent.

# THE CHERRY TREE CAROL

Traditional English Carol

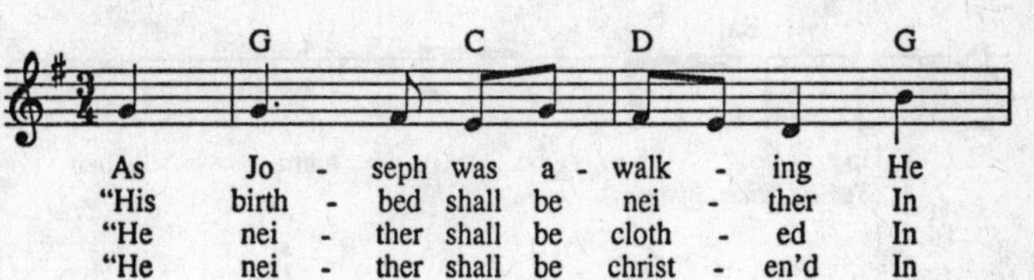
G C D G
As Jo - seph was a - walk - ing He
"His birth - bed shall be nei - ther In
"He nei - ther shall be cloth - ed In
"He nei - ther shall be christ - en'd In

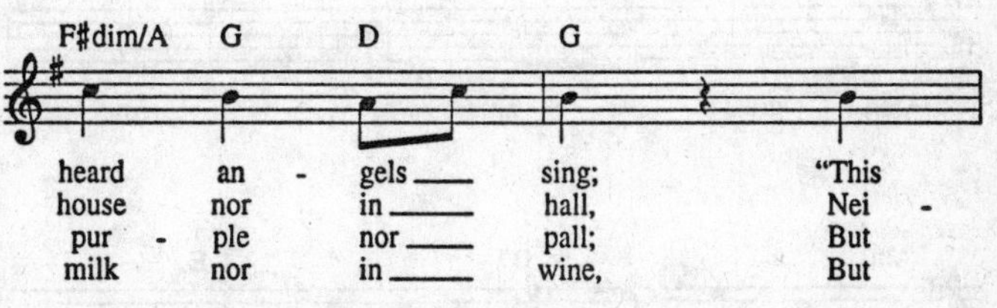
F#dim/A G D G
heard an - gels sing; "This
house nor in hall, Nei -
pur - ple nor pall; But
milk nor in wine, But

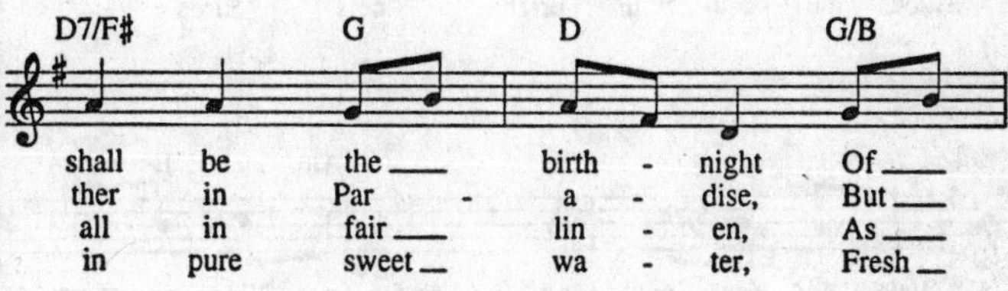
D7/F# G D G/B
shall be the birth - night Of
ther in Par - a - dise, But
all in fair lin - en, As
in pure sweet wa - ter, Fresh

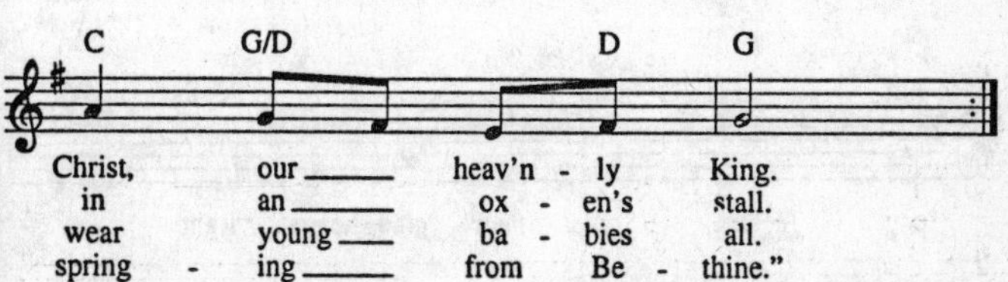
C G/D D G
Christ, our heav'n - ly King.
in an ox - en's stall.
wear young ba - bies all.
spring - ing from Be - thine."

# CAROL OF THE BIRDS

Traditional Catalonian Carol

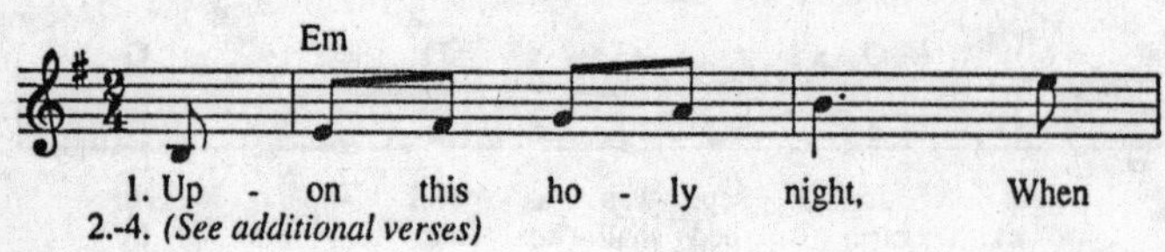
Em
1. Up - on this ho - ly night, When
2.-4. (See additional verses)

B B7 Em
God's great star ap - pears, And

Am B7 E
floods the earth with bright - ness, Birds'

F6 Am B
voic - es rise in song, And, war - bling all night

Em C7 B7sus B7
long, Ex - press their glad hearts' light -

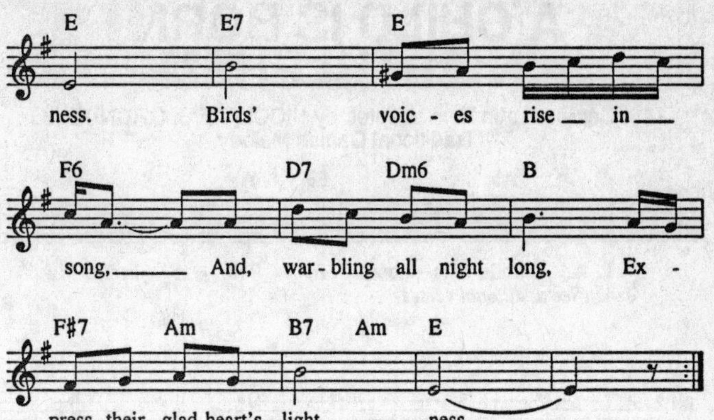
E
E7
E
ness.
Birds'
voic - es
rise
in
F6
D7
Dm6
B
song,
And,
war - bling
all
night
long,
Ex -
F#7
Am
B7
Am
E
press
their
glad
heart's
light
-
ness.

*Additional Verses*

2. The Nightingale is first
To bring his song of cheer,
And tell us of his gladness:
"Jesus, our Lord, is born
To free us from all sin,
And banish ev'ry sadness!
Jesus, our Lord, is born
To free us from all sin,
And banish ev'ry sadness!"

3. The answ'ring Sparrow cries:
"God comes to earth this day
Amid the angels flying."
Trilling in sweetest tones,
The Finch his Lord now owns:
"To Him be all thanksgiving."
Trilling in sweetest tones,
The Finch his Lord now owns:
"To Him be all thanksgiving."

4. The Partridge adds his note:
"To Bethlehem I'll fly,
Where in the stall He's lying.
There, near the manger blest,
I'll build myself a nest,
And sing my love undying.
There, near the manger blest,
I'll build myself a nest,
And sing my love undying."

# A CHILD IS BORN IN BETHLEHEM

14th Century Latin Text adapted by NICOLAI F.S. GRUNDTVIG
Traditional Danish Melody

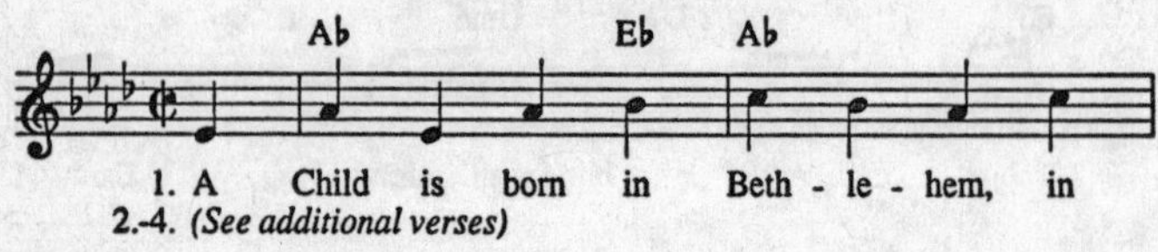
Ab
Eb
Ab
1. A Child is born in Beth - le - hem, in
2.-4. (See additional verses)

Eb
Eb7
Ab
Fm
Eb7
Beth - le - hem; And joy is in Je - ru - sa - lem, Al -

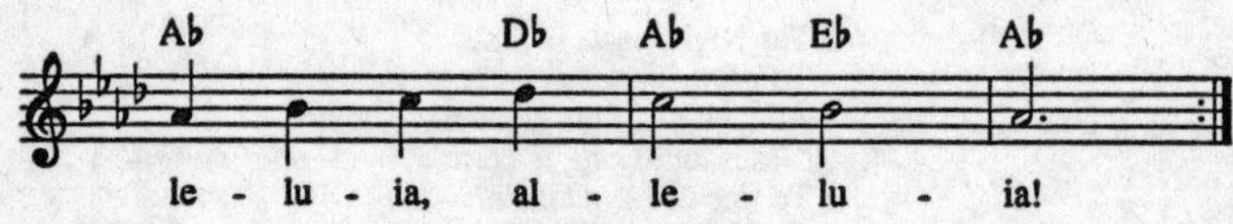
Ab
Db
Ab
Eb
Ab
le - lu - ia, al - le - lu - ia!

*Additional Verses*

2. A lowly maiden all alone,
So all alone,
Gave birth to God's own Holy Son.
Alleluia, alleluia!

3. She chose a manger for His bed,
For Jesus' bed.
God's angels sang for joy o'erhead,
Alleluia, alleluia!

4. Give thanks and praise eternally,
Eternally,
To God, the Holy Trinity.
Alleluia, alleluia!

# CHRIST IS BORN THIS EVENING

Traditional

D G A9 D
Christ is born this eve - ning,
Shep - herds, has - ten yon - der,
Bm Em A7 D G
Let us go re - joic - ing! Though the night is
Where the Babe most ho - ly, In this cold De -
A9 D Bm Em A7 D
gloom - y, Day will soon be dawn - ing!
cem - ber, Lies in man - ger low - ly.
A A7 D
(1.,2.) An - gels from on high are sing - ing
(3.,4.) See, the star on high is gleam - ing,
A A7 D
To the One who comes from Heav - en:
O'er the love - ly In - fant beam - ing!
G F#7
"Glo - ri - a, Glo - ri - a, Glo - ri - a,
2nd time D.C.
Bm Em7 D/A A7 D
In ex - cel - sis De - o!"

# CHILD JESUS

Words by HANS CHRISTIAN ANDERSEN
Music by NIELS GADE

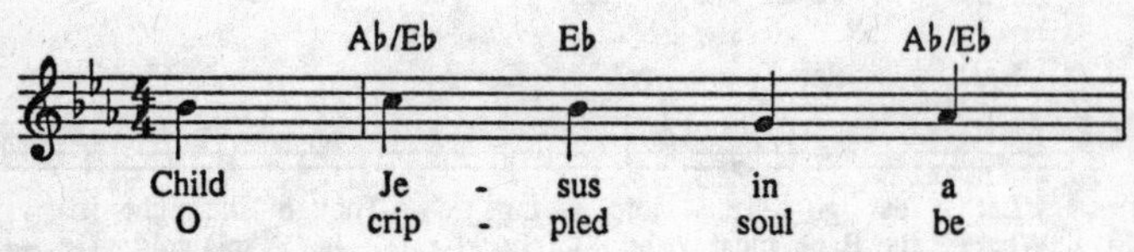
Ab/Eb
Eb
Ab/Eb
Child Je - sus in a
O crip - pled soul be

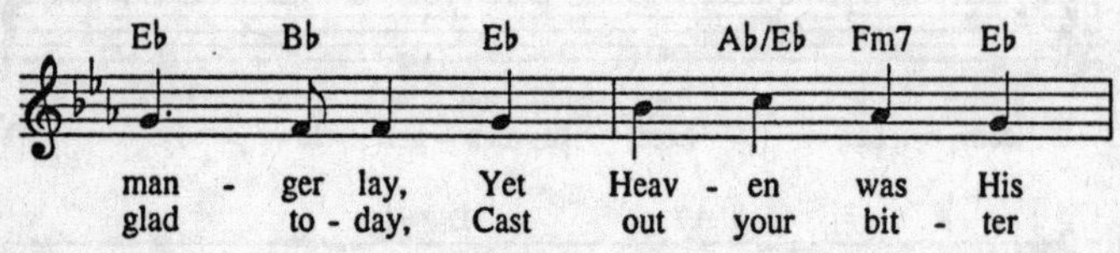
Eb
Bb
Eb
Ab/Eb
Fm7
Eb
man - ger lay, Yet Heav - en was His
glad to - day, Cast out your bit - ter

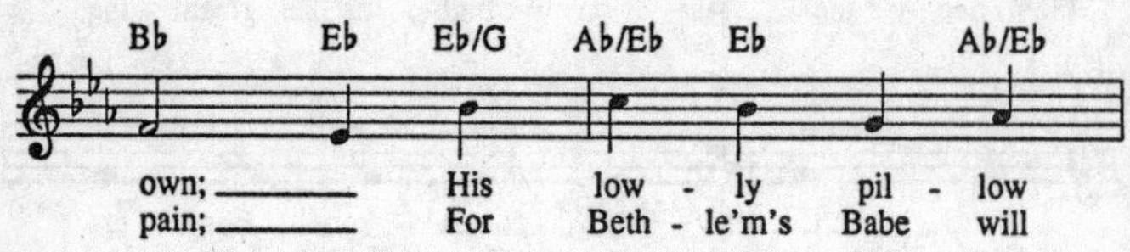
Bb
Eb
Eb/G
Ab/Eb
Eb
Ab/Eb
own; His low - ly pil - low
pain; For Beth - le'm's Babe will

Eb
Bb
Eb
Bb
Cm
Gm
D
was of straw, And 'round Him no light
show the way, We heav'n - ly bliss can

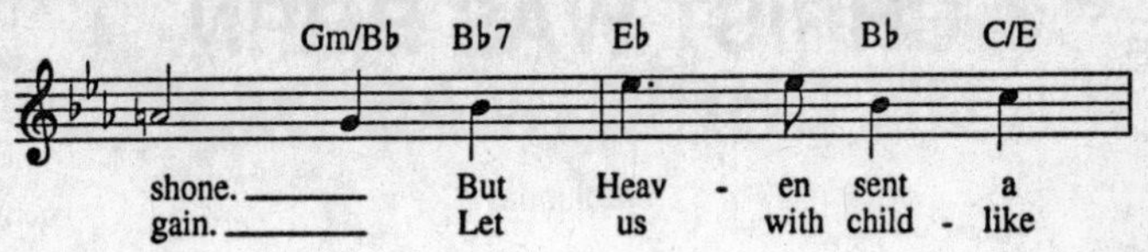
Gm/B♭ B♭7 E♭ B♭ C/E
shone. _______ But Heav - en sent a
gain. _______ Let us with child - like

Fm B♭ E♭ A♭/E♭ Fm7
star so bright, And ox - en kissed his
heart and mind, Seek now the Son of

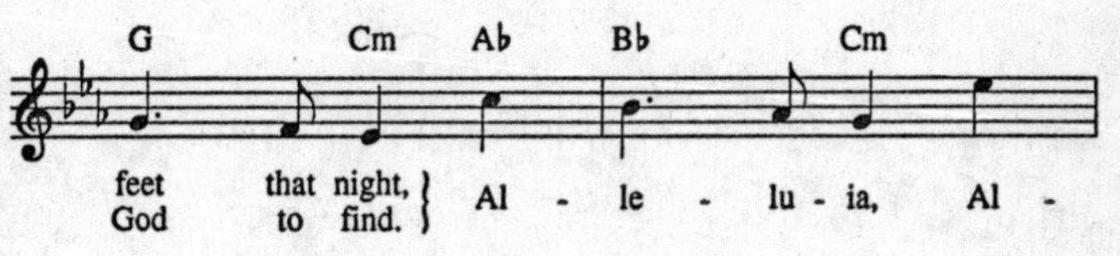
G Cm A♭ B♭ Cm
feet that night,
God to find.
Al - le - lu - ia, Al -

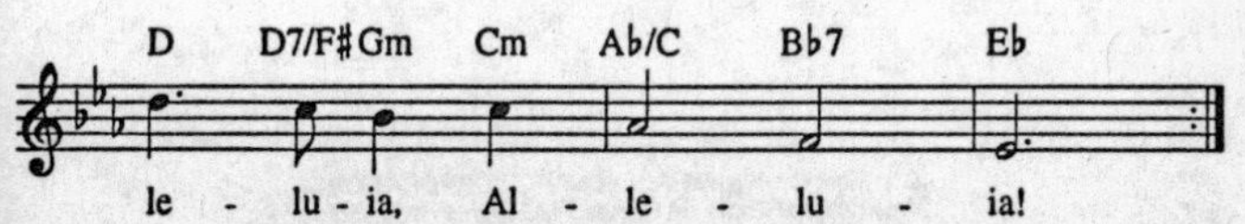
D D7/F♯ Gm Cm A♭/C B♭7 E♭
le - lu - ia, Al - le - lu - ia!

# CHRIST WAS BORN ON CHRISTMAS DAY

Traditional

F
B♭ F
Christ was born on Christ - mas day, Wreath the hol - ly,

B♭ F
Gm
C7
F
C
twine the bay; *Christ - us na - tus ho - di - e;* The

F
B♭
F
C7
F
Babe, the Son, the Ho - ly One of Ma - ry.

# COME, ALL YE CHILDREN

Traditional 17th Century Castilian Melody

F F#dim7 Gm C7
Come, all ye chil - dren, your voic - es raise on this
Wake, all ye chil - dren, your Sav - ior was born this
Rise, all ye chil - dren, a love - ly day is dawn -
F C F
morn, on this morn, Bring the glad tid - ings to
night, born this night, Fol - low the star for its
ing, is dawn - ing, Rouse from your slum - bers and
F#dim7 Gm C7 F C7/F F
men that Je - sus was born, Oh! Re - joice!
beam sends forth a bright light, Oh! Hark - en!
greet this Christ - mas morn - ing, Oh! Laud God!
C C7 F C7/F F
Sweet - ly pro - long what the an - gels pro - claim,
An - gel - ic choirs tell in sweet words of love,
Sing loud, sing well, 'tis the day of Christ's birth;
C C7 F C7/F F
Lift up your voic - es, ac - cent their re - frains,
How the dear God sent his Son from a - bove,
While mor-tals slept, He de - scend - ed to earth;
F#dim7 Gm C7 F
Sing, for Christ's birth will bring peace and joy to the earth.
How Je - sus' birth will re - deem all men up-on earth.
Come, let us sing, for we know that Christ is our King!

# CHRISTIANS, AWAKE! SALUTE THE HAPPY MORN

Traditional

C G C G7 C
1. Chris - tians, a - wake! sa - lute the hap - py
2. Then to the watch - ful shep - herds it was
3.,4. (See additional verses)

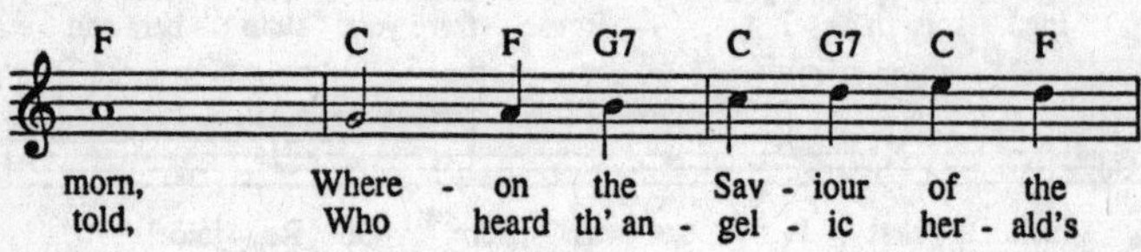
F C F G7 C G7 C F
morn, Where - on the Sav - iour of the
told, Who heard th' an - gel - ic her - ald's

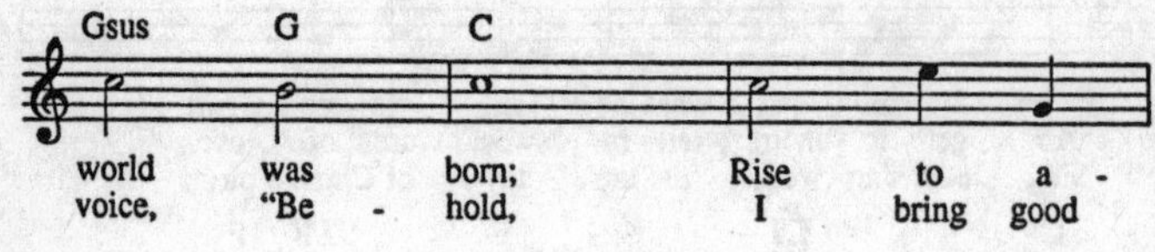
Gsus G C
world was born; Rise to a -
voice, "Be - hold, I bring good

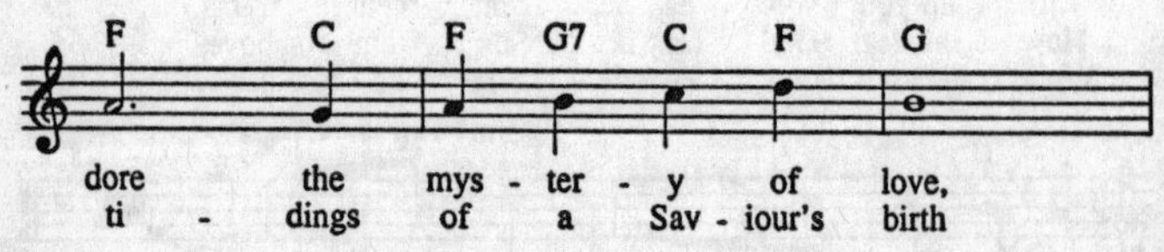
F C F G7 C F G
dore the mys - ter - y of love,
ti - dings of a Sav - iour's birth

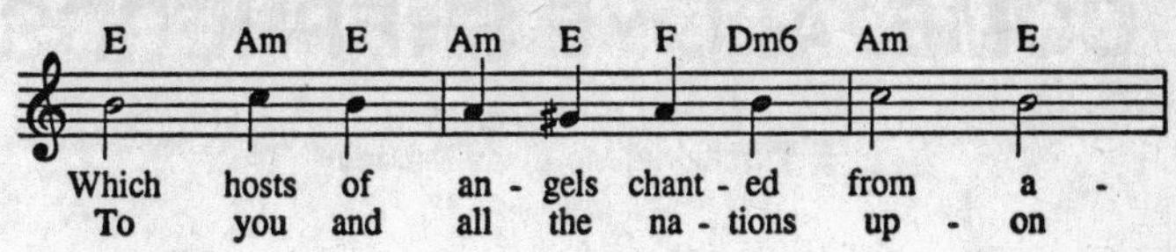
E Am E Am E F Dm6 Am E
Which hosts of an - gels chant - ed from a -
To you and all the na - tions up - on

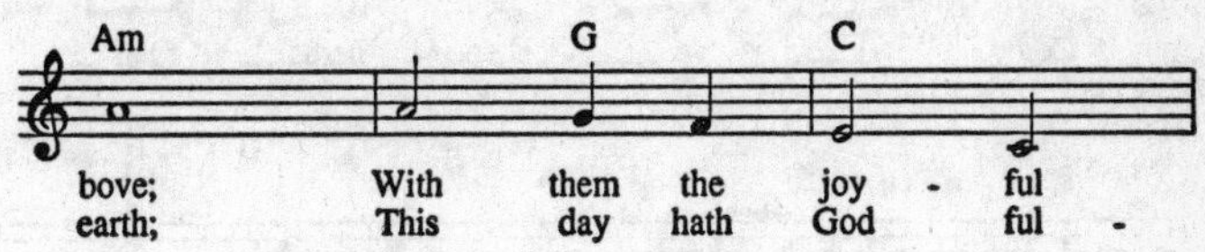
Am G C
bove; With them the joy - ful
earth; This day hath God ful -

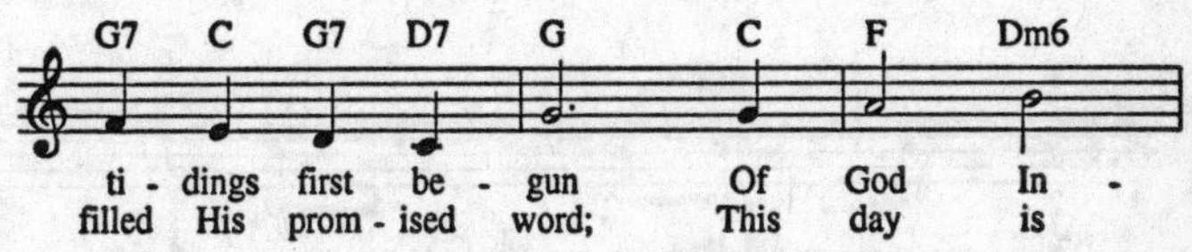
G7 C G7 D7 G C F Dm6
ti - dings first be - gun Of God In -
filled His prom - ised word; This day is

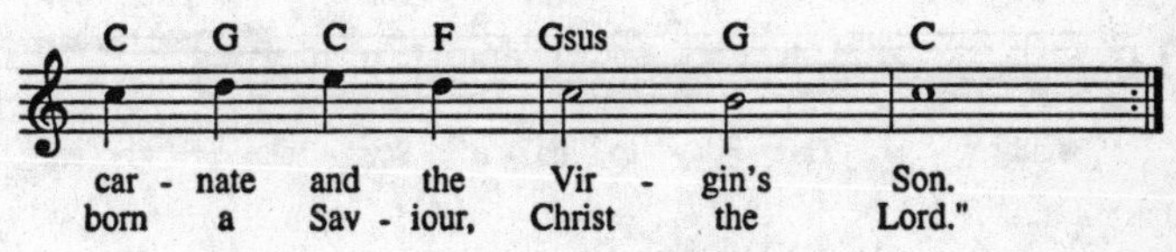
C G C F Gsus G C
car - nate and the Vir - gin's Son.
born a Sav - iour, Christ the Lord."

*Additional Verses*

3. He spake; and straightway the celestial choir
In hymns of joy, unknown before, conspire;
The praises of redeeming love they sang
And heaven's whole orb with alleluias rang;
God's highest glory was their anthem still,
Peace upon earth, and unto men good will.

4. Then may we hope, th' angelic hosts among,
To sing, redeemed, a glad triumphal song;
He that was born upon this joyful day
Around us all His glory shall display;
Saved by His love, incessant we shall sing
Eternal praise to heaven's Almighty King.

# COME, ALL YE SHEPHERDS

Traditional Czech Text
Traditional Moravian Melody

F Bb F Bb
Come, all ye shep - herds such
F C7 F Bb
won - ders en - thrall Come where the
F Bb F C7
young Child is laid in a
F Am Dm C7
stall. This day to us a Sav - iour is giv - en,
F Am Dm C7
Whom God on high hath sent down from heav - en.
F Bb C7 F
Hal - le - lu - jah!

# COVENTRY CAROL

Words by ROBERT CROO
Traditional English Melody

Am E Am Dm E
1. Lul - lay, thou lit - tle ti - ny child,
2. O sis - ters too, how may we do,
3.,4. (See additional verses)
Am Dm E7 Am C
By, by, lul - ly, lul - lay. Lul -
For to pre - serve this day. This
G Am E Am Dm E
lay, Thou lit - tle ti - ny Child,
poor Young - ling for whom we sing,
Am E F Dm E A
By, by, lul - ly lul - lay.
By, by, lul - ly lul - lay.

*Additional Verses*

3. Herod, the King
In his raging,
Charged he hath this day.
His men of might,
In his own sight,
All young children to slay.

4. That woe is me,
Poor child for thee!
And ever morn and day,
For thy parting
Neither say nor sing
By, by, lully, lullay.

# COME RUNNING, YOU SHEPHERDS

Traditional Silesian Carol

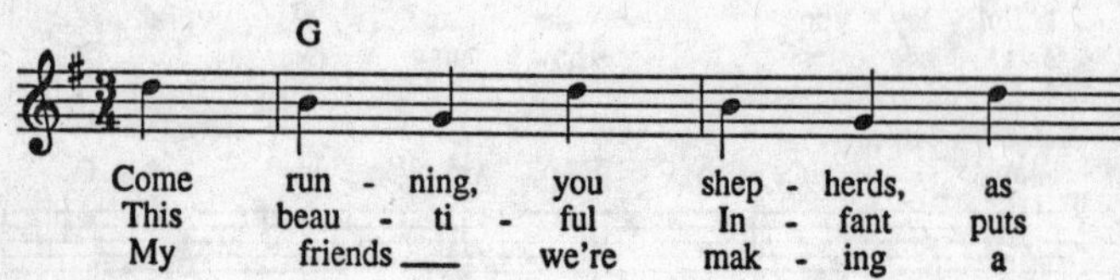
G
Come run - ning, you shep - herds, as
This beau - ti - ful In - fant puts
My friends we're mak - ing a

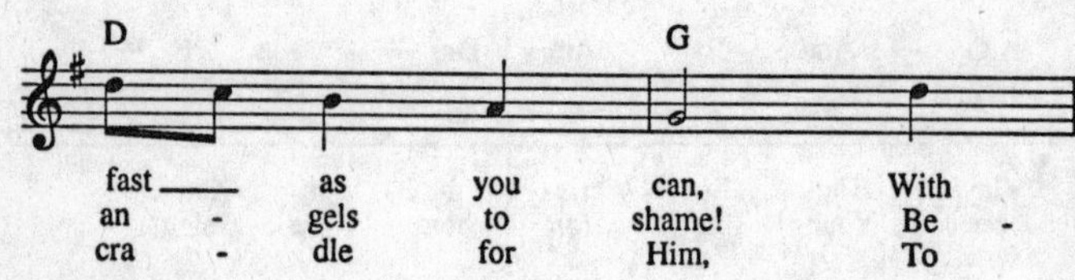
D
G
fast as you can, With
an - gels to shame! Be -
cra - dle for Him, To

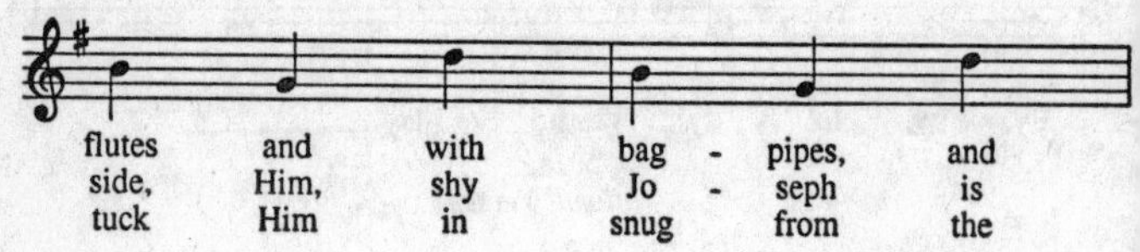
flutes and with bag - pipes, and
side, Him, shy Jo - seph is
tuck Him in snug from the

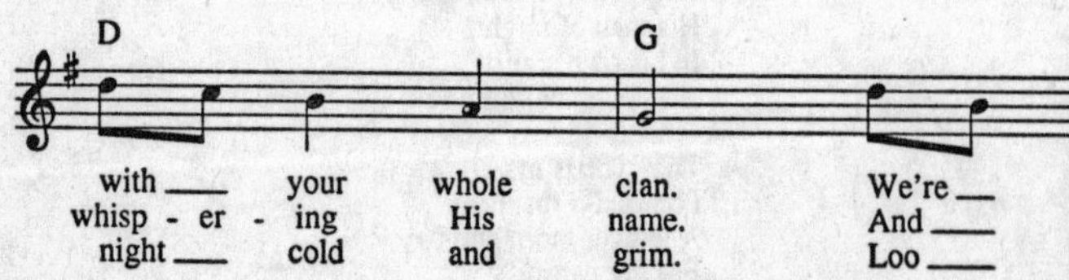
D
G
with your whole clan. We're
whisp - er - ing His name. And
night cold and grim. Loo

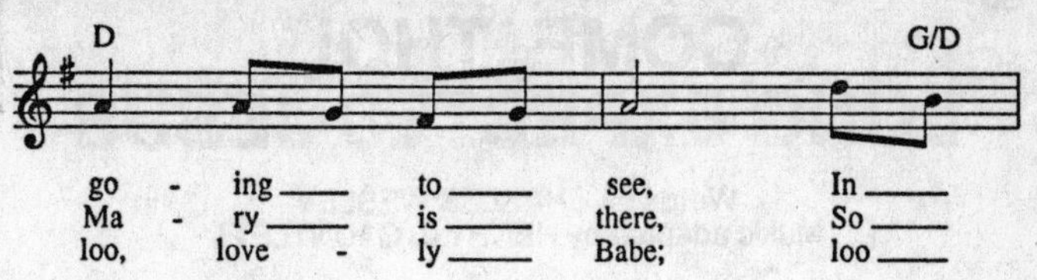
D
G/D
go - ing to see, In
Ma - ry is there, So
loo, love - ly Babe; loo

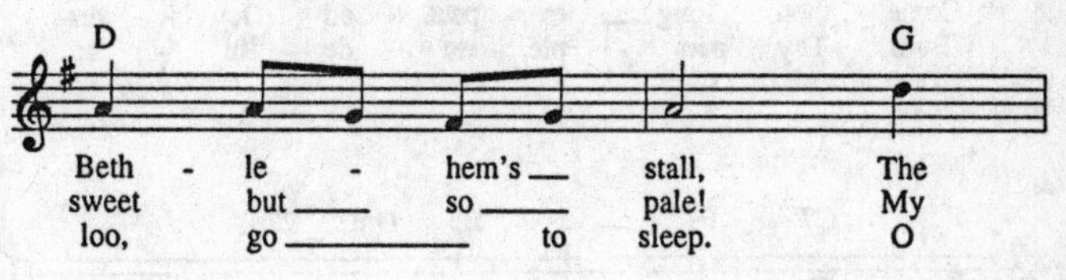
D
G
Beth - le - hem's stall, The
sweet but so pale! My
loo, go to sleep. O

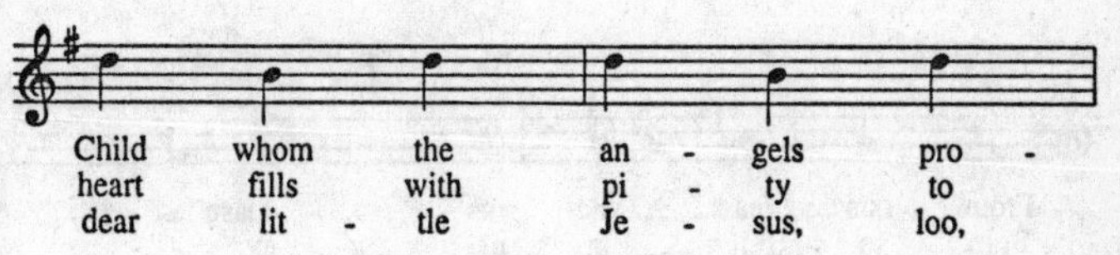
Child whom the an - gels pro -
heart fills with pi - ty to
dear lit - tle Je - sus, loo,

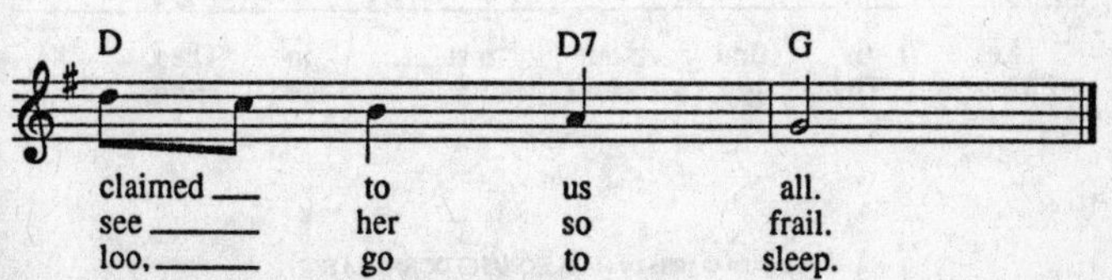
D
D7
G
claimed to us all.
see her so frail.
loo, go to sleep.

# COME, THOU LONG EXPECTED JESUS

Words by CHARLES WESLEY
Music adapted by HENRY J. GAUNTLETT

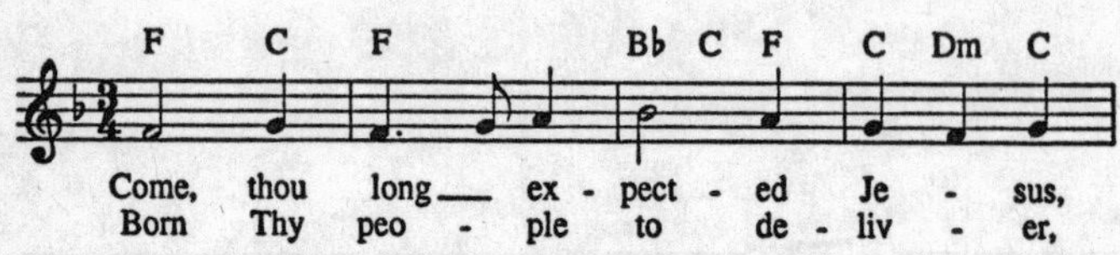
F C F Bb C F C Dm C
Come, thou long ex - pect - ed Je - sus,
Born Thy peo - ple to de - liv - er,

F C7 F Bb Dm C F
Born to set Thy peo - ple free;
Born a child and yet a King.

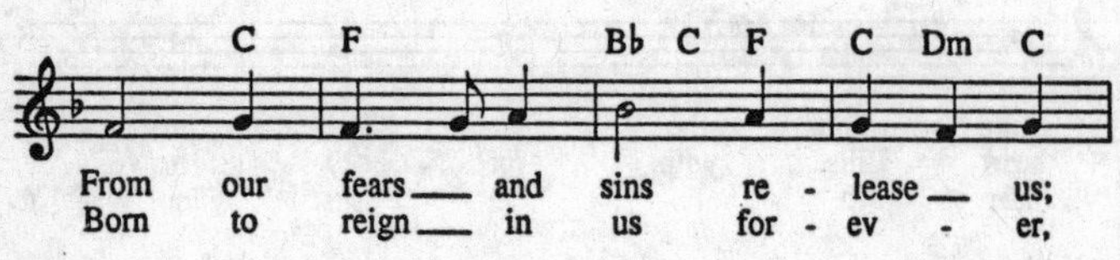
C F Bb C F C Dm C
From our fears and sins re - lease us;
Born to reign in us for - ev - er,

F C7 F Bb Dm C F
Let us find our rest in Thee.
Now Thy gra - cious king - dom bring.

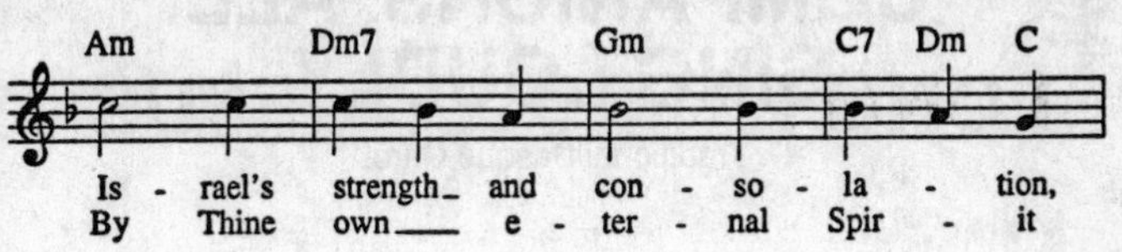
Am Dm7 Gm C7 Dm C
Is - rael's strength_ and con - so - la - tion,
By Thine own ___ e - ter - nal Spir - it

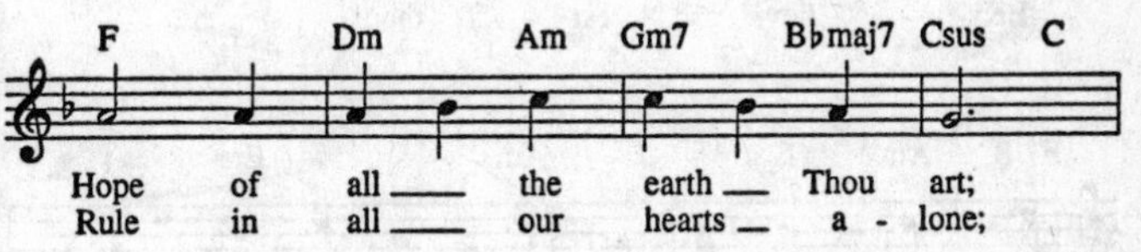
F Dm Am Gm7 B♭maj7 Csus C
Hope of all ___ the earth ___ Thou art;
Rule in all ___ our hearts ___ a - lone;

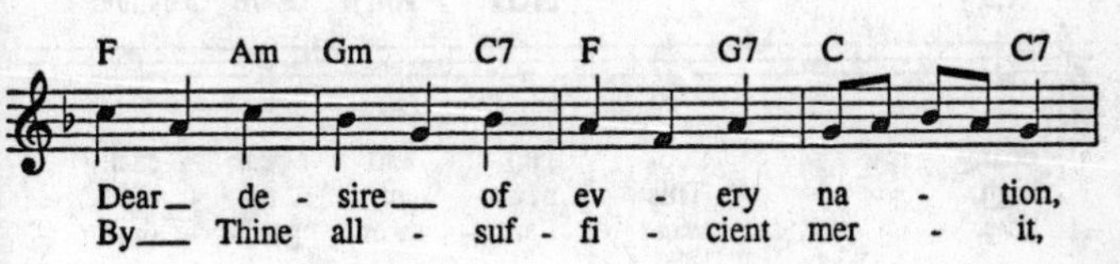
F Am Gm C7 F G7 C C7
Dear ___ de - sire ___ of ev - ery na - tion,
By ___ Thine all - suf - fi - cient mer - it,

F B♭ F C7 F
Joy of ev - ery long - ing heart.
Raise us to ___ Thy glo - rious throne.

# COMPANIONS, ALL SING LOUDLY

Traditional Basque Carol

E/G# Am E7/B Am/C
Com - pan - ions, all sing
Say, Ma - ry, of sal -
Be - liev - est thou the
E7/B Am E Am Em
loud - ly In praise of Ma - ry
va - tion, Who brought these ti - dings
an - gel, O Ma - ry, tell us
Am E/G# Am E7/B Am/C
dear, Look up and bear each
nigh, This news of ex - al -
true, What an - swer gav'st thou
Dm Am/E Em
proud - ly, The day of days is
ta - tion, Whence comes it us a -
Ga - briel Of joy for that ye

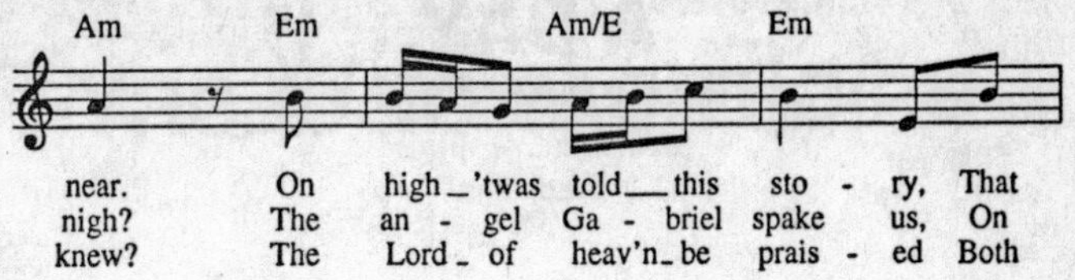
Am Em Am/E Em
near. On high ’twas told this sto - ry, That
nigh? The an - gel Ga - briel spake us, On
knew? The Lord of heav’n be prais - ed Both

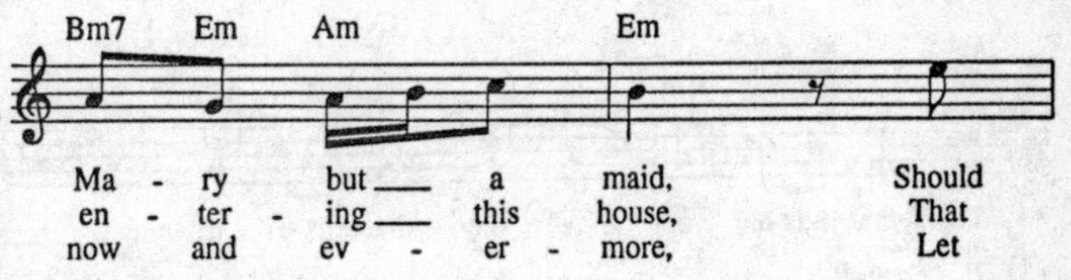
Bm7 Em Am Em
Ma - ry but a maid, Should
en - ter - ing this house, That
now and ev - er - more, Let

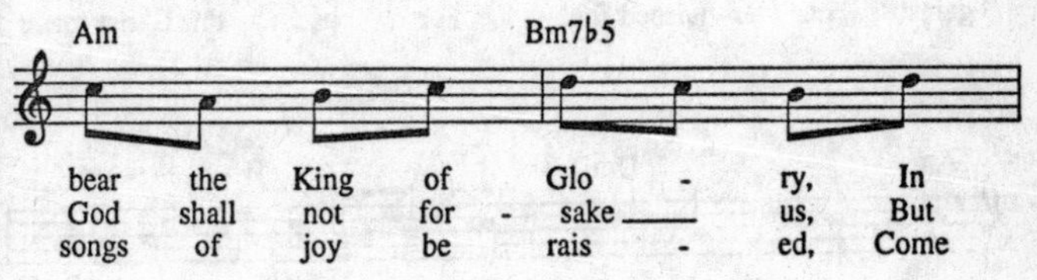
Am Bm7♭5
bear the King of Glo - ry, In
God shall not for - sake us, But
songs of joy be rais - ed, Come

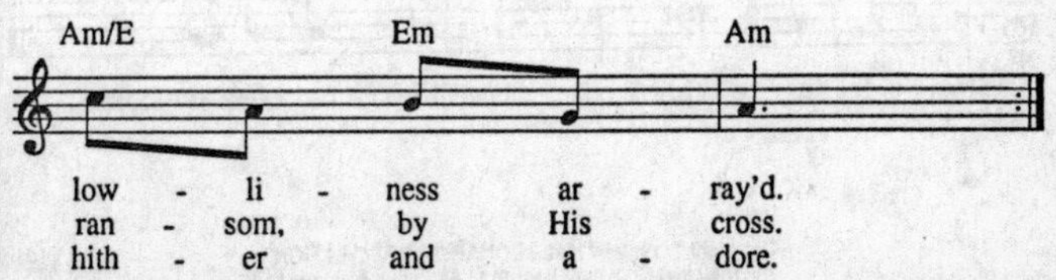
Am/E Em Am
low - li - ness ar - ray’d.
ran - som, by His cross.
hith - er and a - dore.

# A DAY, BRIGHT DAY OF GLORY

Traditional

Am
Dm
A day, bright day of glo - ry! Glad

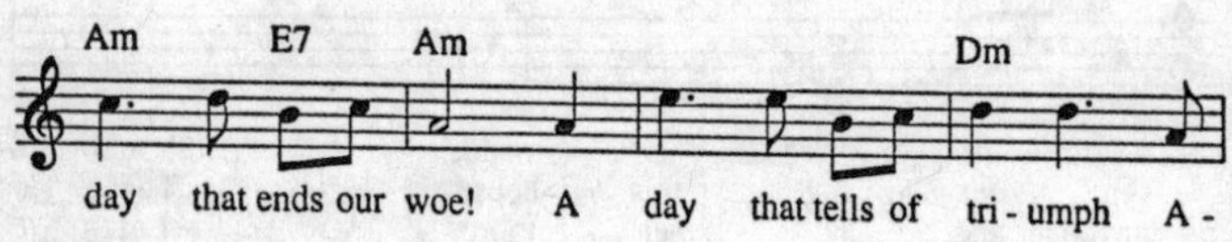
Am
E7
Am
Dm
day that ends our woe! A day that tells of tri - umph A -

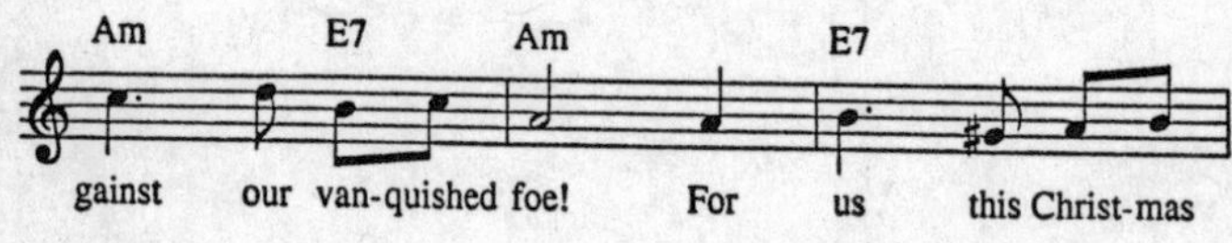
Am
E7
Am
E7
gainst our van-quished foe! For us this Christ-mas

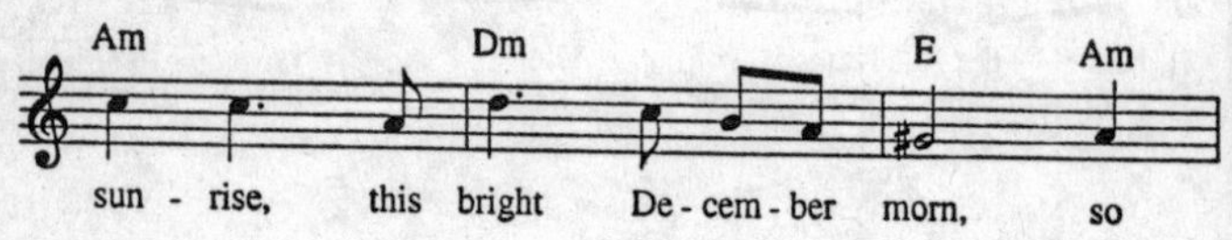
Am
Dm
E
Am
sun - rise, this bright De - cem - ber morn, so

E7
Am
Dm
E7
Am
sing, let us be joy - ous For Christ, our Lord is born!

# DECK THE HALL

Traditional Welsh Carol

F C F C F
1. Deck the hall with boughs of hol - ly,
'Tis the sea - son to be jol - ly,
2.,3. (See additional verses)
C7 F/C C7 F
Fa la la la la, la la la la.
Fa la la la la, la la la la.
C7 F C
Don we now our gay ap - par - rel,
F Dm C/G G7 C F C
Fa — la la — la la la la, Troll the an - cient
F C F B♭ F C7 F
Yule - tide car - ol, Fa la la la la, la la la la.

*Additional Verses*

2. See the blazing Yule before us, Fa la la la la, la la la la.
Strike the harp and join the chorus, Fa la la la la, la la la la.
Follow me in merry measure, Fa la la la la la la,
While I tell of Yuletide treasure, Fa la la la la, la la la la.

3. Fast away the old year passes, Fa la la la la, la la la la.
Hail the new, ye lads and lasses, Fa la la la la, la la la la.
Sing we joyous all together, Fa la la la la la la,
Heedless of the wind and weather, Fa la la la la, la la la la.

# DING DONG! MERRILY ON HIGH!

French Carol

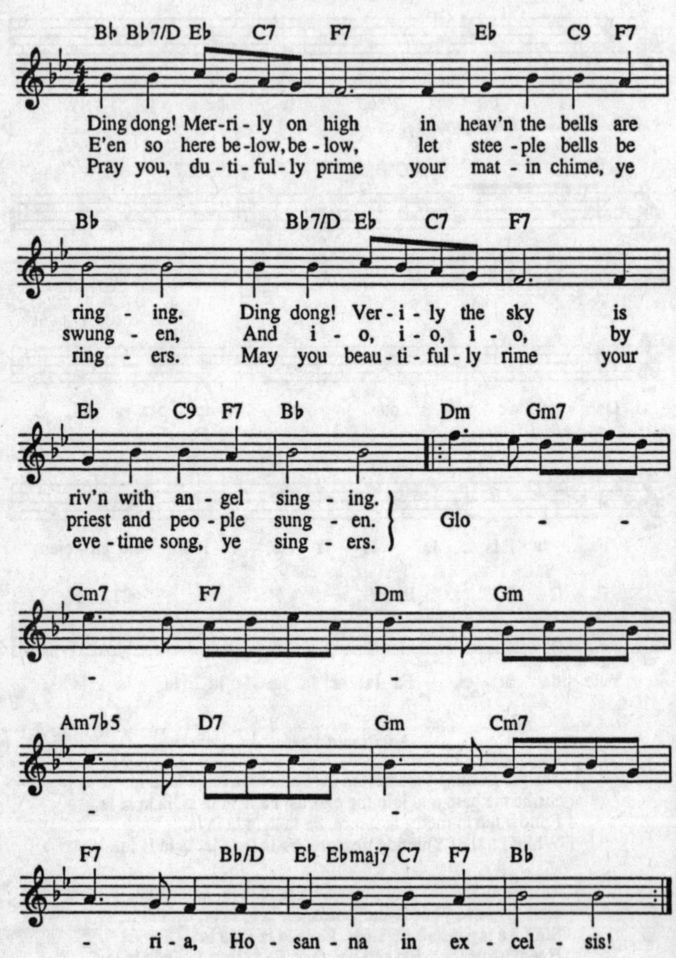
Bb Bb7/D Eb C7 F7 Eb C9 F7
Ding dong! Mer-ri-ly on high in heav'n the bells are
E'en so here be-low, be-low, let stee-ple bells be
Pray you, du-ti-ful-ly prime your mat-in chime, ye
Bb Bb7/D Eb C7 F7
ring-ing. Ding dong! Ver-i-ly the sky is
swung-en, And i-o, i-o, i-o, by
ring-ers. May you beau-ti-ful-ly rime your
Eb C9 F7 Bb Dm Gm7
riv'n with an-gel sing-ing.
priest and peo-ple sung-en.
eve-time song, ye sing-ers.
Glo-
Cm7 F7 Dm Gm
Am7b5 D7 Gm Cm7
F7 Bb/D Eb Ebmaj7 C7 F7 Bb
-ri-a, Ho-san-na in ex-cel-sis!

# EVERYWHERE, EVERYWHERE, CHRISTMAS TONIGHT

By LEWIS H. REDNER and PHILLIP BROOKS

G
Christ - mas in lands of the
Christ - mas where chil - dren are
D7 G D7
fir tree and pine, Christ - mas in
hope - ful and gay, Christ - mas where
G A7 D
lands of the palm tree and vine,
old men are pa - tient and gray,
D7 G B7
Christ - mas where snow peaks stand sol - emn and
Christ - mas where peace like a dove in its
Em C G
white Christ - mas where corn - fields lie
flight Broods o'er brave men in the
D7 G
sun - ny and bright.
thick of the fight.
Ev - 'ry-where,
C G/D D7 G
ev - 'ry-where, Christ - mas to - night.

# A FIRE IS STARTED IN BETHLEHEM

Traditional Castilian Carol

Gm
D
Here in Beth - le - hem this
In a cold and hum - ble
Wash - ing swad - dling clothes for
D7
Gm
Cm
D7
eve - ning, Springs a might - y Flame from
sta - ble, Blooms a per - fect white car -
Je - sus, Ma - ry by a stream is
Gm
C7
D7
Heav - en, Whom our self - ish - ness will be con -
na - tion, That be - comes a love - ly pur - ple
sing - ing. Spar-rows chirp to hear a joy - ful
Gm
D
C#dim7
Dm
Dm/A
A
sum - ing, And through whom we are for -
Li - ly, Sac - ri - ficed for our re -
greet - ing, And the rip - pling brook is

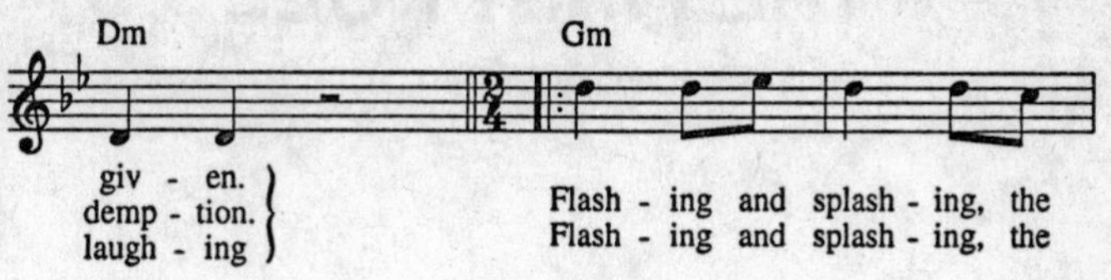
Dm
Gm
giv - en.
demp - tion.
laugh - ing
Flash - ing and splash - ing, the
Flash - ing and splash - ing, the

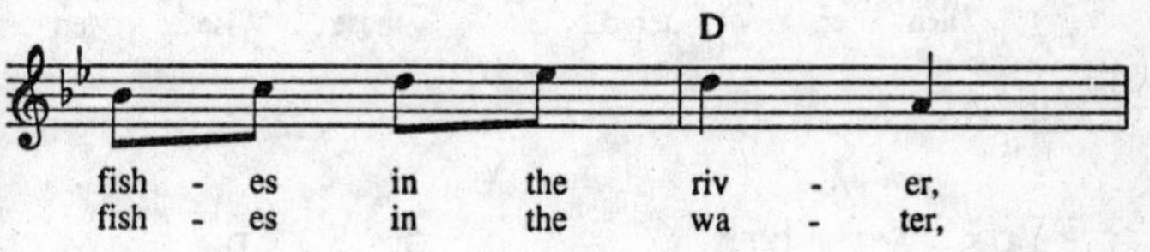
D
fish - es in the riv - er,
fish - es in the wa - ter,

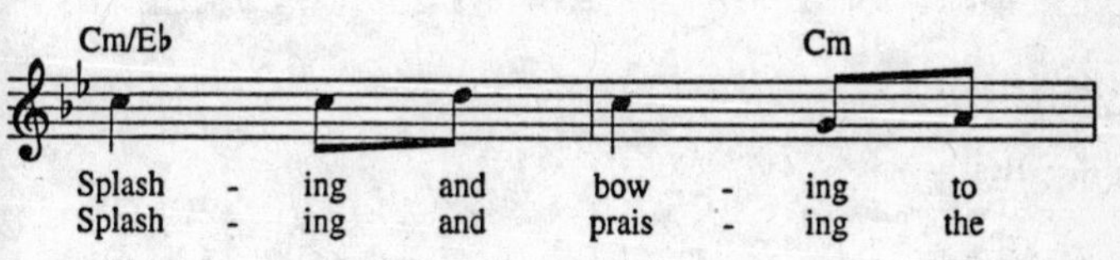
Cm/E♭
Cm
Splash - ing and bow - ing to
Splash - ing and prais - ing the

Gm
D
Gm
Christ from Heav - en com - ing;
Light from Heav - en dawn - ing.

# THE FIRST NOEL

17th Century English Carol

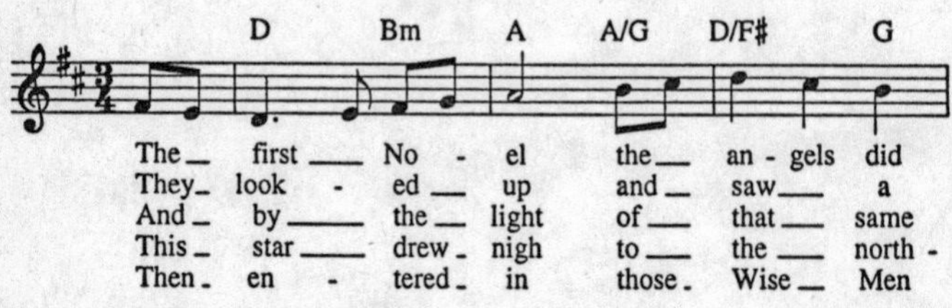
D Bm A A/G D/F# G
The first No - el the an - gels did
They look - ed up and saw a
And by the light of that same
This star drew nigh to the north -
Then en - tered in those Wise Men

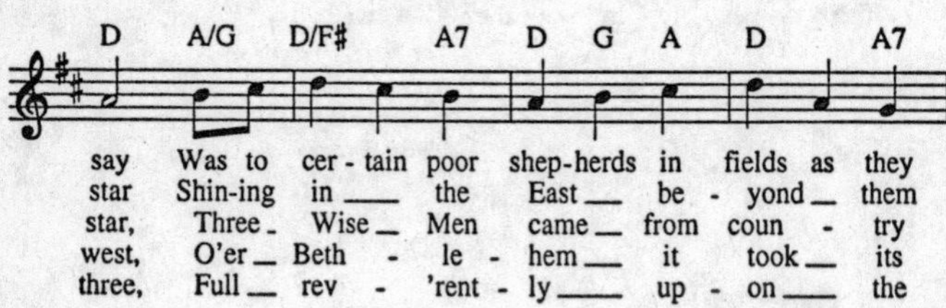
D A/G D/F# A7 D G A D A7
say Was to cer - tain poor shep-herds in fields as they
star Shin-ing in the East be - yond them
star, Three Wise Men came from coun - try
west, O'er Beth - le - hem it took its
three, Full rev - 'rent - ly up - on the

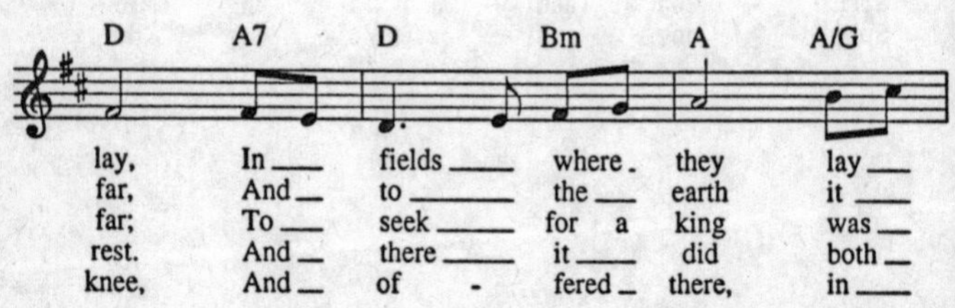
D A7 D Bm A A/G
lay, In fields where they lay
far, And to the earth it
far; To seek for a king was
rest. And there it did both
knee, And of - fered there, in

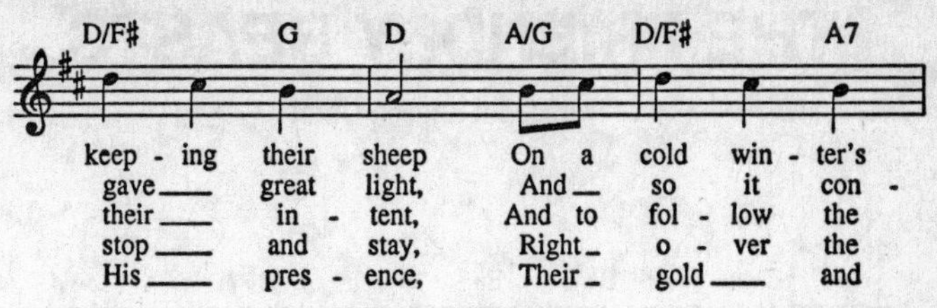
D/F# G D A/G D/F# A7
keep - ing their sheep On a cold win - ter's
gave great light, And so it con -
their in - tent, And to fol - low the
stop and stay, Right o - ver the
His pres - ence, Their gold and

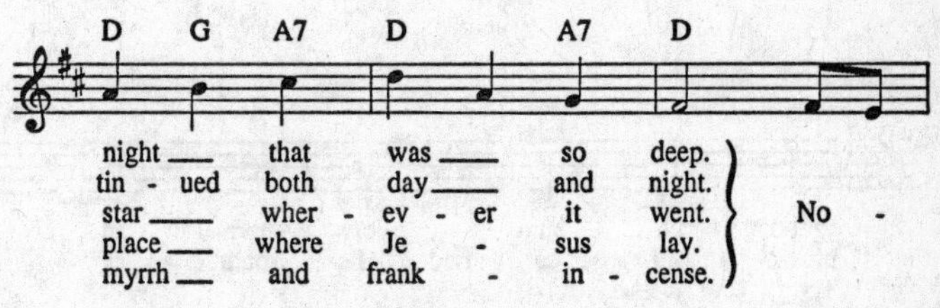
D G A7 D A7 D
night that was so deep.
tin - ued both day and night.
star wher - ev - er it went.
place where Je - sus lay.
myrrh and frank - in - cense.
No -

Bm F#m D G D A/C#
el, No - el, No - el, No - el,

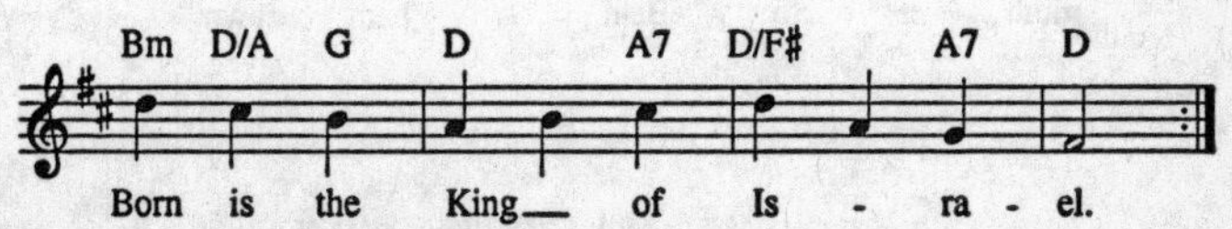
Bm D/A G D A7 D/F# A7 D
Born is the King of Is - ra - el.

# THE FRIENDLY BEASTS

Traditional English Carol

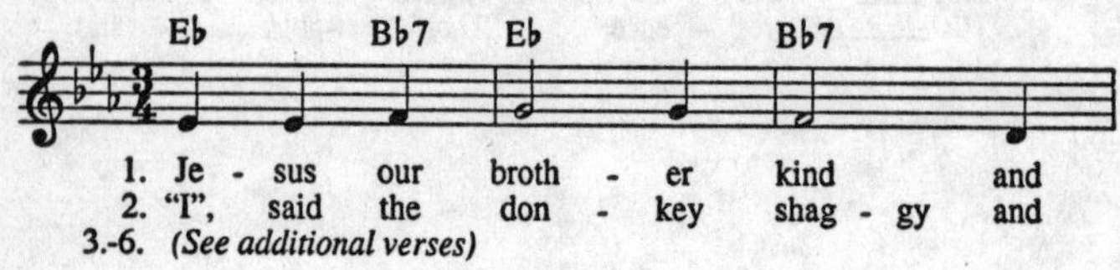
Eb
Bb7
Eb
Bb7
1. Je - sus our broth - er kind and
2. "I", said the don - key shag - gy and
3.-6. (See additional verses)

Eb
Ab
good Was hum - bly born in a
brown, "I car - ried His moth - er

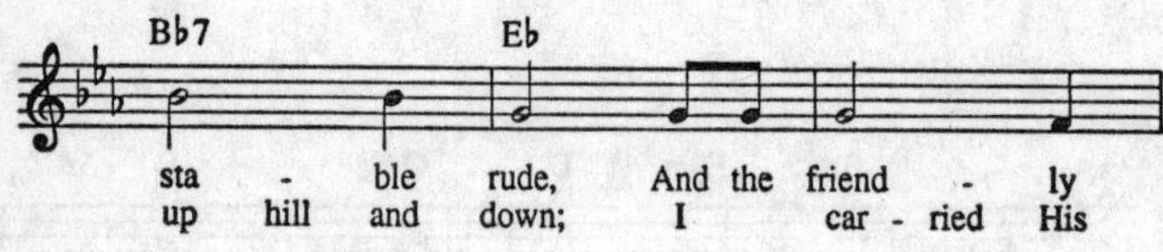
Bb7
Eb
sta - ble rude, And the friend - ly
up hill and down; I car - ried His

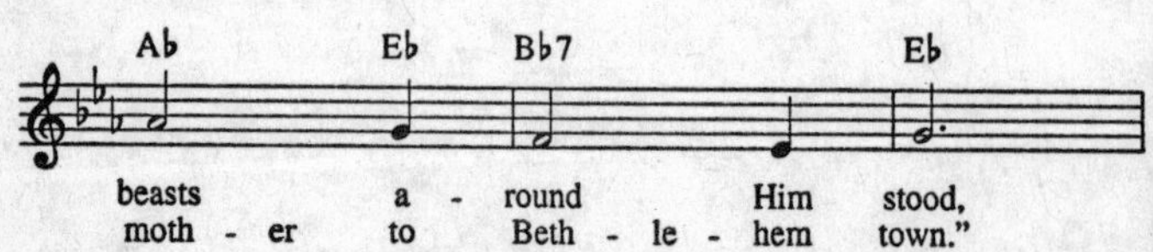
Ab
Eb
Bb7
Eb
beasts a - round Him stood,
moth - er to Beth - le - hem town."

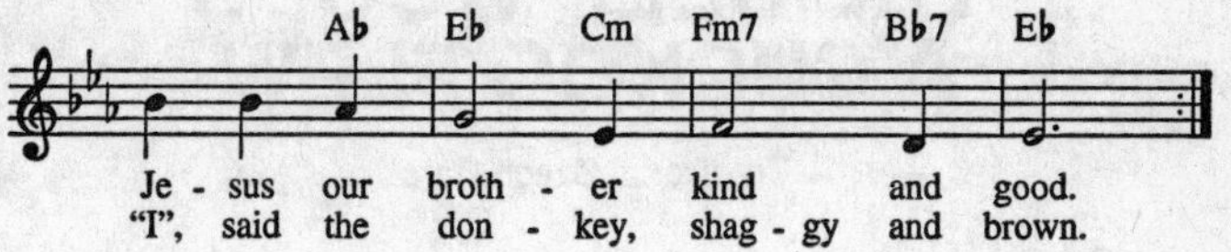
Ab Eb Cm Fm7 Bb7 Eb
Je - sus our broth - er kind and good.
"I", said the don - key, shag - gy and brown.

*Additional Verses*

3. "I," said the cow all white and red,
"I gave Him my manger for His bed;
I gave Him my hay to pillow His head."
"I," said the cow all white and red.

4. "I," said the sheep with the curly horn,
"I gave Him my wool for His blanket warm;
He wore my coat on Christmas morn."
"I," said the sheep with the curly horn.

5. "I," said the dove from the rafters high,
"I cooed Him to sleep that He would not cry;
We cooed Him to sleep, my mate and I."
"I," said the dove from the rafters high.

6. Thus every beast by some good spell,
In the stable dark was glad to tell
Of the gift he gave Emmanuel,
The gift he gave Emmanuel.

# FROM OUT THE DEEP WOODS A CUCKOO FLEW

Traditional Czech Carol

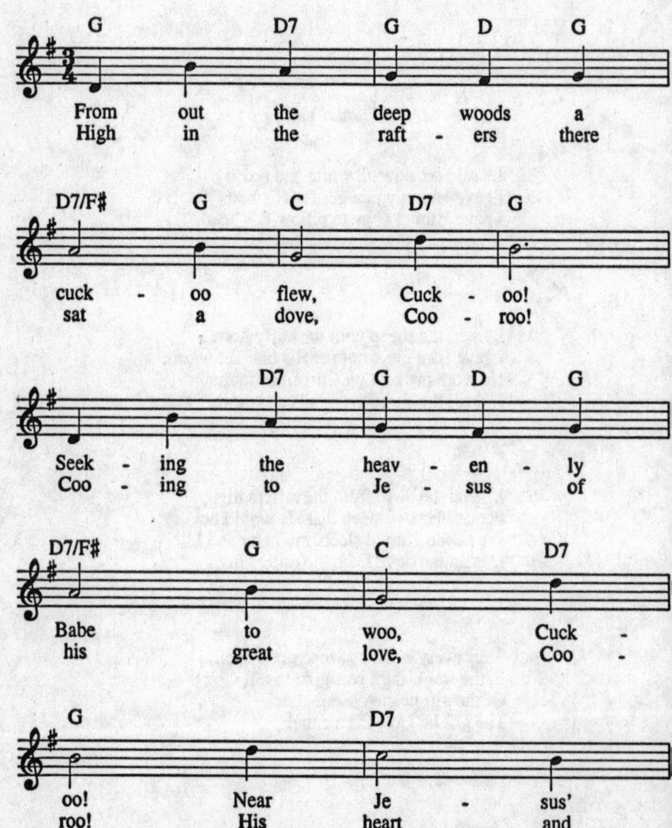
G D7 G D G
From out the deep woods a
High in the raft - ers there
D7/F# G C D7 G
cuck - oo flew, Cuck - oo!
sat a dove, Coo - roo!
D7 G D G
Seek - ing the heav - en - ly
Coo - ing to Je - sus of
D7/F# G C D7
Babe to woo, Cuck -
his great love, Coo -
G D7
oo! Near Je - sus'
roo! His heart and

Edim7/D
bed, he gave in
voice so full of

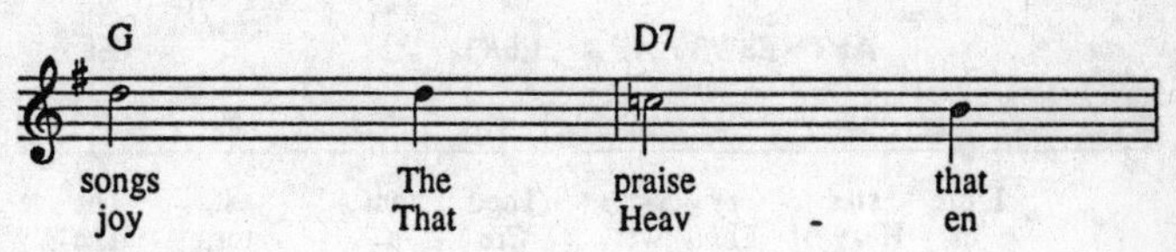
G
D7
songs The praise that
joy That Heav - en

Edim7/D
to our God be -
sent this love - ly

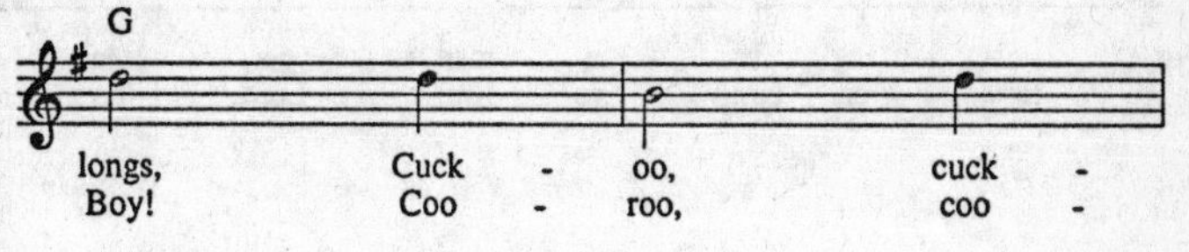
G
longs, Cuck - oo, cuck -
Boy! Coo - roo, coo -

D7
G
oo, cuck - oo!
roo, coo - roo!

# FROM STARRY SKIES THOU COMEST

Words and Music by
ALPHONSUS LIGUORI

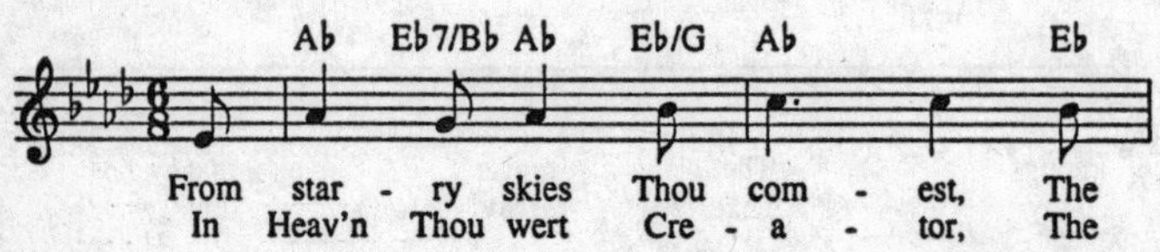
Ab Eb7/Bb Ab Eb/G Ab Eb
From star - ry skies Thou com - est, The
In Heav'n Thou wert Cre - a - tor, The

Ab Eb Ab/Eb
King of Heav - en fore - told, Ap -
True and On - ly Word, Yet

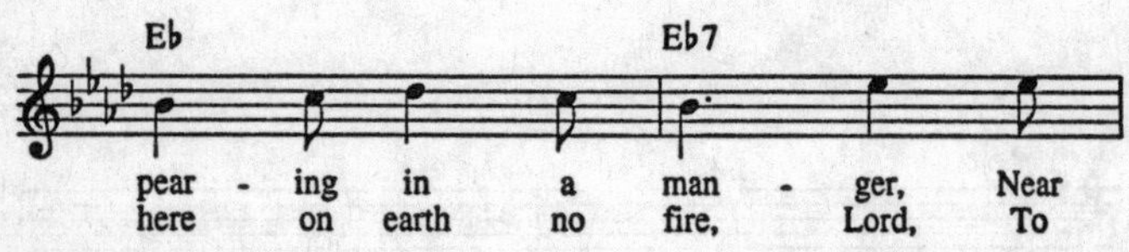
Eb Eb7
pear - ing in a man - ger, Near
here on earth no fire, Lord, To

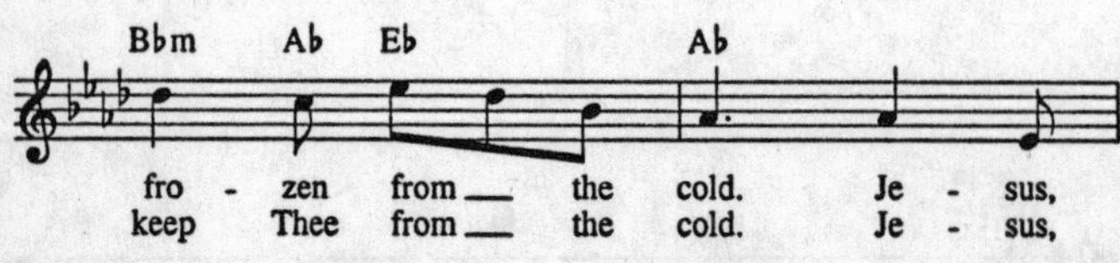
Bbm Ab Eb Ab
fro - zen from the cold. Je - sus,
keep Thee from the cold. Je - sus,

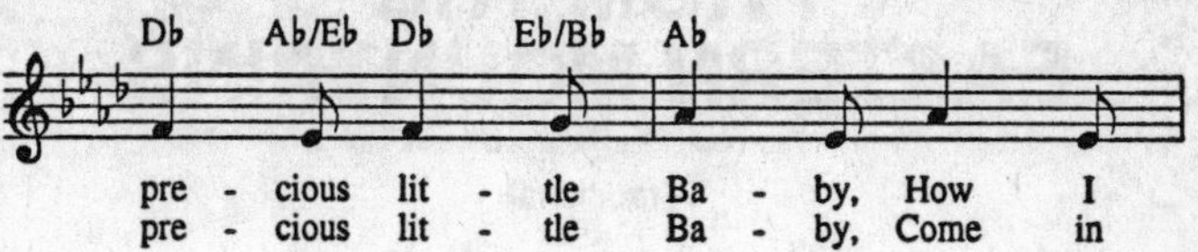
Db Ab/Eb Db Eb/Bb Ab
pre - cious lit - tle Ba - by, How I
pre - cious lit - tle Ba - by, Come in

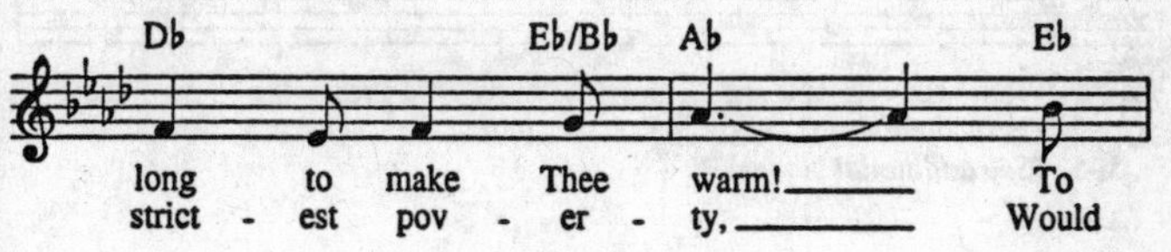
Db Eb/Bb Ab Eb
long to make Thee warm! To
strict - est pov - er - ty, Would

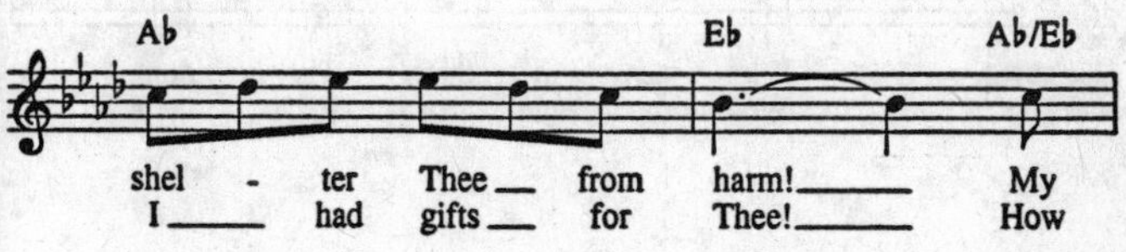
Ab Eb Ab/Eb
shel - ter Thee from harm! My
I had gifts for Thee! How

Eb Eb7
heart is filled with pit - y,
won - der - ful God's love that

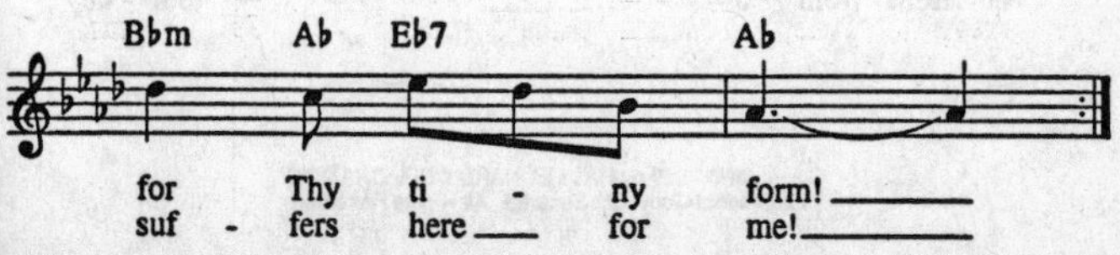
Bbm Ab Eb7 Ab
for Thy ti - ny form!
suf - fers here for me!

# FROM THE EASTERN MOUNTAINS

Traditional

F C7/G F/A C7 F/A B♭
1. From the East - ern moun - tains Press - ing on they
2. There their Lord and Sav - iour Meek and low - ly
3.-5. (See additional verses)

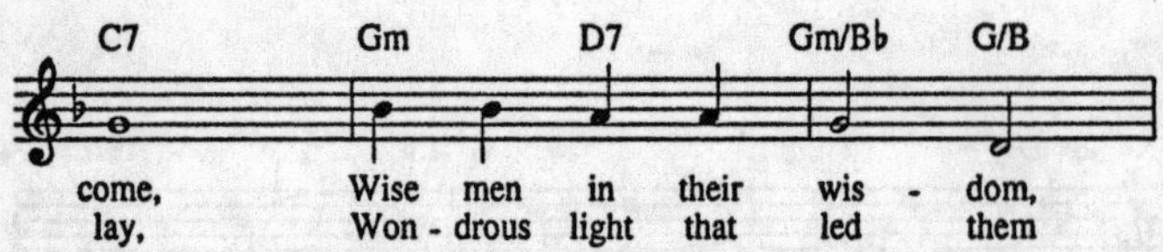
C7 Gm D7 Gm/B♭ G/B
come, Wise men in their wis - dom,
lay, Won - drous light that led them

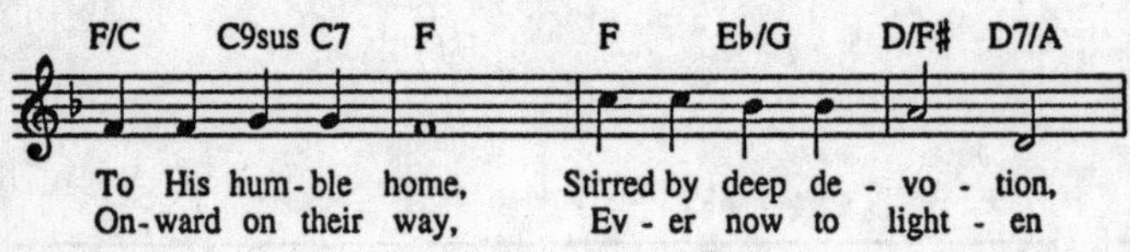
F/C C9sus C7 F F E♭/G D/F♯ D7/A
To His hum - ble home, Stirred by deep de - vo - tion,
On - ward on their way, Ev - er now to light - en

Gm B♭6 C9sus C7 Gm C7
Hast - ing from a - far,
Na - tions from a - far,
Ev - er jour - n'ing
As they jour - ney

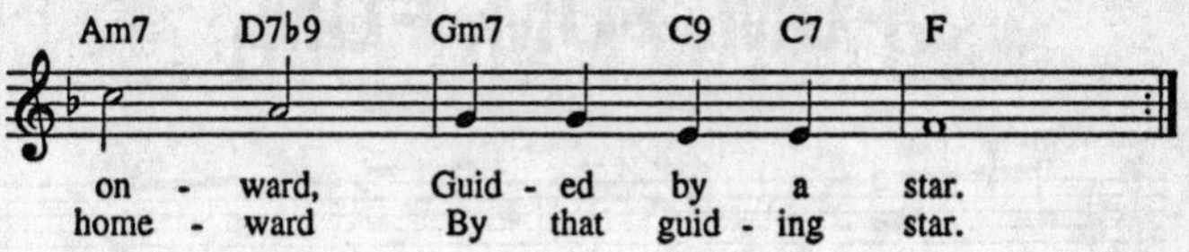
Am7
D7♭9
Gm7
C9
C7
F
on - ward, Guid - ed by a star.
home - ward By that guid - ing star.

*Additional Verses*

3. Thou who in a manger
Once hast lowly lain,
Who dost now in glory
O'er all kingdoms reign,
Gather in the heathen
Who in lands afar
Ne'er have seen the brightness
Of Thy guiding star.

4. Gather in the outcasts,
All who have astray,
Throw Thy radiance o'er them,
Guide them on their way,
Those who never knew Thee,
Those who have wandered far,
Guide them by the brightness
Of Thy guiding star.

5. Onward through the darkness
Of the lonely night,
Shining still before, them
With Thy kindly light,
Guide them, Jew and Gentile,
Homeward from afar,
Young and old together,
By Thy guiding star.

# FUM, FUM, FUM

Traditional Catalonian Carol

Am Dm E7
On this joy - ful Christ - mas day sing
Thanks to God for hol - i - days sing
Am E7 Am
Fum, Fum, Fum. On this joy - ful
Fum, Fum, Fum. Thanks to God for
Dm E7 Am E7
Christ - mas day sing Fum, Fum,
hol - i - days, sing Fum, Fum,
Am C G7
Fum. For a bless - ed Babe was
Fum. Now we all our voic - es
C G7
born up - on this day at break of
raise, and sing a song of grate - ful
C F Dm
morn. In a man - ger poor and
praise, Cel - e - brate in song and
E7 Am E Am Dm
low - ly lay the Son of God most
sto - ry, all the won - ders of his
E7 Am E7 Am
ho - ly, Fum, Fum, Fum.
glo - ry, Fum, Fum, Fum.

# GLAD CHRISTMAS BELLS

Traditional American Carol

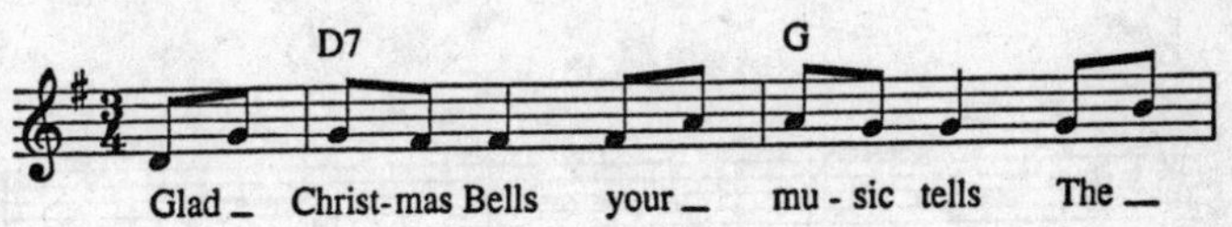
D7
G
Glad Christ-mas Bells your mu - sic tells The

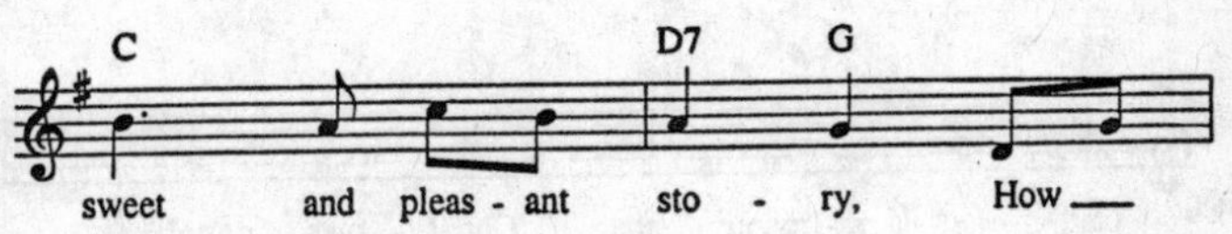
C
D7
G
sweet and pleas - ant sto - ry, How

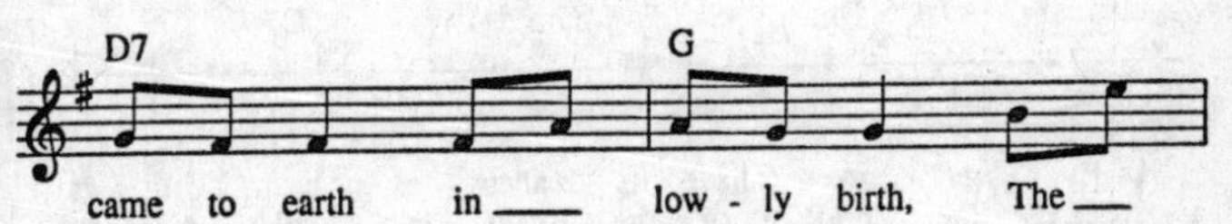
D7
G
came to earth in low - ly birth, The

D7
G
Lord of life and glo - ry.

# GATHER AROUND THE CHRISTMAS TREE

By JOHN H. HOPKINS

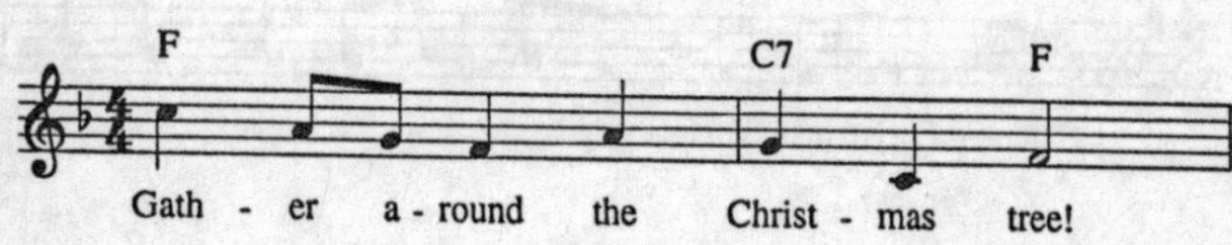
F
C7
F
Gath - er a - round the Christ - mas tree!

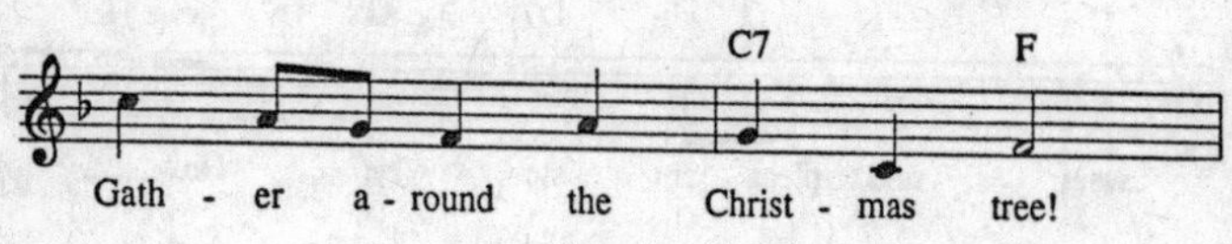
C7
F
Gath - er a - round the Christ - mas tree!

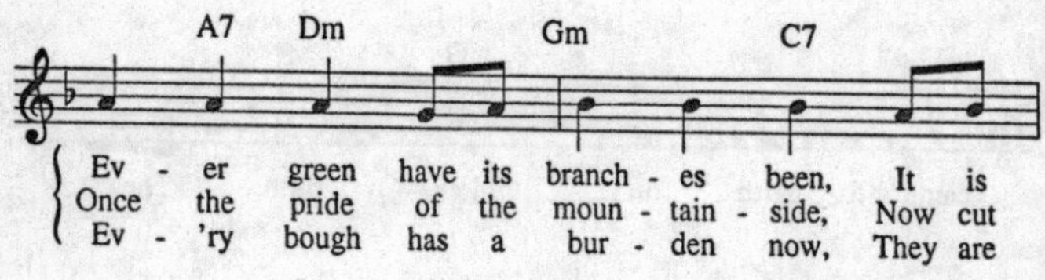
A7
Dm
Gm
C7
Ev - er green have its branch - es been, It is
Once the pride of the moun - tain - side, Now cut
Ev - 'ry bough has a bur - den now, They are

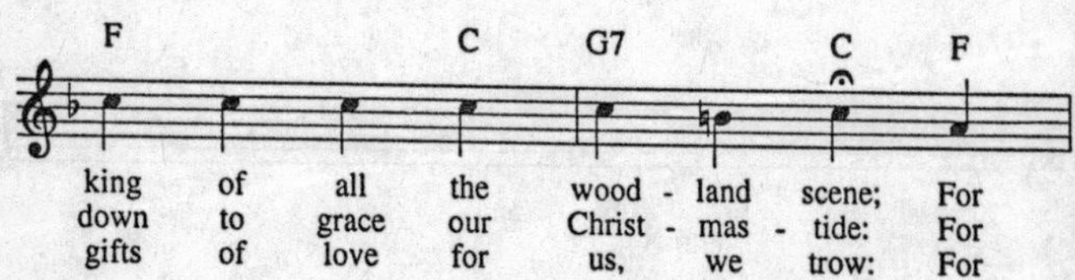
F
C
G7
C
F
king of all the wood - land scene; For
down to grace our Christ - mas - tide: For
gifts of love for us, we trow: For

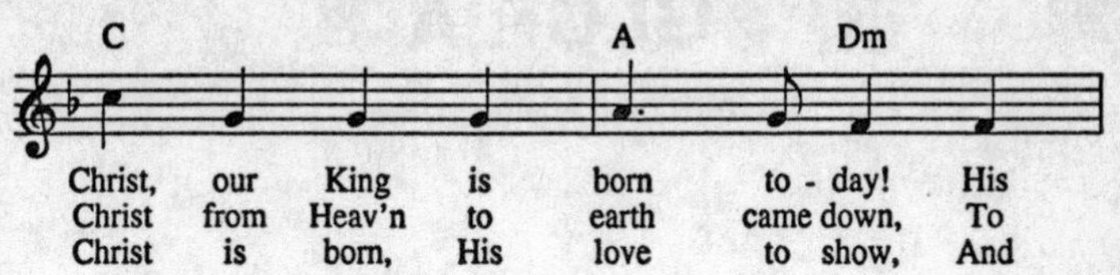
C A Dm
Christ, our King is born to - day! His
Christ from Heav'n to earth came down, To
Christ is born, His love to show, And

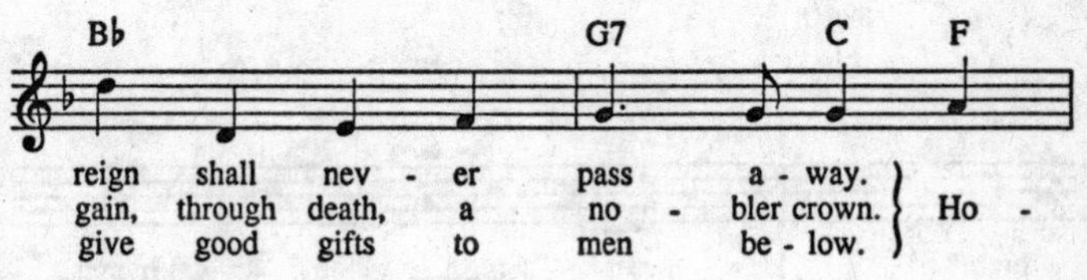
B♭ G7 C F
reign shall nev - er pass a - way.
gain, through death, a no - bler crown. Ho -
give good gifts to men be - low.

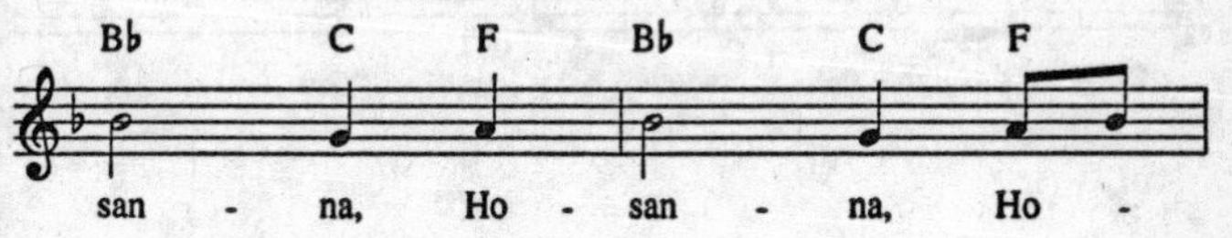
B♭ C F B♭ C F
san - na, Ho - san - na, Ho -

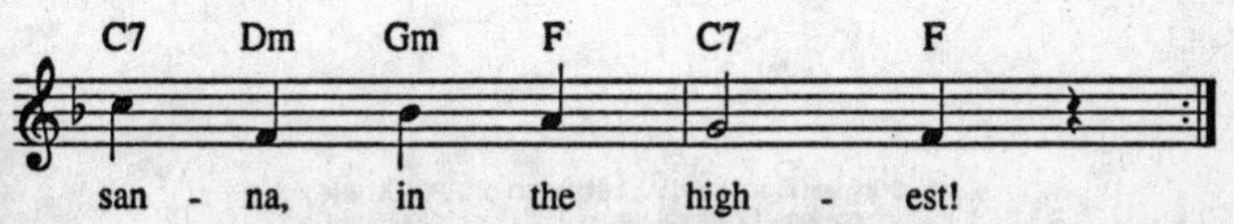
C7 Dm Gm F C7 F
san - na, in the high - est!

# GLORIA

Traditional Austrian Carol

C
G
"Glo - ri - a, Glo - ri - a, To God on

C
G
C
high!" How sweet - ly__ an - gel hymns

G
C
G
Ring through_ the__ snow - y sky: "Glo - ri - a,

C
G
C
Dm7
G
C
Glo - ri - a, To God on High!"

# GO TELL IT ON THE MOUNTAIN

African-American Spiritual

F Bb F C
Go, tell it on the moun - tain, O - ver the hills and
F Bb
ev - 'ry - where; Go, tell it on the
Last time
F Dm Bb C F Fine
moun - tain That Je - sus Christ is born.
While
The
Down
shep - herds kept their watch - ing O'er
shep - herds feared and trem - bled When,
in a low - ly man - ger Our
C Dm C F
si - lent flocks by night, Be - hold, through-out the
lo! a - bove the earth Rang out the an - gel
hum - ble Christ was born, And God sent us sal -
G7 C C7 D.C.
heav - ens There shone a ho - ly light.
cho - rus That hailed our Sav - ior's birth.
va - tion That bless - ed Christ - mas morn.

# GOD REST YE MERRY, GENTLEMEN

19th Century English Carol

Em
B7/F#
Em/G
Am
God rest ye mer - ry, gen - tle - men, Let
In Beth - le - hem, in Jew - ry, This
From God our Heav'n - ly Fa - ther, A

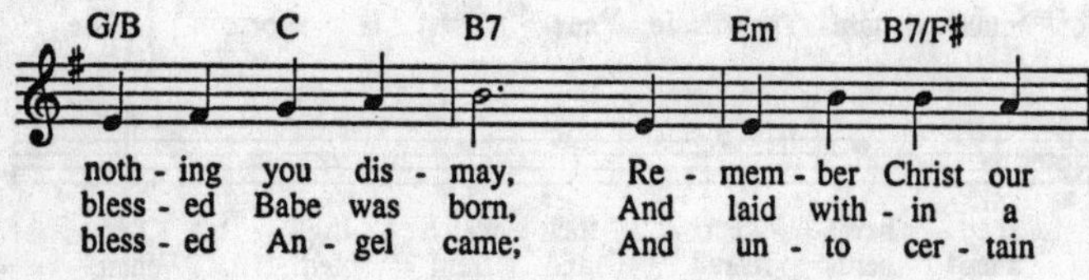
G/B
C
B7
Em
B7/F#
noth - ing you dis - may, Re - mem - ber Christ our
bless - ed Babe was born, And laid with - in a
bless - ed An - gel came; And un - to cer - tain

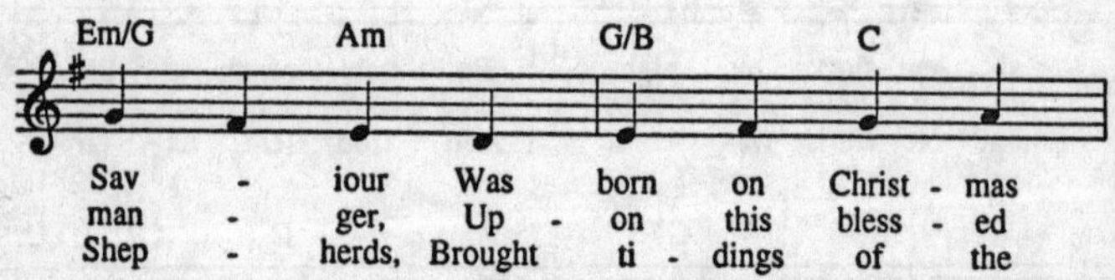
Em/G
Am
G/B
C
Sav - iour Was born on Christ - mas
man - ger, Up - on this bless - ed
Shep - herds, Brought ti - dings of the

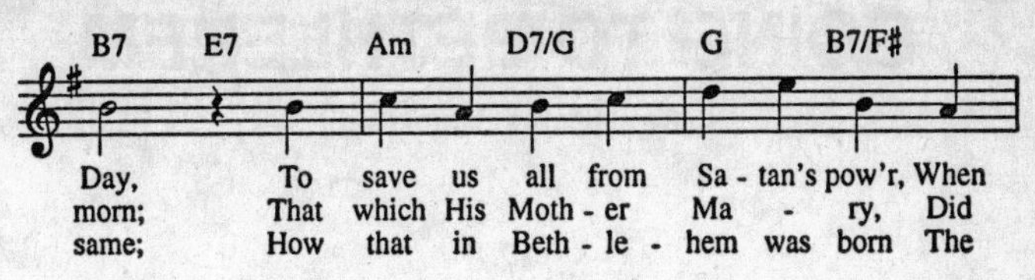
B7 E7 Am D7/G G B7/F#
Day, To save us all from Sa - tan's pow'r, When
morn; That which His Moth - er Ma - ry, Did
same; How that in Beth - le - hem was born The

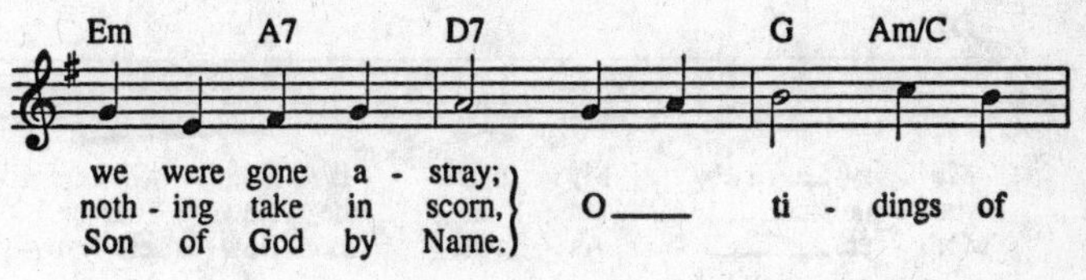
Em A7 D7 G Am/C
we were gone a - stray;
noth - ing take in scorn,
Son of God by Name.
O ti - dings of

D7 B7/D# Em A7 D
com - fort and joy, com-fort and joy, O

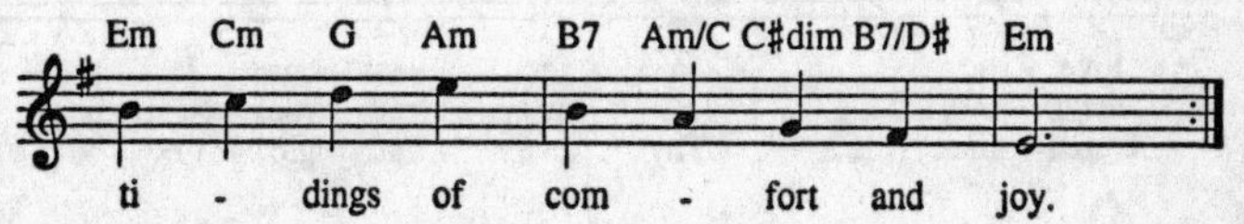
Em Cm G Am B7 Am/C C#dim B7/D# Em
ti - dings of com - fort and joy.

# GOING TO BETHLEHEM

Traditional Chilean Carol

G
Good eve - ning, dear, gen - tle
Good - bye to you lit - tle
O Ma - ry, Ho - li - est
D7
Ma - ry, My heart is filled with de -
Man - uel, Un - til the New Year be -
Moth - er, As pure as flow - ers un -
G
D7
G
vo - tion, My heart is filled with de -
gin - ning, Un - til the New Year be -
fold - ing, As pure as flow - ers un -
D7
vo - tion; For you and Je - sus so
gin - ning; I'll see you af - ter the
fold - ing; I come on this eve of
G
love - ly, A fer - vent prayer I am
shear - ing, So rich from wool you'll be
Christ - mas, Thy love and glo - ry be -

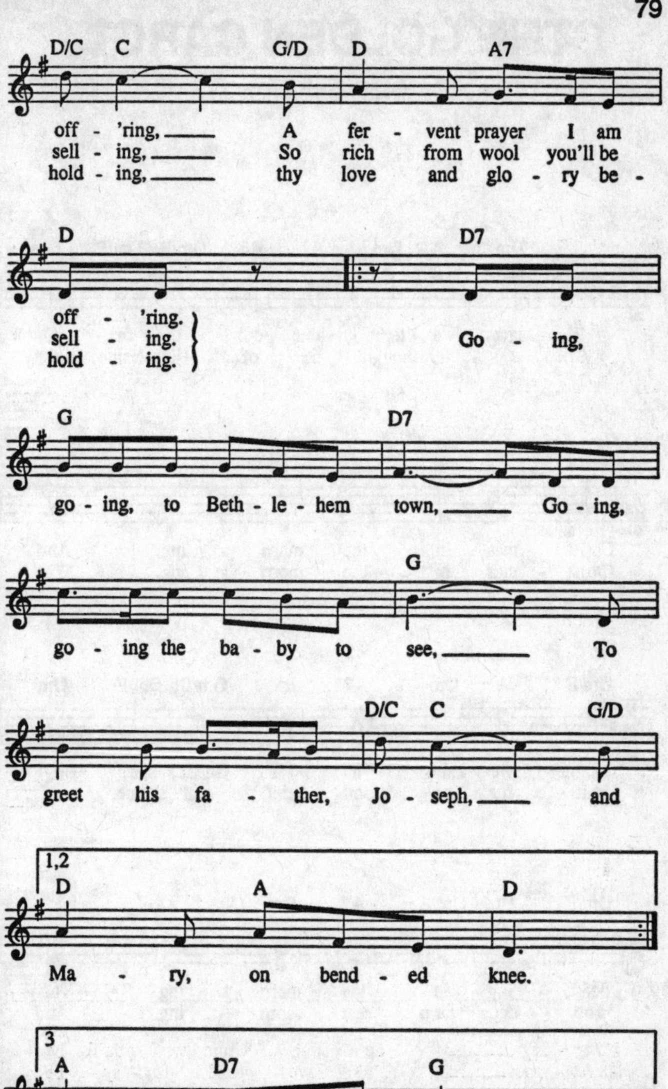
D/C C G/D D A7
off - 'ring, A fer - vent prayer I am
sell - ing, So rich from wool you'll be
hold - ing, thy love and glo - ry be -
D D7
off - 'ring.
sell - ing.
hold - ing.
Go - ing,
G D7
go - ing, to Beth - le - hem town, Go - ing,
G
go - ing the ba - by to see, To
D/C C G/D
greet his fa - ther, Jo - seph, and
1,2
D A D
Ma - ry, on bend - ed knee.
3
A D7 G
Ma - ry, on bend - ed knee.

# THE GOLDEN CAROL

Old English Carol

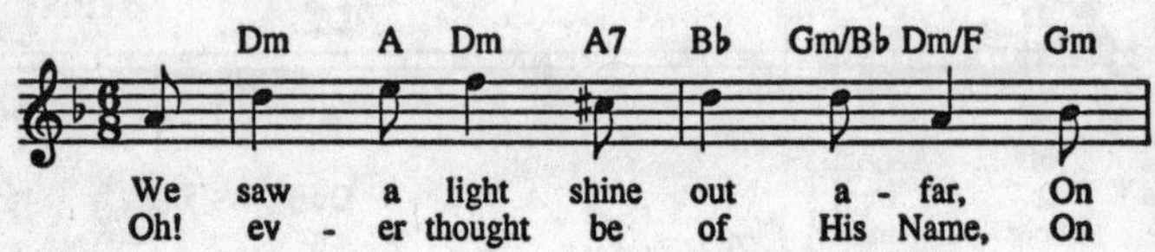
Dm A Dm A7 B♭ Gm/B♭ Dm/F Gm
We saw a light shine out a - far, On
Oh! ev - er thought be of His Name, On

Dm/A A Dm
Christ - mas in the morn - ing, And
Christ - mas in the morn - ing, Who

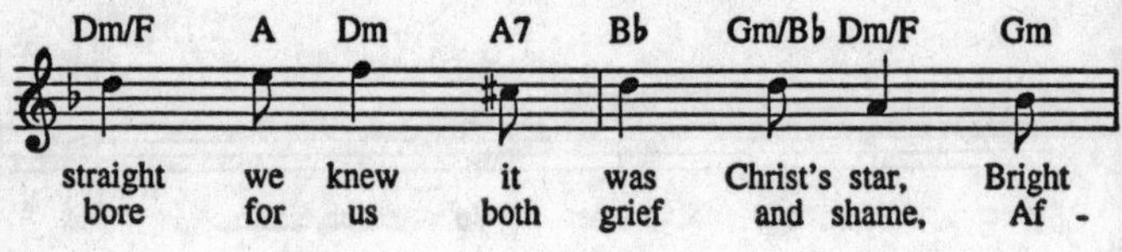
Dm/F A Dm A7 B♭ Gm/B♭ Dm/F Gm
straight we knew it was Christ's star, Bright
bore for us both grief and shame, Af -

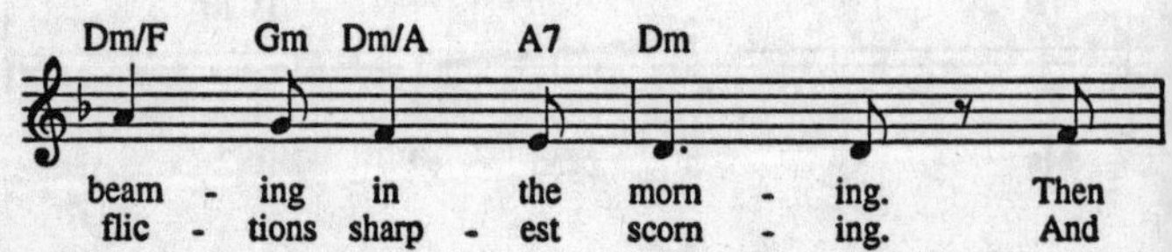
Dm/F Gm Dm/A A7 Dm
beam - ing in the morn - ing. Then
flic - tions sharp - est scorn - ing. And

Gm6
Bb/F Em7b5
A
Dm
A
did we fall on bend - ed knee, On
may we die (when death shall come), On

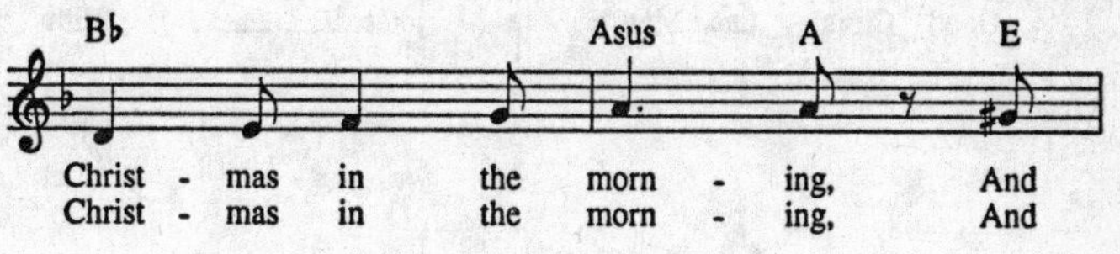
Bb
Asus
A
E
Christ - mas in the morn - ing, And
Christ - mas in the morn - ing, And

A
Dm
A
Dm
prais'd the Lord, who'd let us see His
see in heav'n, our glo - ri'us home, That

Gm
A
Dm
glo - ry at its dawn - ing.
Star of Christ - mas morn - ing.

# GOOD CHRISTIAN MEN, REJOICE

14th Century German Melody

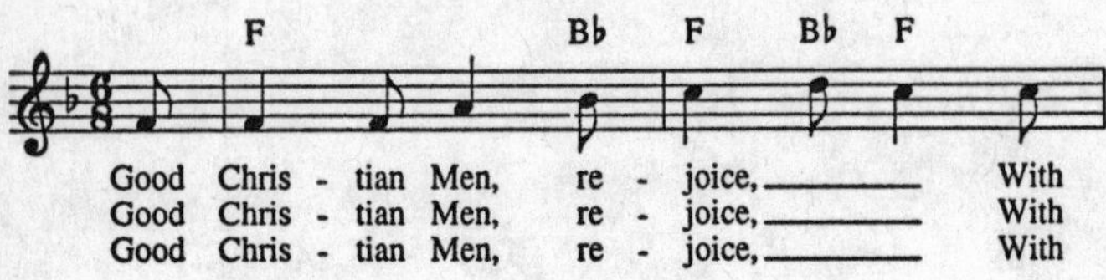
F
B♭
F
B♭
F
Good Chris - tian Men, re - joice, With
Good Chris - tian Men, re - joice, With
Good Chris - tian Men, re - joice, With

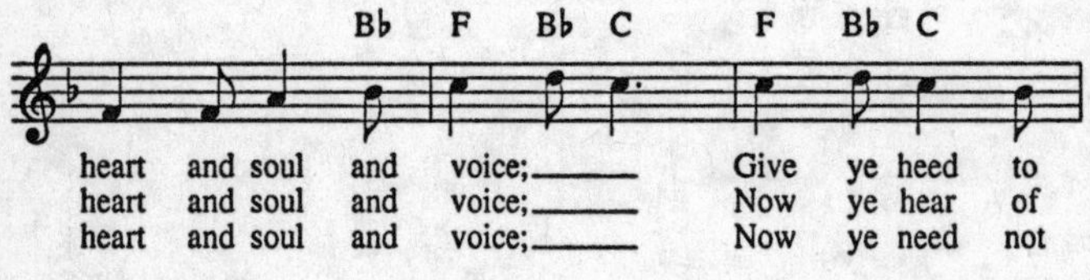
B♭
F
B♭ C
F
B♭ C
heart and soul and voice; Give ye heed to
heart and soul and voice; Now ye hear of
heart and soul and voice; Now ye need not

F/C
C♯dim Dm
B♭
F/A
Gm
C7
what we say: News! News! Je - sus Christ is
end - less bliss; Joy! Joy! Je - sus Christ was
fear the grave; Peace! Peace! Je - sus Christ was

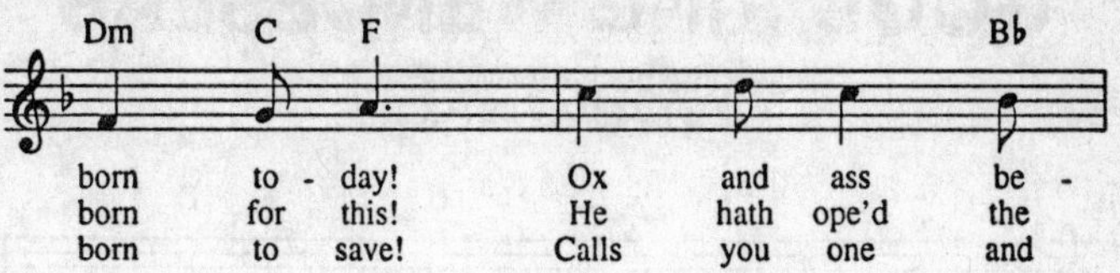
Dm C F Bb
born to - day! Ox and ass be -
born for this! He hath ope'd the
born to save! Calls you one and

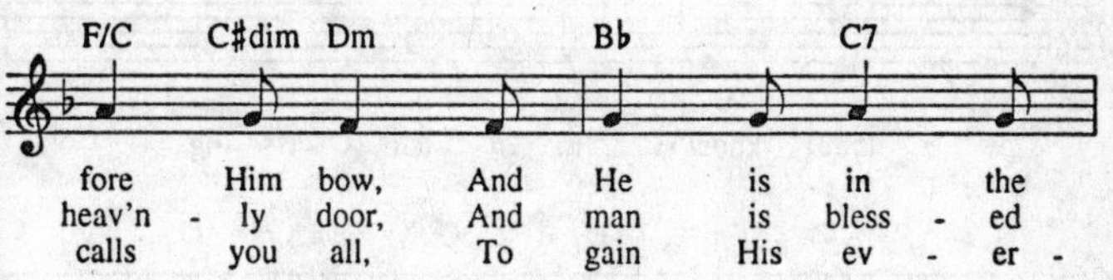
F/C C#dim Dm Bb C7
fore Him bow, And He is in the
heav'n - ly door, And man is bless - ed
calls you all, To gain His ev - er -

Dm C F Bb C7/G
man - ger now; Christ is born to -
ev - er - more. Christ was born for
last - ing hall. Christ was born to

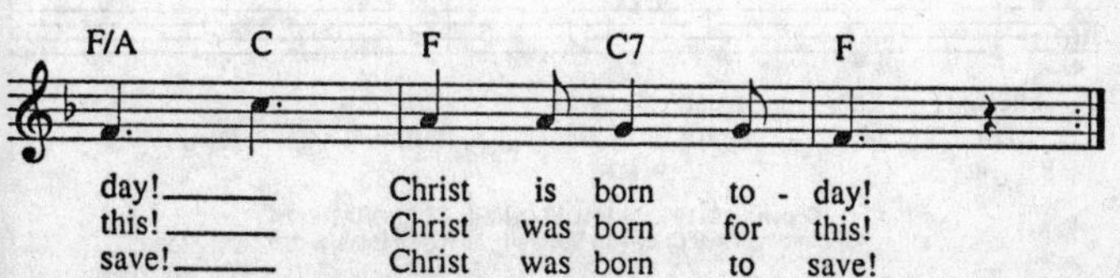
F/A C F C7 F
day! Christ is born to - day!
this! Christ was born for this!
save! Christ was born to save!

# GOOD KING WENCESLAS

Words by JOHN M. NEALE
Music by PIAE CANTIONES

G Em D G D
1. Good King Wen - ces - las looked out
2. "Hith - er, page, and stand by me,
3.-5. (See additional verses)
C G C D7 G
On the feast of Ste - phen,
If thou know'st it, tell - ing,
Em D G D
When the snow lay 'round a - bout,
Yon - der pea - sant, who is he?
C G C D7 G
Deep, and crisp, and e - ven;
Where and what his dwell - ing?"
D7 G D7 Em
Bright - ly shone the moon that night,
'Sire, he lives a good league hence,
C G C D7 G
Though the frost was cru - el,
Un - der - neath the moun - tain,

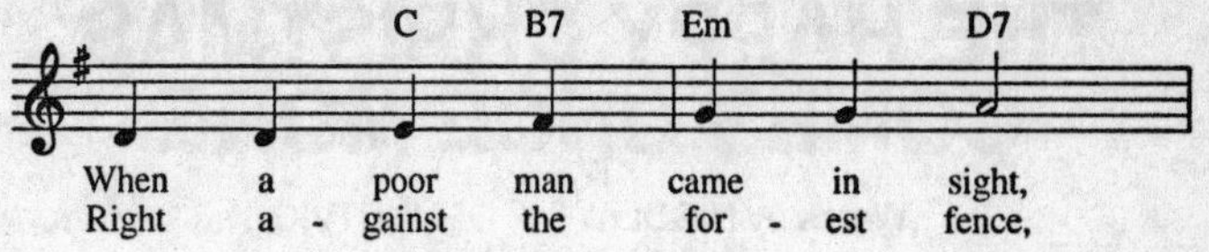
C B7 Em D7
When a poor man came in sight,
Right a - gainst the for - est fence,

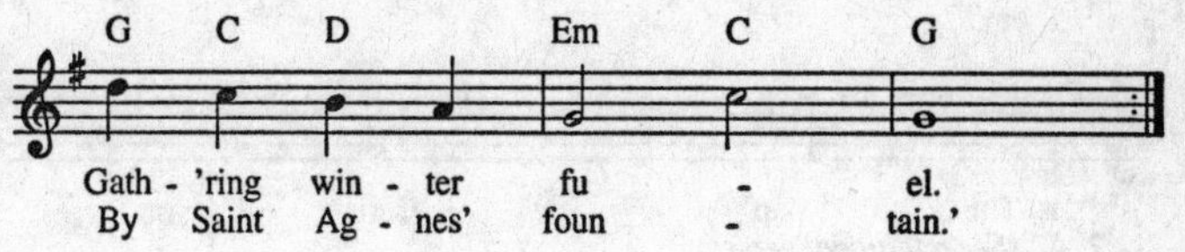
G C D Em C G
Gath - 'ring win - ter fu - el.
By Saint Ag - nes' foun - tain.'

*Additional Verses*

3. 'Bring me flesh, and bring me wine,
Bring me pine-logs hither:
Thou and I will see him dine,
When we bear them thither.'
Page and monarch, forth they went,
Forth they went together;
Through the rude wind's wild lament
And the bitter weather.

4. 'Sire, the night is darker now,
And the wind blows stronger;
Fails my heart, I know not how;
I can go no longer.'
'Mark my footsteps good, my page;
Tread thou in them boldly:
Thou shalt find the winter's rage
Freeze thy blood less coldly.'

5. In his master's steps he trod,
Where the snow lay dinted;
Heat was in the very sod
Which the saint had printed.
Therefore, Christian men, be sure,
Wealth or rank possessing,
Ye who now will bless the poor,
Shall yourselves find blessing.

# THE HAPPY CHRISTMAS COMES ONCE MORE

Words by NICOLAI F.S. GRUNDTVIG
Music by C. BALLE

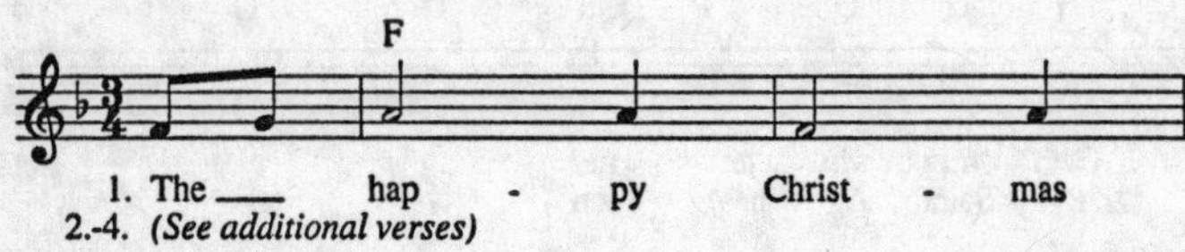
F
1. The hap - py Christ - mas
2.-4. (See additional verses)

C
comes once more, The heav'n - ly

F
Guest is at the

C
F
door, The bless - ed words the

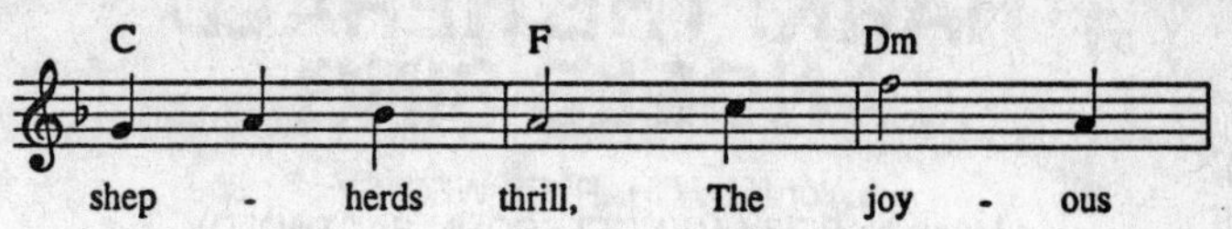
C
F
Dm
shep - herds thrill, The joy - ous

B♭6
F
C7
F
ti - dings, peace, good — will.

*Additional Verses*

2. To David's city let us fly,
   Where angels sing beneath the sky,
   Through plain and village pressing near,
   And news from God with shepherds hear.

3. O, let us go with quiet mind,
   The gentle Babe with shepherds find,
   To gaze on Him who gladdens them,
   The loveliest flow'r on Jesse's stem.

4. Come, Jesus glorious heav'nly guest,
   Keep Thine own Christmas in our breast;
   Then David's harp-string, hushed so long
   Shall swell our jubilee of song.

# HARK! THE HERALD ANGELS SING

Words by CHARLES WESLEY
Music by FELIX MENDELSSOHN-BARTHOLDY

G
D7
Hark! the her - ald an - gels sing.
Christ, by high - est heav'n a - dored,
Mild He lays His glo - ry by,
G
C
G
D7
G
Glo - ry to the new - born King;
Christ, the ev - er - last - ing Lord;
Born that man no more may die,
Em
A7
Peace on earth, and mer - cy mild.
Late in time be - hold Him come,
Born to raise the sons of earth,
D
A7
D
A7
D
God and sin - ners re - con - ciled!
Off - spring of the vir - gin's womb.
Born to give them sec - ond birth.
G
D7
G
D7
Joy - ful all ye na - tions, rise,
Veil'd in flesh the God - head see:
Ris'n with heal - ing in His wings,

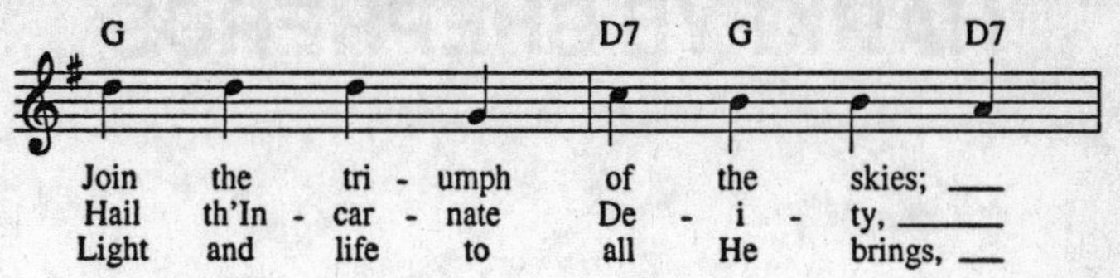
G D7 G D7
Join the tri - umph of the skies; ___
Hail th'In - car - nate De - i - ty, ___
Light and life to all He brings, ___

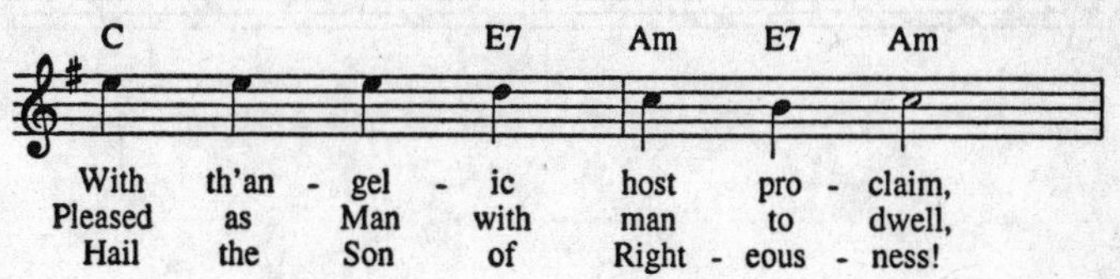
C E7 Am E7 Am
With th'an - gel - ic host pro - claim,
Pleased as Man with man to dwell,
Hail the Son of Right - eous - ness!

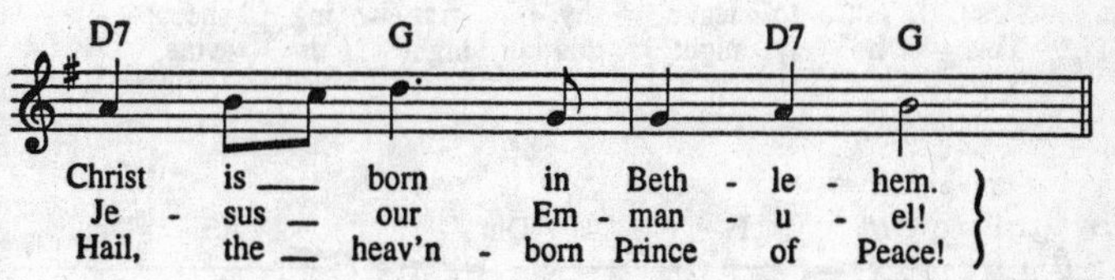
D7 G D7 G
Christ is ___ born in Beth - le - hem.
Je - sus ___ our Em - man - u - el!
Hail, the ___ heav'n - born Prince of Peace!

C E7 Am E7 Am
Hark! the her - ald an - gels sing,

D7 G D7 G
Glo - ry ___ to the new - born King.

# HARK! YE SHEPHERDS

Traditional Italian Carol

F C7/F F Dm A/E Dm
Hark! ye ___ shep - herds, has - ten to the man - ger,
Haste ye ___ shep - herds, from the vale and moun - tain,

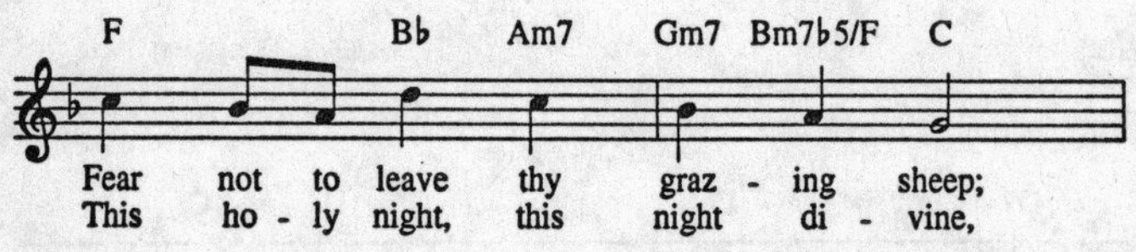
F B♭ Am7 Gm7 Bm7♭5/F C
Fear not to leave thy graz - ing sheep;
This ho - ly night, this night di - vine,

F C7/F F Dm A/E Dm
Hear the ___ host of heav - en loud pro - claim - ing,
Thus spake _ an - gels, tell - ing the glad ti - dings,

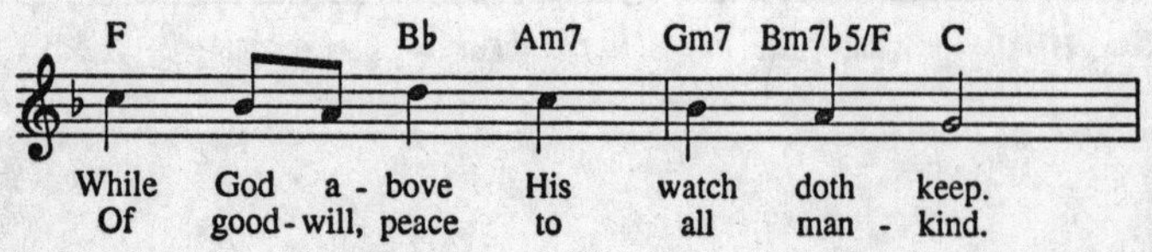
F B♭ Am7 Gm7 Bm7♭5/F C
While God a - bove His watch doth keep.
Of good - will, peace to all man - kind.

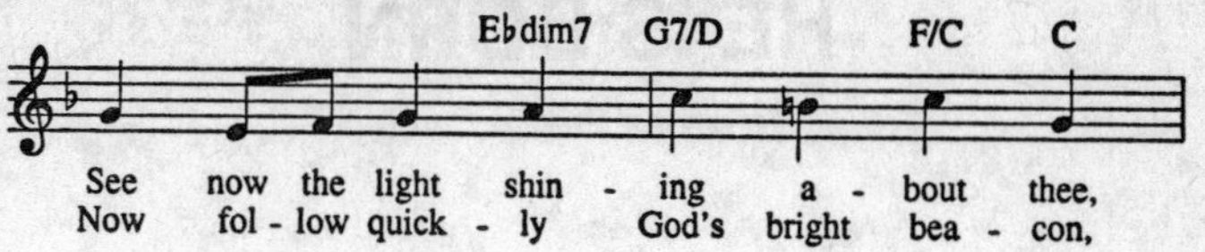
E♭dim7
G7/D
F/C
C
See now the light shin - ing a - bout thee,
Now fol - low quick - ly God's bright bea - con,

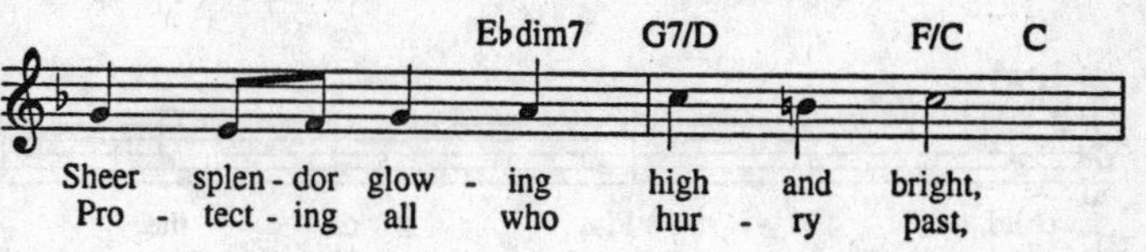
E♭dim7
G7/D
F/C
C
Sheer splen - dor glow - ing high and bright,
Pro - tect - ing all who hur - ry past,

F
F♯dim7
Gm
C7
B♭/F
F
It was fore - told by men ho - ly, ye would
Ba - by Je - sus waits thy hum - ble greet - ing

C7
Dm
B♭
C7
F
See Je - sus our dear Lord to - night.
And of - fer - ing of all thou hast.

# HE IS BORN

Traditional French Carol

G
C/G
G
He is born, the di - vine Christ

C/G
G
child. Play on the

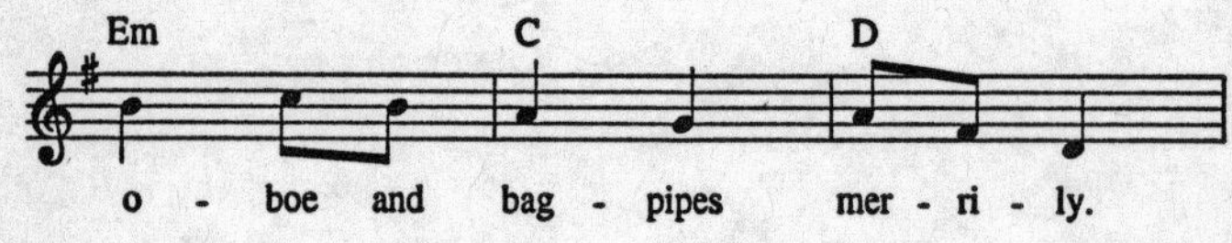
Em
C
D
o - boe and bag - pipes mer - ri - ly.

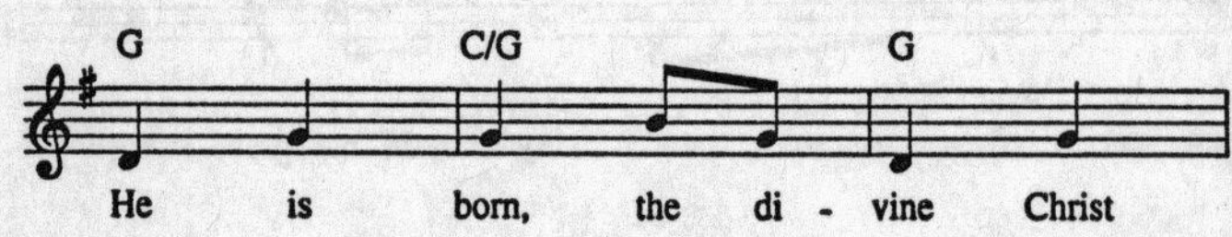
G
C/G
G
He is born, the di - vine Christ

C/G
G
Bm7/F#
Em
child. Sing we all of the

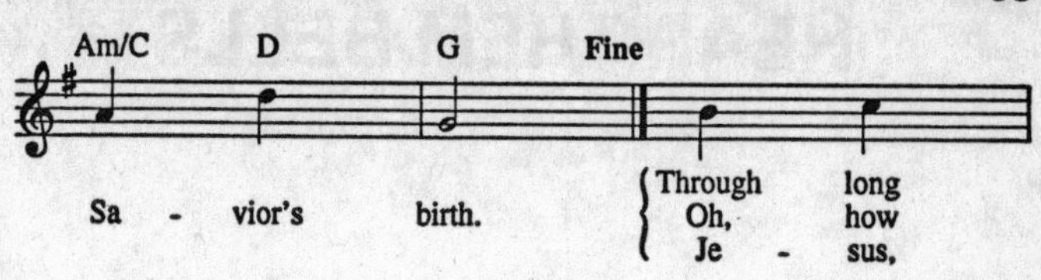
Am/C
D
G
Fine
Sa - vior's birth.
Through long
Oh, how
Je - sus,

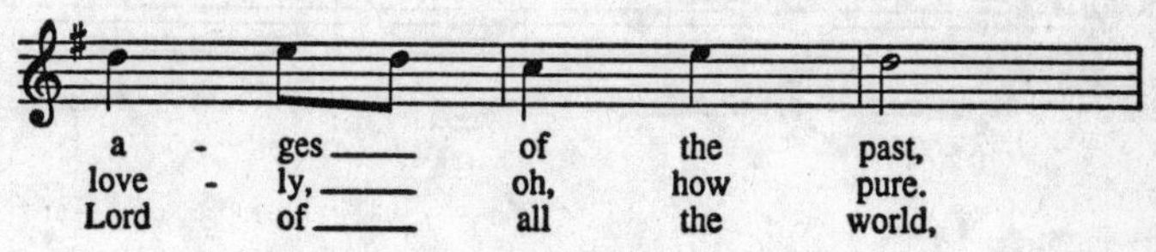
a - ges of the past,
love - ly, oh, how pure.
Lord of all the world,

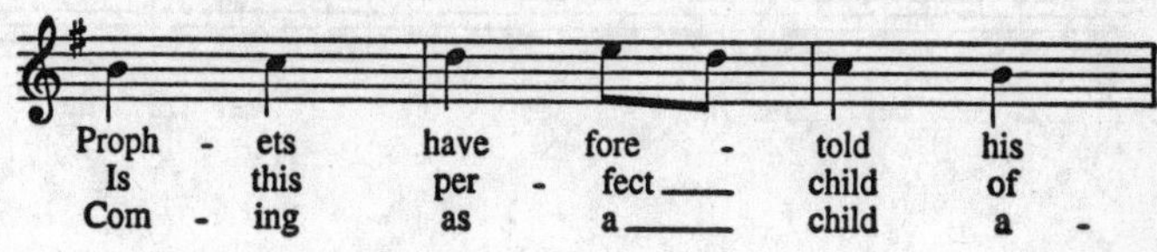
Proph - ets have fore - told his
Is this per - fect child of
Com - ing as a child a -

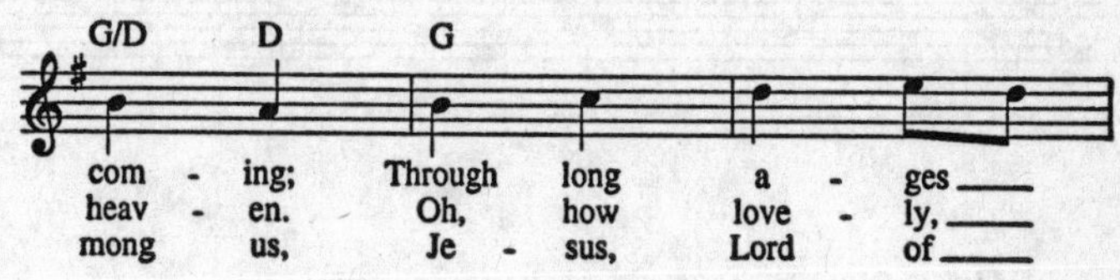
G/D
D
G
com - ing; Through long a - ges
heav - en. Oh, how love - ly,
mong us, Je - sus, Lord of

of the past, Now the
oh, how pure, Gra - cious
all the world, Grant to

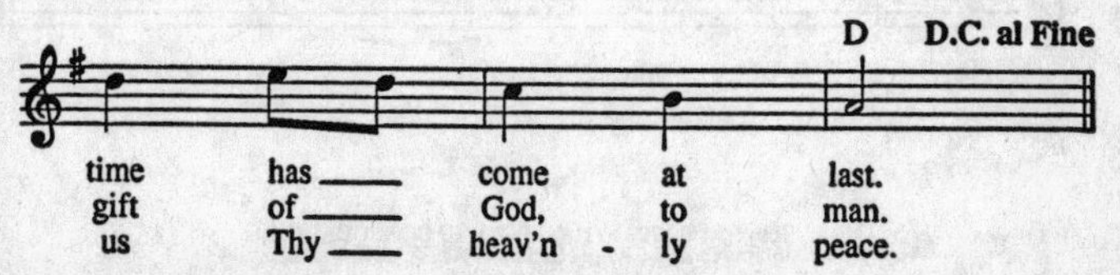
D
D.C. al Fine
time has come at last.
gift of God, to man.
us Thy heav'n - ly peace.

# HEAR THEM BELLS

Words and Music by D.S. McCOSH

G D7 G
Hear them bells! Mer - ry Christ-mas bells!

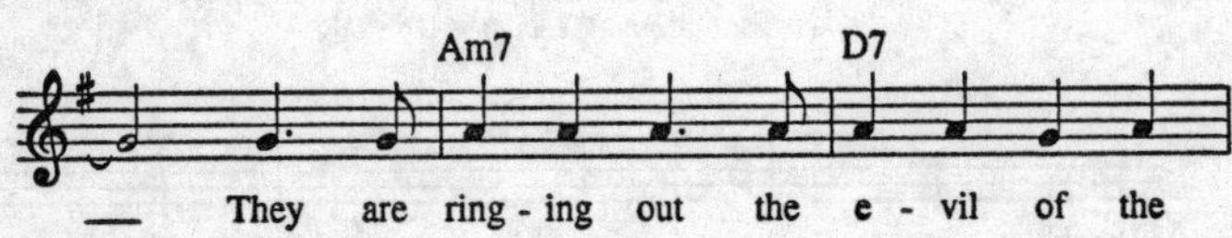
Am7 D7
They are ring - ing out the e - vil of the

G D7
sword; Hear them bells! Mer - ry

G Am7
Christ-mas bells! They are ring - ing in the

D7 G
glo - ry of the Lord!

# HEAR, O SHEPHERDS

Traditional Croatian Carol

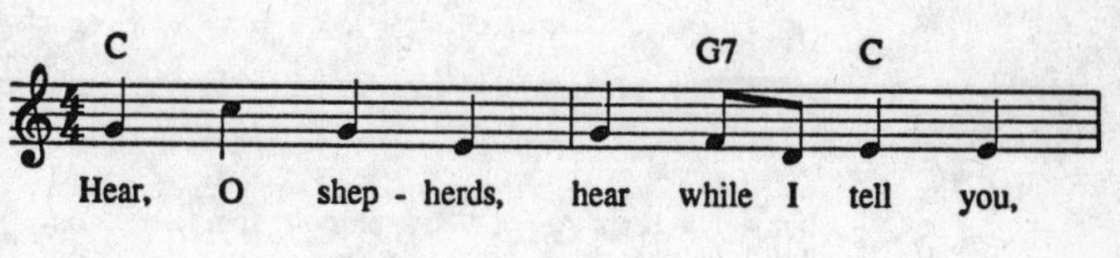
C
G7
C
Hear, O shep - herds, hear while I tell you,

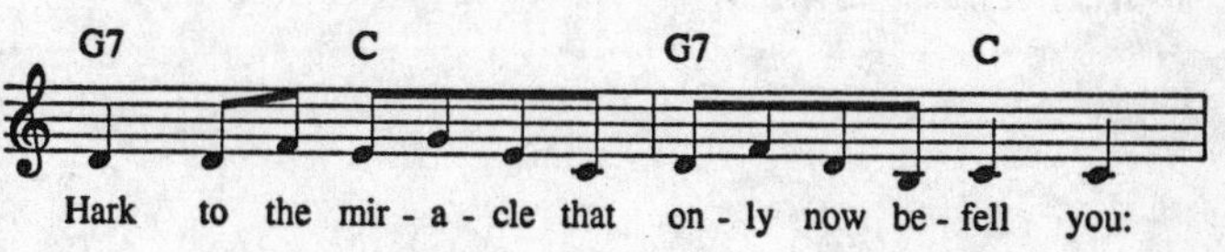
G7
C
G7
C
Hark to the mir - a - cle that on - ly now be - fell you:

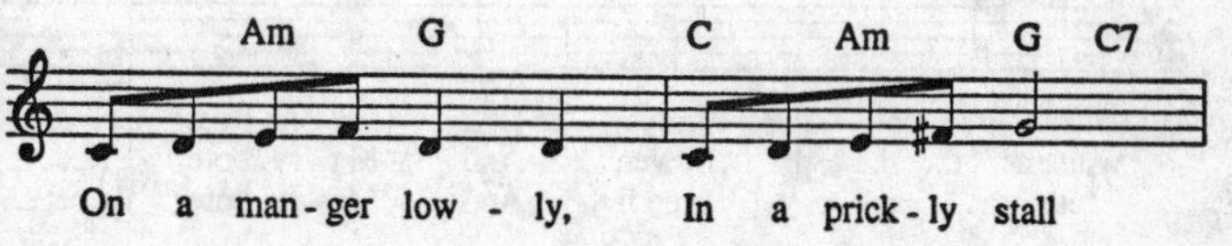
Am
G
C
Am
G
C7
On a man - ger low - ly, In a prick - ly stall

F
Em/G
Am
C
G7
C7
Lies the ba - by ho - ly Who will save us all.

F
Em/G
Am
C/G
G7
C
Lies the ba - by ho - ly Who will save us all.

# THE HOLLY AND THE IVY

18th Century English Carol

G C G
1.,6.The hol - ly and the i - vy, When
2.The hol - ly bears a blos - som, As
3.The hol - ly bears a ber - ry, As
4.,5. (See additional verses)

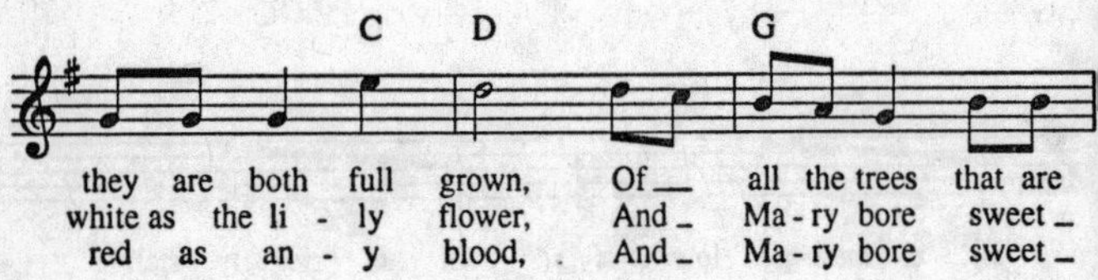
C D G
they are both full grown, Of all the trees that are
white as the li - ly flower, And Ma - ry bore sweet
red as an - y blood, And Ma - ry bore sweet

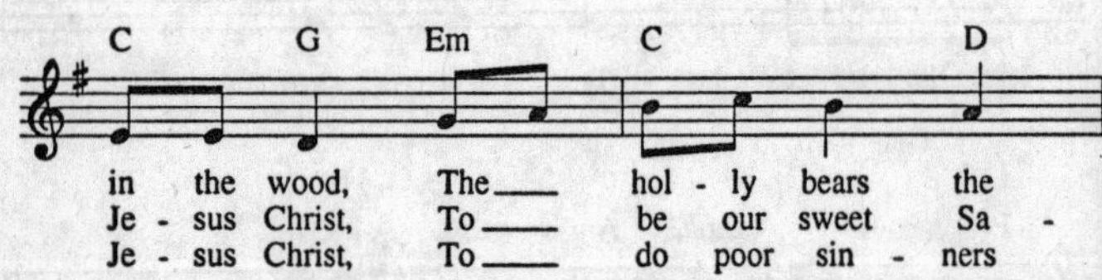
C G Em C D
in the wood, The hol - ly bears the
Je - sus Christ, To be our sweet Sa -
Je - sus Christ, To do poor sin - ners

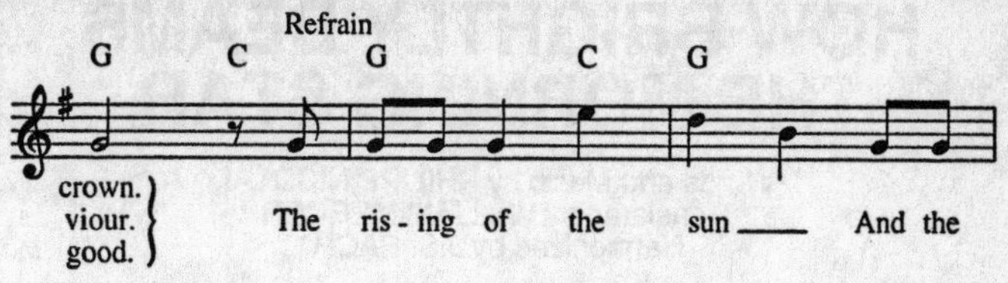
Refrain
G C G C G
crown.
viour.
good.
The ris - ing of the sun And the

C D G
run-ning of the deer, The play-ing of the

C G Em C D G
mer - ry or - gan, Sweet sing - ing in the choir.

*Additional Verses*

4. The holly bears a prickle,
As sharp as any thorn,
And Mary bore sweet Jesus Christ,
On Christmas Day in the morn.
*(Refrain)*

5. The holly bears a bark,
As bitter as any gall,
And Mary bore sweet Jesus Christ,
For to redeem us all.
*(Refrain)*

# HOW BRIGHTLY BEAMS THE MORNING STAR

Words and Music by PHILIPP NICOLAI
Translated by WILLIAM MERCER
Harmonized by J.S. BACH

D A D Bm F♯m
1. How bright - ly beams the
ray of God that
2.,3. (See additional verses)
D6 E A D G A7 D E7 A
morn - ing star! What sud - den ra - diance
breaks our night And fills the dark - en'd
D6 E7 A D G D Em D
from a - far Doth glad us with its
souls with light, Who long for truth were
1
Asus A7 D
shin - ing? The
2
Asus A7 D
pin - ing.
A D A Bm
Thy word Je - sus,

Em7 D A7 D G A7 D A B7
tru - ly feeds us, Right - ly leads us,

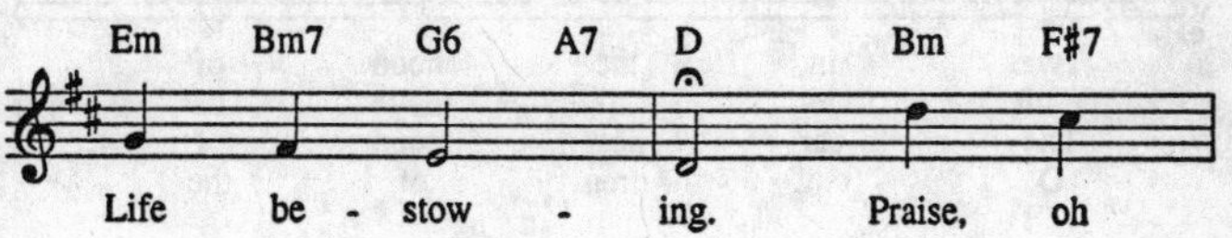
Em Bm7 G6 A7 D Bm F#7
Life be - stow - ing. Praise, oh

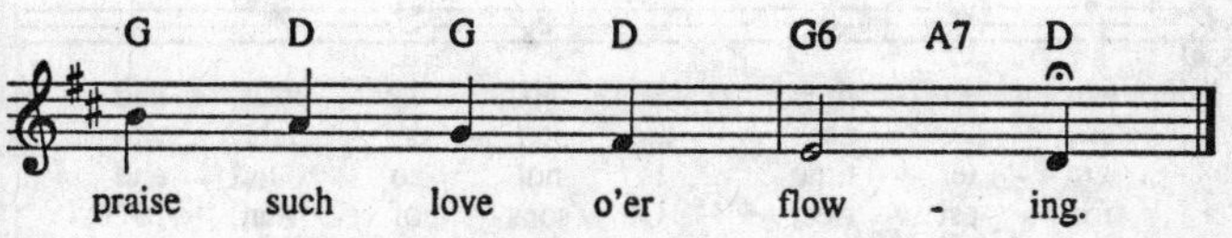
G D G D G6 A7 D
praise such love o'er flow - ing.

*Additional Verses*

2. Through thee alone can we be blest;
Then deep be on our hearts impress
The love that thou hast borne us;
So make us ready to fulfil
With burning zeal thy holy will,
Though men may vex or scorn us;
Saviour, let us never lose thee,
For we choose thee,
Thirst to know thee
All we are and have we owe thee!

3. O praise to him who came to save,
Who conquer'd death and burst the grave;
Each day new praise resoundeth
To him the Lamb who once was slain,
The friend whom none shall trust in vain,
Whose grace for ay aboundeth;
Sing, ye heavens, tell the story
Of his glory,
Till his praises
Flood with light earth's darkest places!

# THE HURON CAROL

Traditional French-Canadian Text
Traditional Canadian-Indian Melody

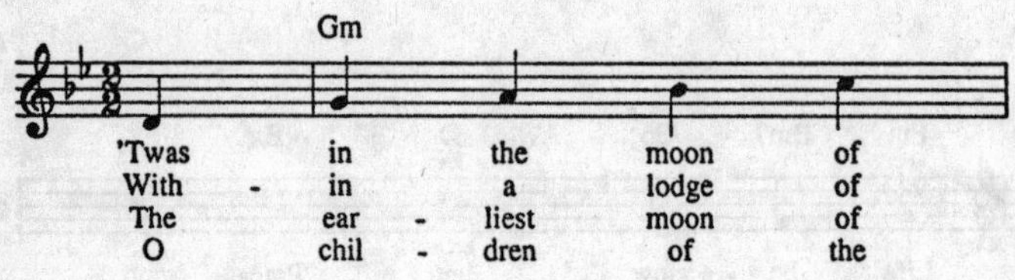
Gm
'Twas in the moon of
With - in a lodge of
The ear - liest moon of
O chil - dren of the

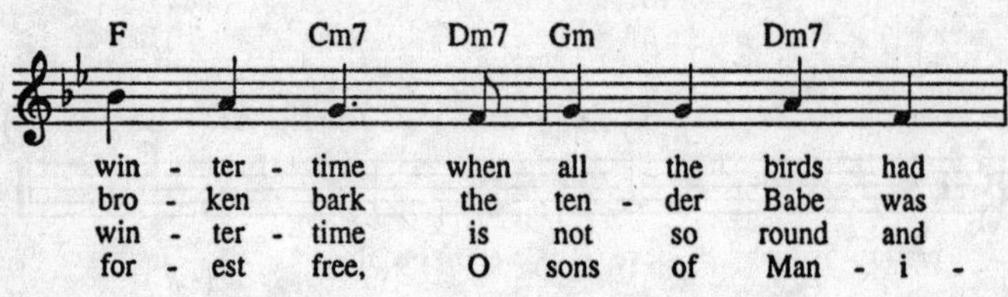
F Cm7 Dm7 Gm Dm7
win - ter - time when all the birds had
bro - ken bark the ten - der Babe was
win - ter - time is not so round and
for - est free, O sons of Man - i -

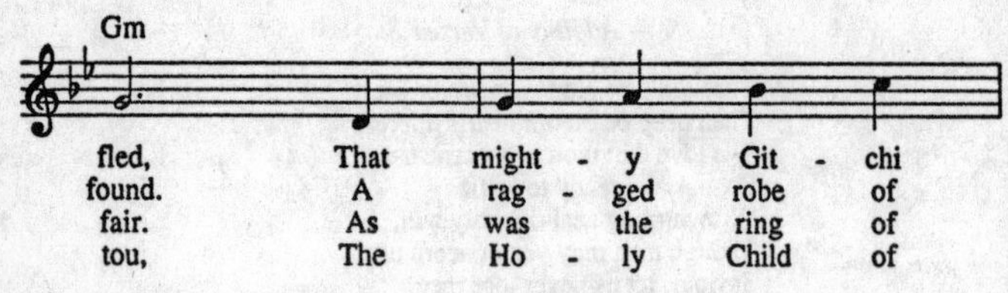
Gm
fled, That might - y Git - chi
found. A rag - ged robe of
fair. As was the ring of
tou, The Ho - ly Child of

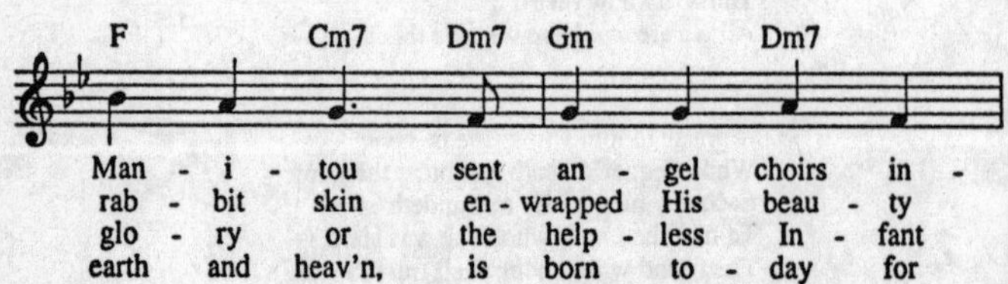
F Cm7 Dm7 Gm Dm7
Man - i - tou sent an - gel choirs in -
rab - bit skin en - wrapped His beau - ty
glo - ry or the help - less In - fant
earth and heav'n, is born to - day for

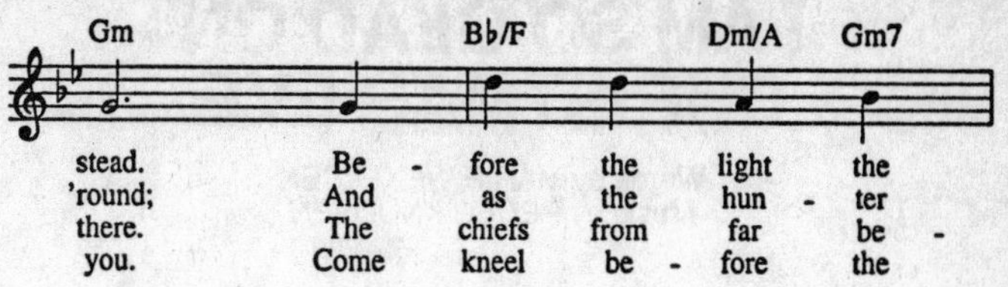
Gm Bb/F Dm/A Gm7
stead. Be - fore the light the
'round; And as the hun - ter
there. The chiefs from far be -
you. Come kneel be - fore the

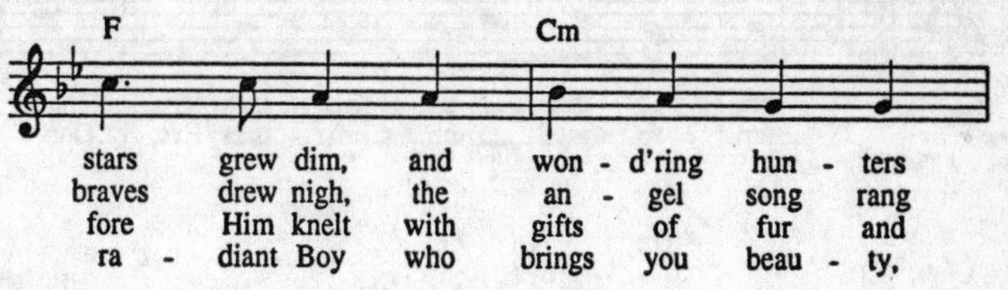
F Cm
stars grew dim, and won - d'ring hun - ters
braves drew nigh, the an - gel song rang
fore Him knelt with gifts of fur and
ra - diant Boy who brings you beau - ty,

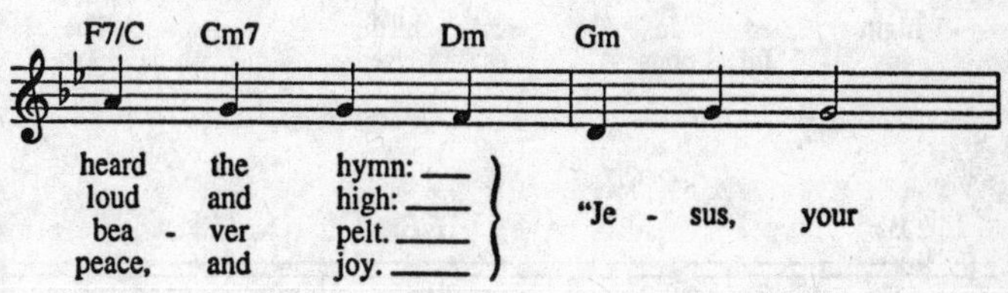
F7/C Cm7 Dm Gm
heard the hymn:
loud and high:
bea - ver pelt.
peace, and joy.
"Je - sus, your

Dm7 Eb Gm Dm
King, is born. Je - sus is

Eb Gm/D Dm Gm Cm/G D Gm
born. In ex - cel - sis glo - ri - a!"

# I AM SO GLAD ON CHRISTMAS EVE

Words by MARIE WEXELSEN
Music by PEDER KNUDSEN

Bb
F
I am so glad on Christ - mas Eve, The
I am so glad on Christ - mas Eve, Our

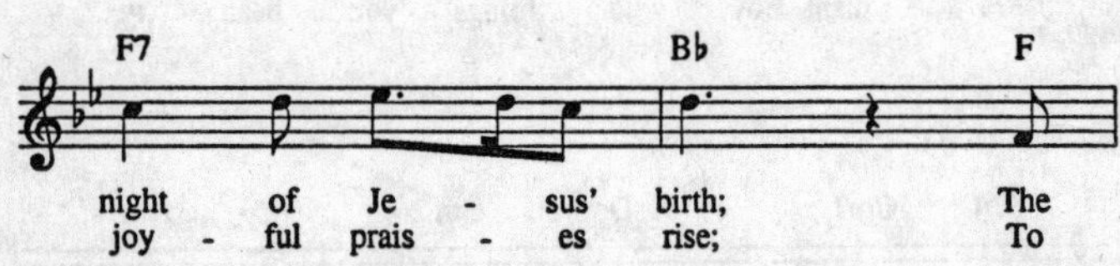
F7
Bb
F
night of Je - sus' birth; The
joy - ful prais - es rise; To

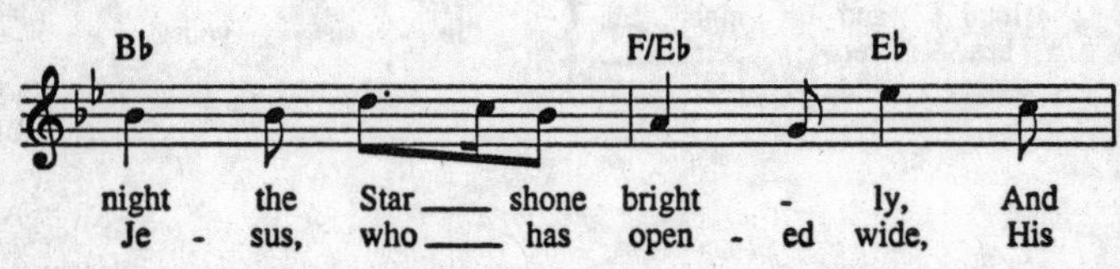
Bb
F/Eb
Eb
night the Star shone bright - ly, And
Je - sus, who has open - ed wide, His

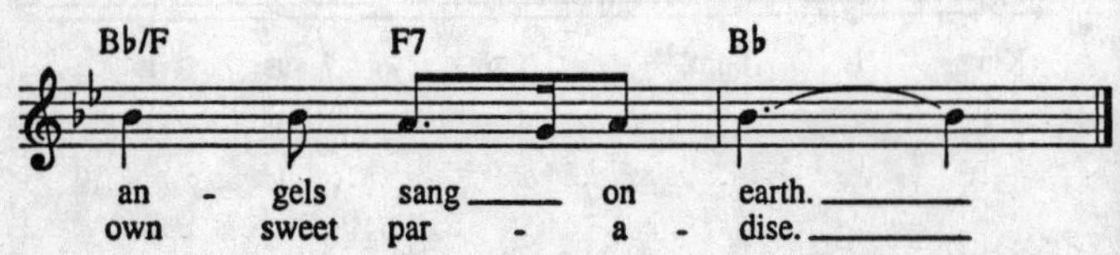
Bb/F
F7
Bb
an - gels sang on earth.
own sweet par - a - dise.

# I GO TO BETHLEHEM

Traditional Czech Carol

Eb Bb7/D Bb7
I go to Beth - le - hem,
Roos - ter will crow a - way
Eb Bb Bb7
To see the ti - ny child;
Mak - ing the Ba - by gay;
Eb Bb7/D Bdim7
My black roos - ter, trim and sleek,
Cuck - oo perch - ing near His lit - tle head,
Cm7 Bb/D Fm Bb
My cuck - oo with song so sweet:
Call - ing, soft - ly will make His heart glad:
Eb Bb7 Eb
These will I give Him.
These will I give Him.
Coo, coo-coo! Coo coo-coo
Bb7 Eb Bb Eb
Je - sus, He sings for you! Coo, coo-coo!
Bb7 Eb Bb Eb
Coo coo-coo Je - sus, He sings for you!

# I HEARD THE BELLS ON CHRISTMAS DAY

Words by HENRY WADSWORTH LONGFELLOW
Music by JOHN BAPTISTE CALKIN

Eb
Edim
Bb7
F#dim
1. I heard the bells on Christ - mas Day Their
2. I thought how, as the day had come, The
3.-5. (See additional verses)
Eb/G
Bb7
Eb
old fa - mil - iar car - ols play; And
bel - fries of all Christ - ten - dom Had
Ab
Eb
G7
Cm
wild and sweet the words re - peat Of
roll'd a - long th'un - bro - ken song Of
Eb
Ab
Eb
Bb7
Eb
peace on earth, good will to men.
peace on earth, good will to men.

*Additional Verses*

3. And in despair I bow'd my head:
"There is no peace on earth," I said,
"For hate is strong, and mocks the song
Of peace on earth, good will to men."

4. Then pealed the bells more loud and deep:
"God is not dead, nor doth He sleep;
The wrong shall fail, the right prevail,
With peace on earth good will to men."

5. Till, ringing, singing on its way,
The world revolved from night to day,
A voice, a chime, a chant sublime,
Of peace on earth, good will to men!

# I SAW THREE SHIPS

Traditional English Carol

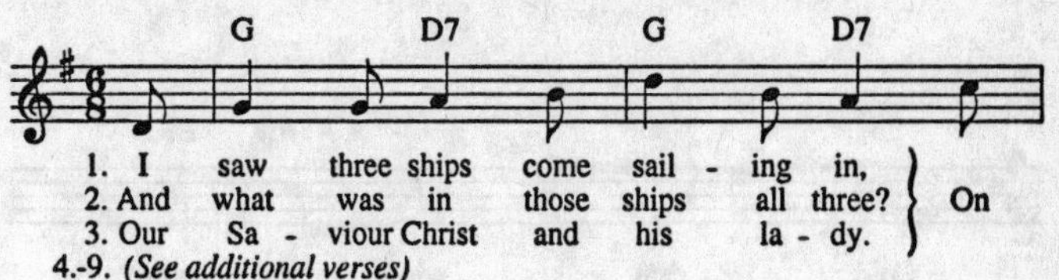
G
D7
G
D7
1. I saw three ships come sail - ing in,
2. And what was in those ships all three?
3. Our Sa - viour Christ and his la - dy.
On
4.-9. (See additional verses)

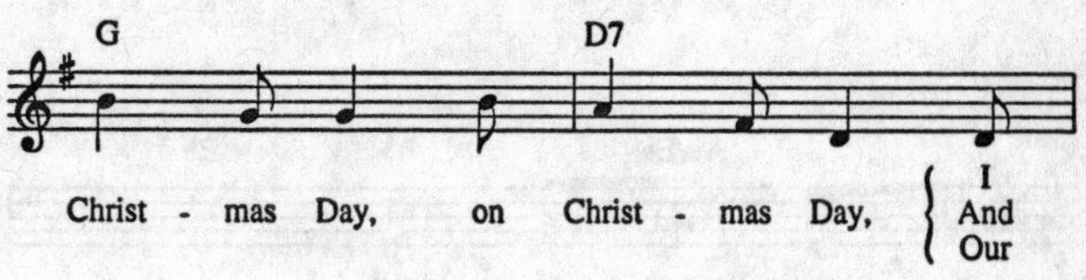
G
D7
Christ - mas Day, on Christ - mas Day,
I
And
Our

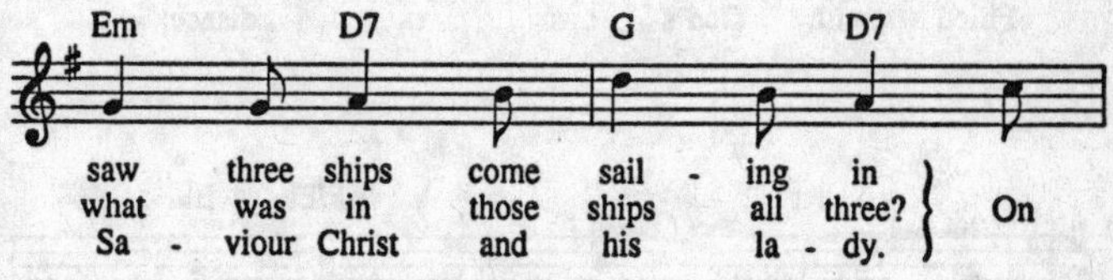
Em
D7
G
D7
saw three ships come sail - ing in
what was in those ships all three?
Sa - viour Christ and his la - dy.
On

G
Em
C
D7
G
Christ - mas Day in the morn - ing.

*Additional Verses*

4. Pray, whither sailed those ships all three?
5. O, they sailed into Bethlehem.
6. And all the bells on earth shall ring,
7. And all the angels in heaven shall sing,
8. And all the souls on earth shall sing.
9. Then let us all rejoice amain!

# THE ICY DECEMBER

Traditional Catalonian Carol

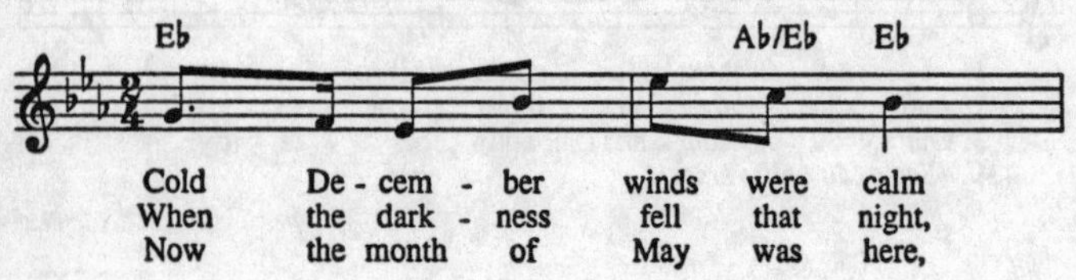
Eb
Ab/Eb
Eb
Cold De - cem - ber winds were calm
When the dark - ness fell that night,
Now the month of May was here,

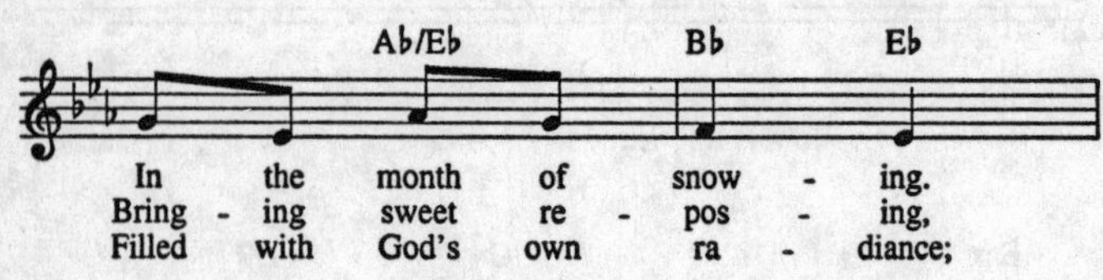
Ab/Eb
Bb
Eb
In the month of snow - ing.
Bring - ing sweet re - pos - ing,
Filled with God's own ra - diance;

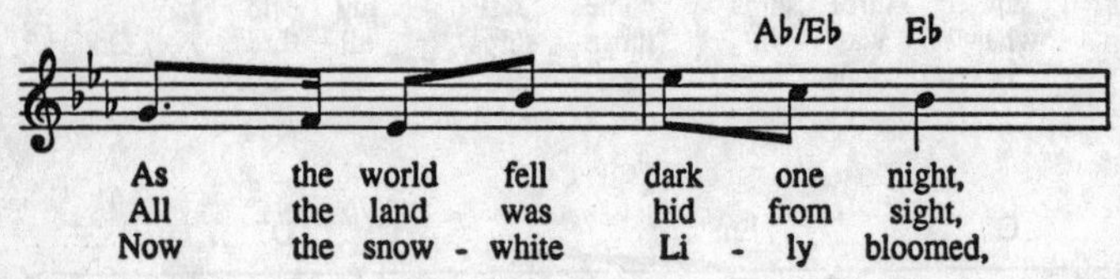
Ab/Eb
Eb
As the world fell dark one night,
All the land was hid from sight,
Now the snow - white Li - ly bloomed,

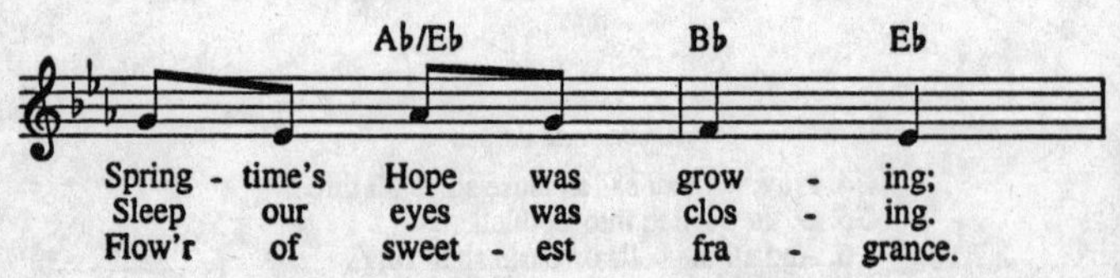
Ab/Eb
Bb
Eb
Spring - time's Hope was grow - ing;
Sleep our eyes was clos - ing.
Flow'r of sweet - est fra - grance.

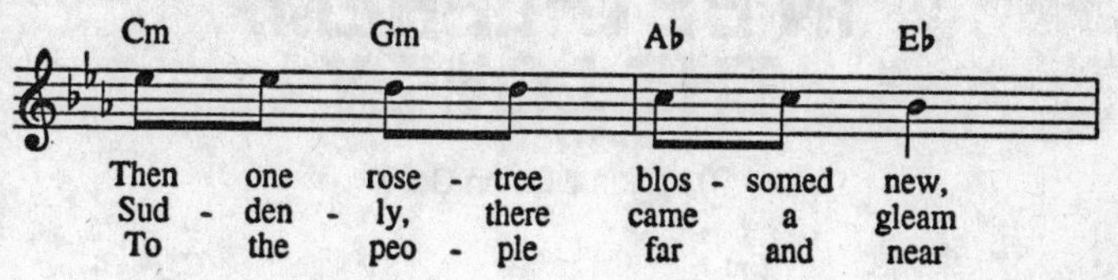
Cm
Gm
Ab
Eb
Then one rose - tree blos - somed new,
Sud - den - ly, there came a gleam
To the peo - ple far and near

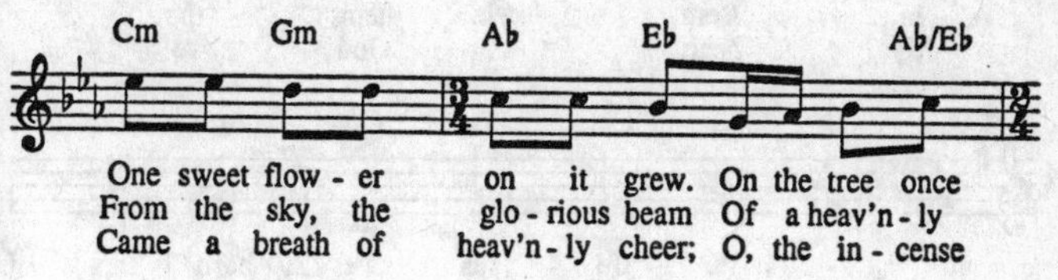
Cm
Gm
Ab
Eb
Ab/Eb
One sweet flow - er on it grew. On the tree once
From the sky, the glo - rious beam Of a heav'n - ly
Came a breath of heav'n - ly cheer; O, the in - cense

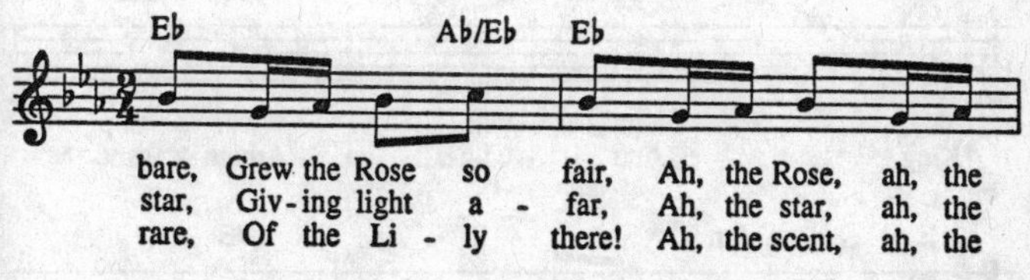
Eb
Ab/Eb
Eb
bare, Grew the Rose so fair, Ah, the Rose, ah, the
star, Giv - ing light a - far, Ah, the star, ah, the
rare, Of the Li - ly there! Ah, the scent, ah, the

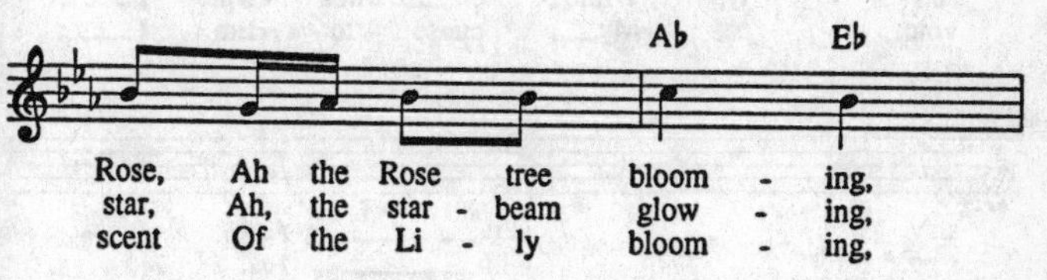
Ab
Eb
Rose, Ah the Rose tree bloom - ing,
star, Ah, the star - beam glow - ing,
scent Of the Li - ly bloom - ing,

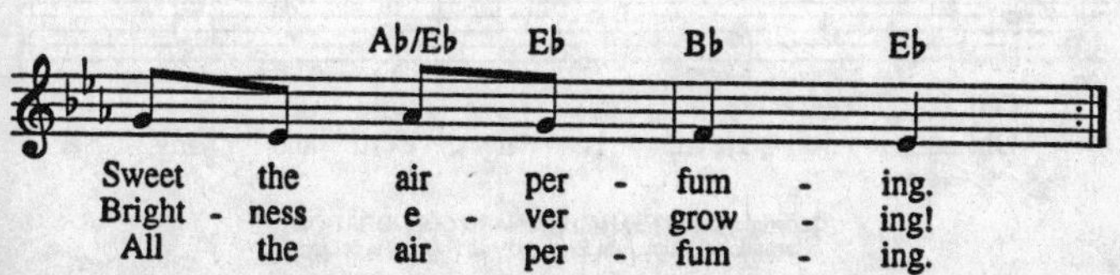
Ab/Eb
Eb
Bb
Eb
Sweet the air per - fum - ing.
Bright - ness e - ver grow - ing!
All the air per - fum - ing.

# IN BETHLEHEM, THE LOWLY

Traditional Dutch Carol

Em D G C
In Beth - le - hem, the
My heart in God re -
G/D D G Em D G Am G
low - ly, Je - sus was born this
joic - es, He is my Lord and
D D/F# G Am Dm/F
day, Him will I wor - ship
King, And with a thou - sand
E Am D G/B
on - ly, While on this earth I
voic - es, My praise to Him I
D G/B D
stay. Oh! Yes!
sing. Oh! Yes!
G/B D G C/E G/D D7 G
Oh! Yes! Je - sus was born this day.
Oh! Yes! He is my Lord and King.

# INFANT HOLY, INFANT LOWLY

Traditional Polish Carol

G D D7
In - fant ho - ly, In - fant low - ly, For His
Flocks are sleep - ing; Shep-herds keep - ing Vig - il
Bm C6 D7 G D
bed a cat - tle stall; Ox - en low - ing, Lit - tle
till the morn-ing new Saw the glo - ry, Heard the
D7 Bm C6 D7 G
know - ing Christ the Babe is Lord of all. Swift are
sto - ry, Ti-dings of a gos-pel true. Thus re -
C Am D B Em Am7
wing - ing An-gels sing - ing, No-els ring - ing, Ti-dings
joic - ing, Free from sor - row, Prais-es voic - ing Greet the
D D7 Bm C6 D7 G
bring - ing: Christ the Babe is Lord of all.
mor - row: Christ the Babe was born for you.

# IN BETHLEHEM'S CRADLE

Traditional Puerto Rican Carol

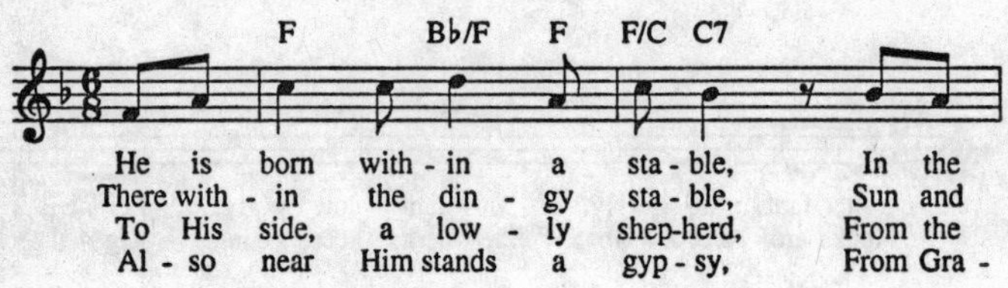
F Bb/F F F/C C7
He is born with - in a sta - ble, In the
There with - in the din - gy sta - ble, Sun and
To His side, a low - ly shep-herd, From the
Al - so near Him stands a gyp - sy, From Gra -

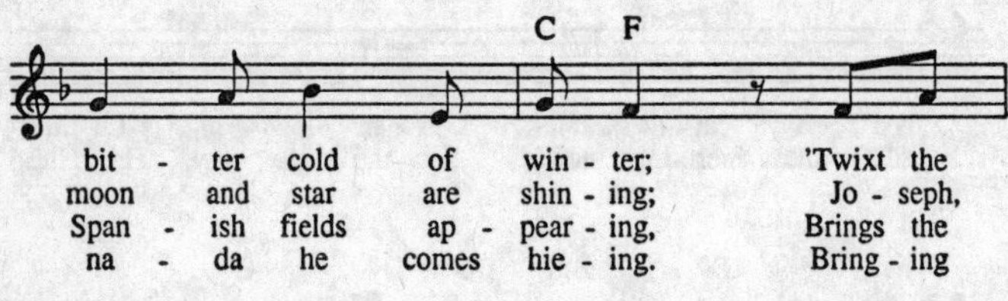
C F
bit - ter cold of win - ter; 'Twixt the
moon and star are shin - ing; Jo - seph,
Span - ish fields ap - pear - ing, Brings the
na - da he comes hie - ing. Bring - ing

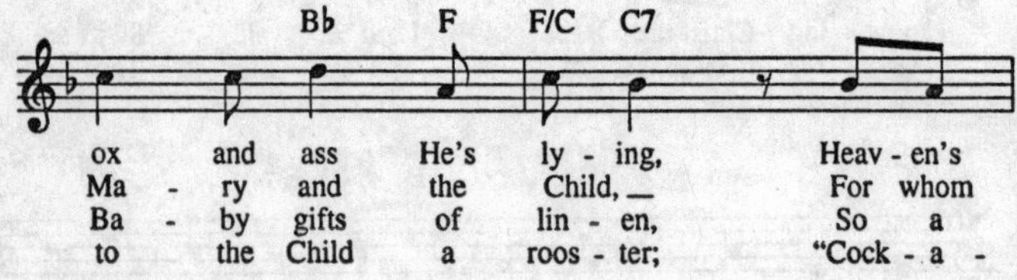
Bb F F/C C7
ox and ass He's ly - ing, Heav - en's
Ma - ry and the Child, For whom
Ba - by gifts of lin - en, So a
to the Child a roos - ter; "Cock - a -

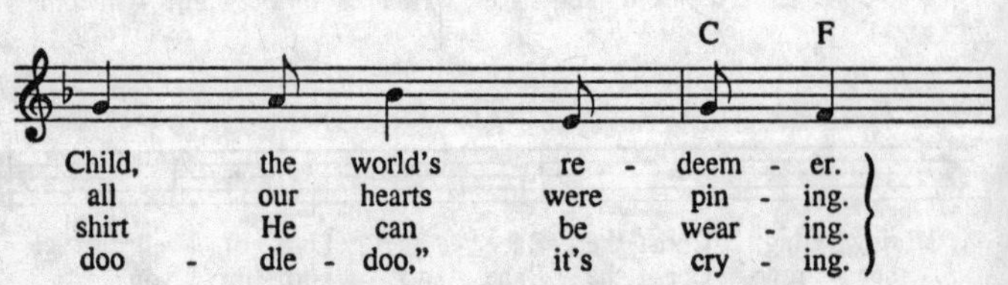
C F
Child, the world's re - deem - er.
all our hearts were pin - ing.
shirt He can be wear - ing.
doo - dle - doo," it's cry - ing.

C7
Sing now of Je - sus, of the dear

F
C7
ba - by, O what a glo - rious gift from a -

F
C7
bove! He has our hearts and all of our

F
C7
love! He has our hearts and all of our

F
love! Le - rum, le - rum, le - rum,

la! ¡Que vi - va!

# IN THE BLEAK MIDWINTER

Poem by CHRISTINA ROSSETTI
Music by GUSTAV HOLST

F Dm

In the bleak mid - win - ter,
God, heaven can - not hold him,
An - gels and arch - an - gels
What ______ can I give him,

B♭6 F6/A Gm7 C7

frost - y wind made moan,
nor ______ earth sus - tain;
may have gath - ered there,
poor ______ as I am?

F Dm

earth stood hard as i - ron,
heaven and earth shall flee a - way
cher - u - bim and ser - a - phim
If I were a shep - herd,

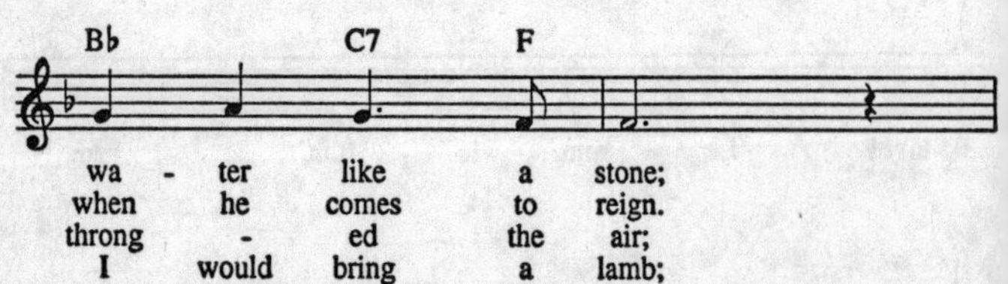
B♭ C7 F
wa - ter like a stone;
when he comes to reign.
throng - ed the air;
I would bring a lamb;

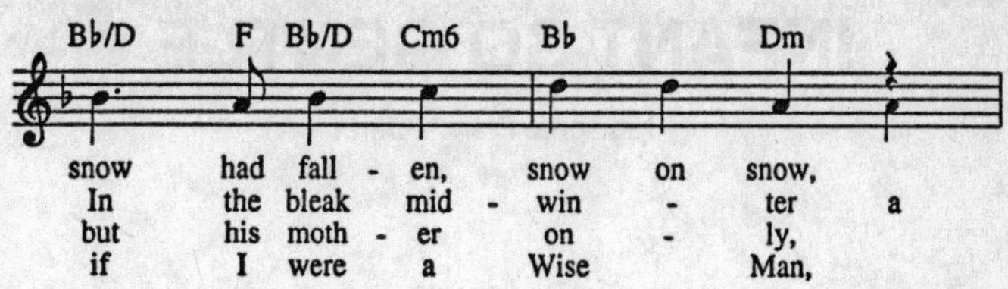
B♭/D F B♭/D Cm6 B♭ Dm
snow had fall - en, snow on snow,
In the bleak mid - win - ter a
but his moth - er on - ly,
if I were a Wise Man,

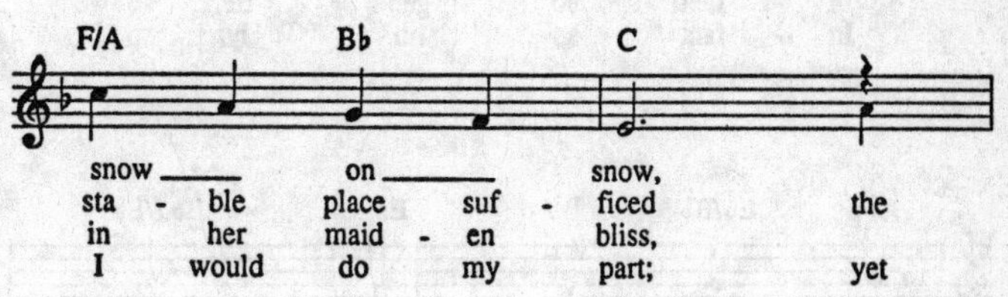
F/A B♭ C
snow on snow,
sta - ble place suf - ficed the
in her maid - en bliss,
I would do my part; yet

F Dm
in the bleak mid - win - ter,
Lord God Al - might - y,
wor - shipped the be - lov - ed
what can I give him:

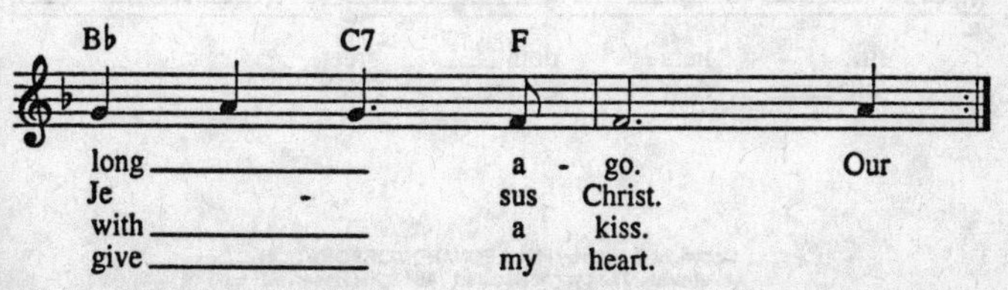
B♭ C7 F
long a - go. Our
Je - sus Christ.
with a kiss.
give my heart.

# INFANT SO GENTLE

Traditional French Carol

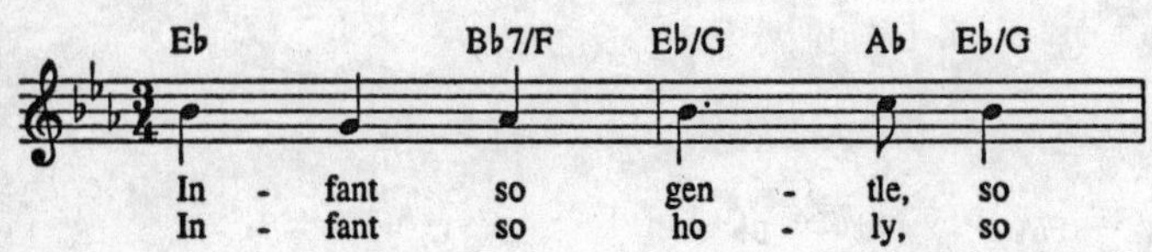
Eb
Bb7/F
Eb/G
Ab
Eb/G
In - fant so gen - tle, so
In - fant so ho - ly, so

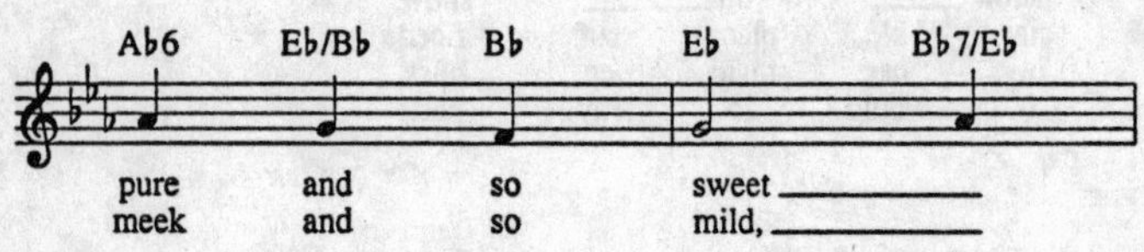
Ab6
Eb/Bb
Bb
Eb
Bb7/Eb
pure and so sweet
meek and so mild,

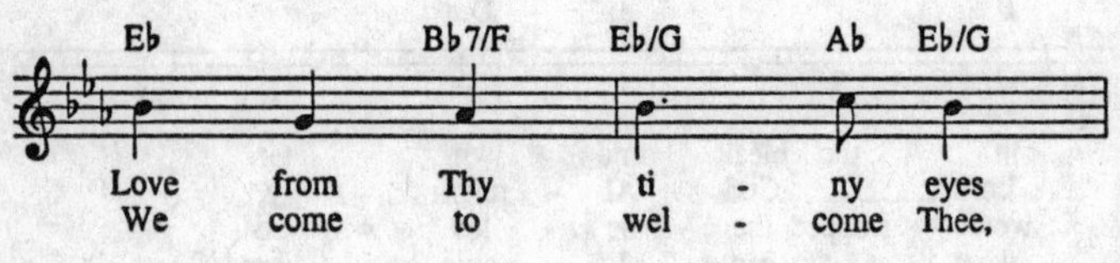
Eb
Bb7/F
Eb/G
Ab
Eb/G
Love from Thy ti - ny eyes
We come to wel - come Thee,

Ab6
Eb/Bb
Bb
Eb
sin - ners doth greet,
our dear Christ Child.

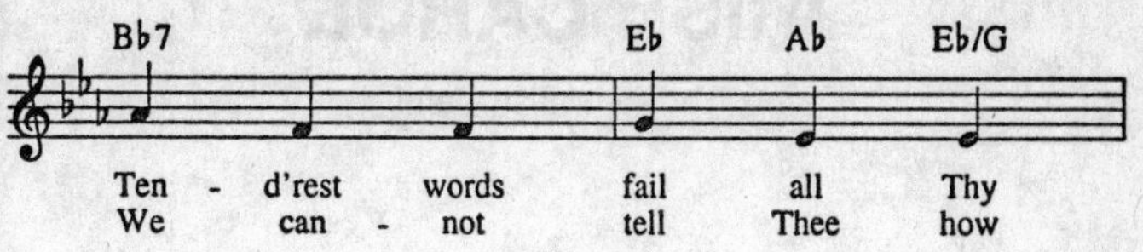
Bb7
Eb
Ab
Eb/G
Ten - d'rest words fail all Thy
We can - not tell Thee how

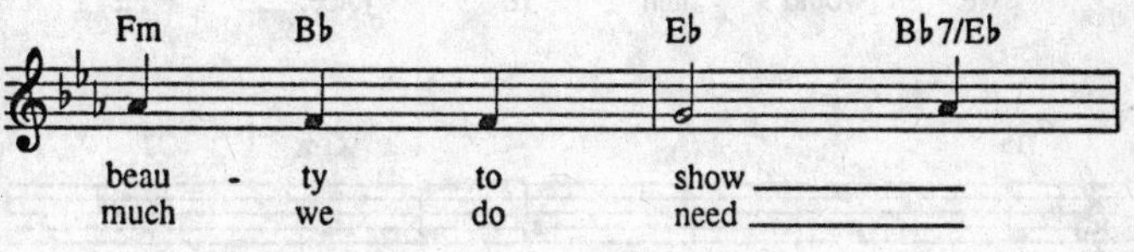
Fm
Bb
Eb
Bb7/Eb
beau - ty to show
much we do need

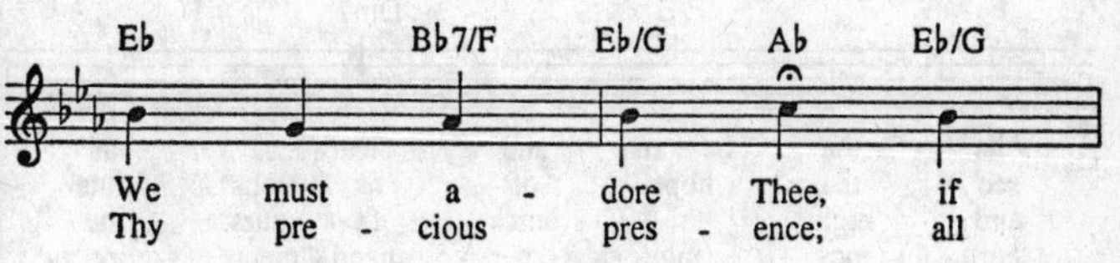
Eb
Bb7/F
Eb/G
Ab
Eb/G
We must a - dore Thee, if
Thy pre - cious pres - ence; all

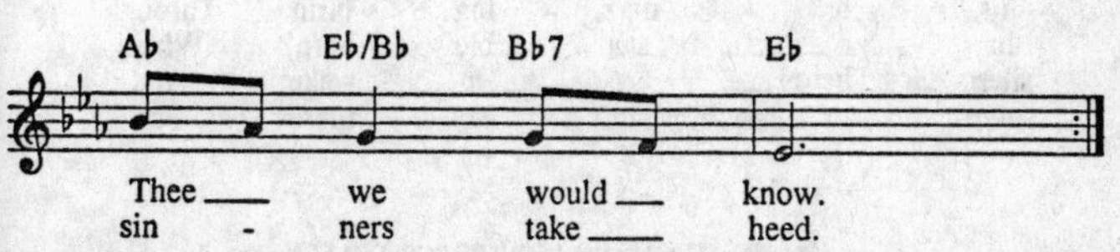
Ab
Eb/Bb
Bb7
Eb
Thee we would know.
sin - ners take heed.

# IRISH CAROL

Traditional Irish Carol

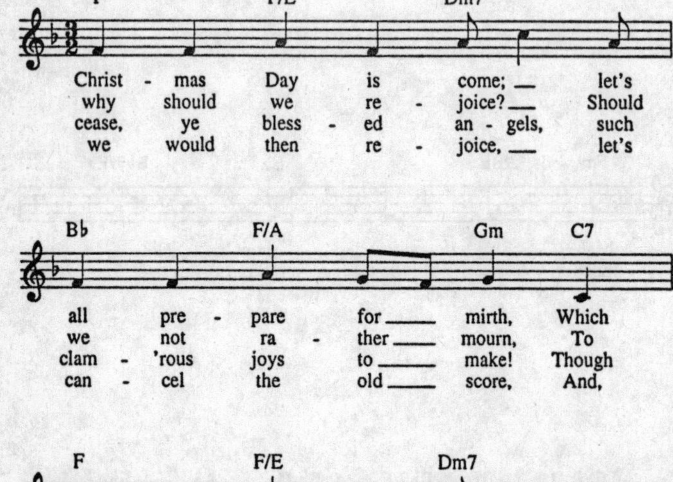
F F/E Dm7
Christ - mas Day is come; let's
why should we re - joice? Should
cease, ye bless - ed an - gels, such
we would then re - joice, let's
B♭ F/A Gm C7
all pre - pare for mirth, Which
we not ra - ther mourn, To
clam - 'rous joys to make! Though
can - cel the old score, And,

F F/E Dm7
fills the heav'ns and earth at
see the hope of na - tions thus
mid - night si - lence fa - vours, the
pur - pos - ing a - mend - ment, re -

B♭ C Dm Gm/B♭ F C
this a - maz - ing birth, Through
in a sta - ble born? Where
shep - herds are a - wake; And
solve to sin no more; For

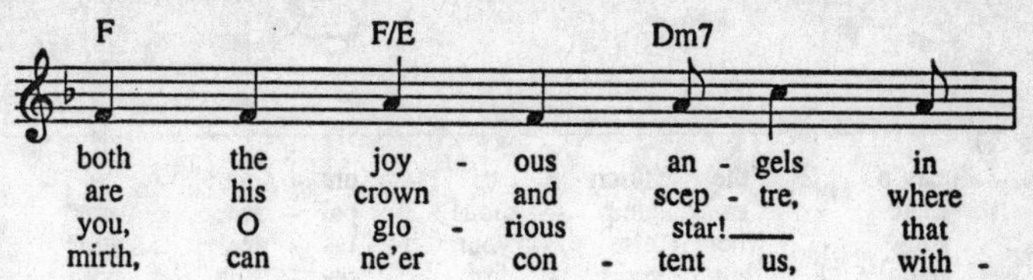
F F/E Dm7
both the joy - ous an - gels in
are his crown and scep - tre, where
you, O glo - rious star! that
mirth, can ne'er con - tent us, with -

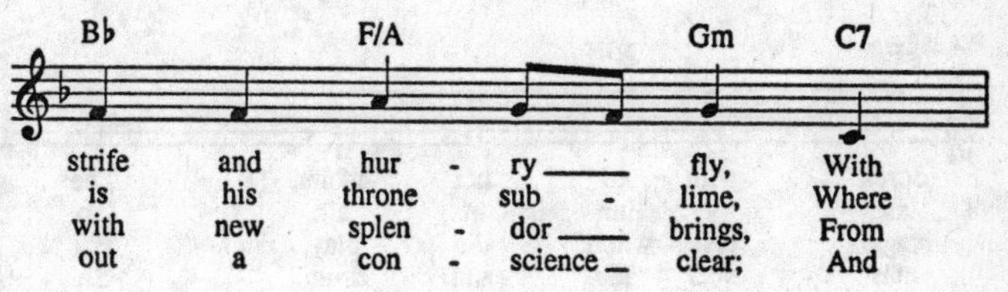
B♭ F/A Gm C7
strife and hur - ry fly, With
is his throne sub - lime, Where
with new splen - dor brings, From
out a con - science clear; And

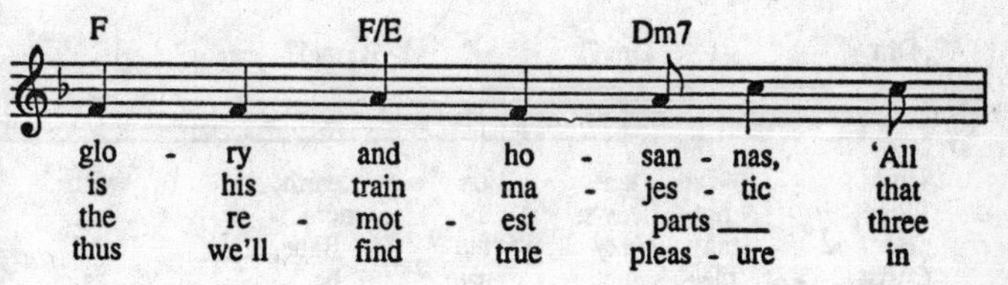
F F/E Dm7
glo - ry and ho - san - nas, 'All
is his train ma - jes - tic that
the re - mot - est parts three
thus we'll find true pleas - ure in

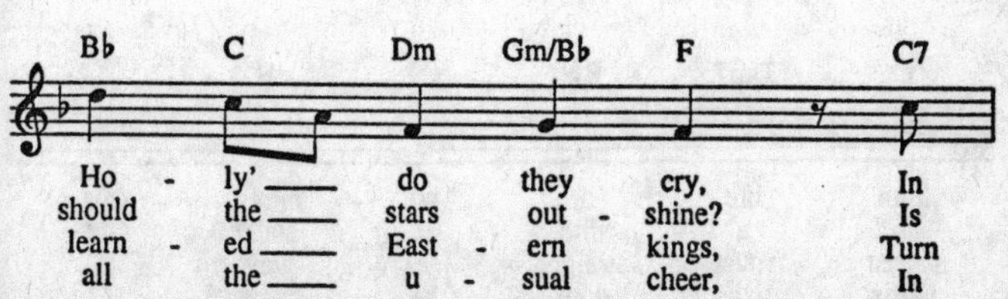
B♭ C Dm Gm/B♭ F C7
Ho - ly' do they cry, In
should the stars out - shine? Is
learn - ed East - ern kings, Turn
all the u - sual cheer, In

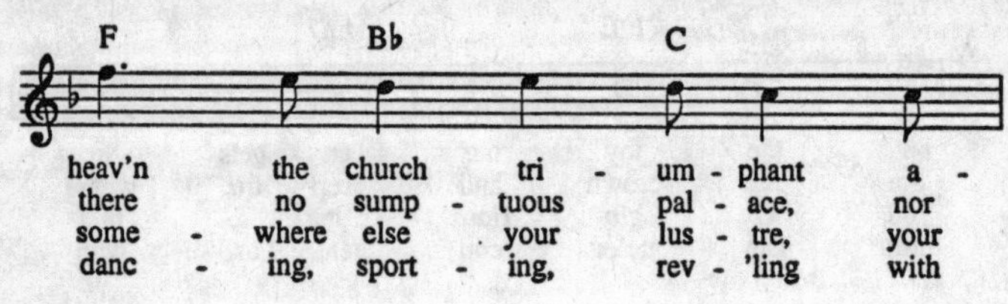
F Bb C
heav'n the church tri - um - phant a -
there no sump - tuous pal - ace, nor
some - where else your lus - tre, your
danc - ing, sport - ing, rev - 'ling with

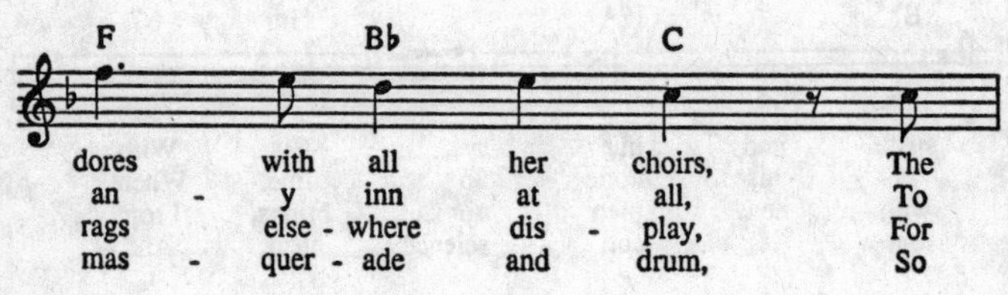
F Bb C
dores with all her choirs, The
an - y inn at all, To
rags else - where dis - play, For
mas - quer - ade and drum, So

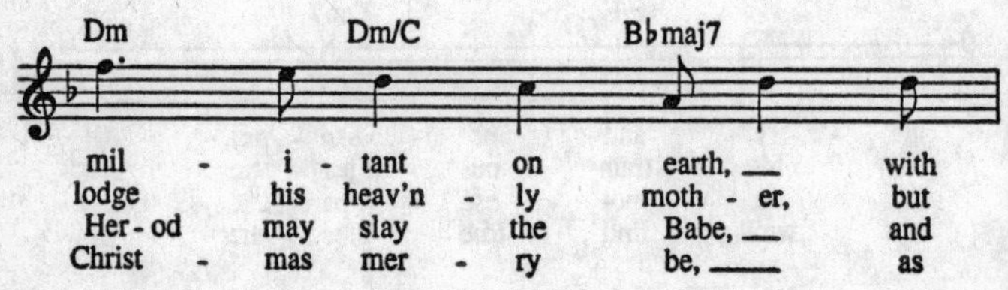
Dm Dm/C Bbmaj7
mil - i - tant on earth, with
lodge his heav'n - ly moth - er, but
Her - od may slay the Babe, and
Christ - mas mer - ry be, as

C Dm7 Bb C9 F
hum - ble faith ad - mires. But
in a filth - y stall? Oh!
Christ must straight a - way. If
Chris - tians doth be - come.

# LOVE CAME DOWN AT CHRISTMAS

Text by CHRISTINA ROSSETTI
Traditional Irish Melody

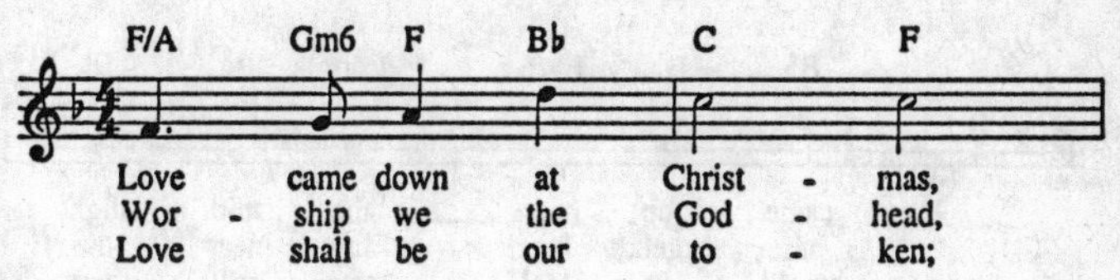
F/A Gm6 F B♭ C F
Love came down at Christ - mas,
Wor - ship we the God - head,
Love shall be our to - ken;

F/A C7/G F B♭/F C/E F F/C C
love all love - ly, love di - vine;
love in - car - nate, love di - vine;
love be yours and love be mine,

Dm B♭/D F/C B♭ F/A C7/G F
love was born at Christ - mas;
wor - ship we our Je - sus,
love to God and neigh - bor,

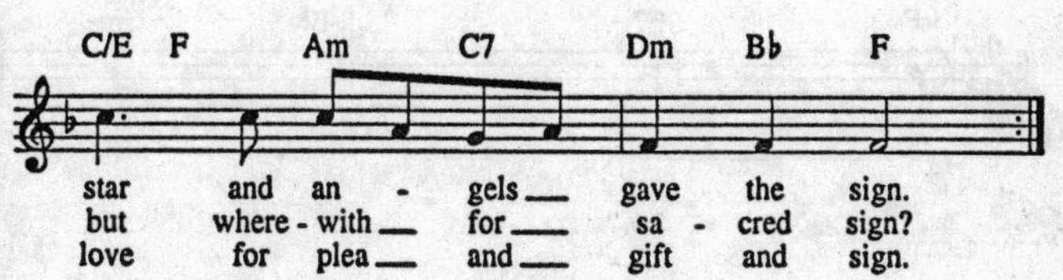
C/E F Am C7 Dm B♭ F
star and an - gels gave the sign.
but where - with for sa - cred sign?
love for plea and gift and sign.

# IT CAME UPON THE MIDNIGHT CLEAR

Words by EDMUND H. SEARS
Music by RICHARD STORRS WILLIS

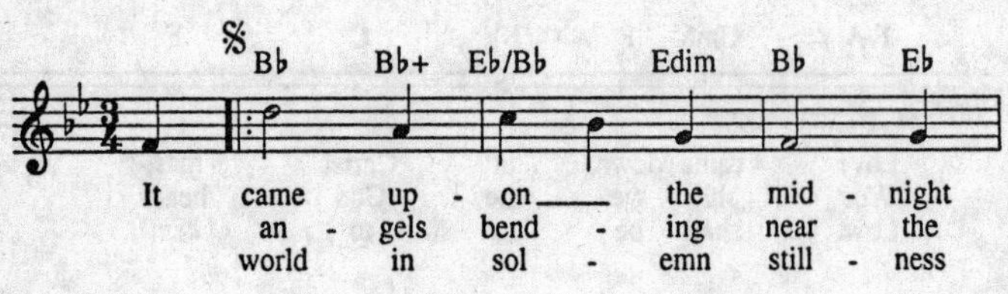
Bb
Bb+
Eb/Bb
Edim
Bb
Eb
It came up - on the mid - night
an - gels bend - ing near the
world in sol - emn still - ness

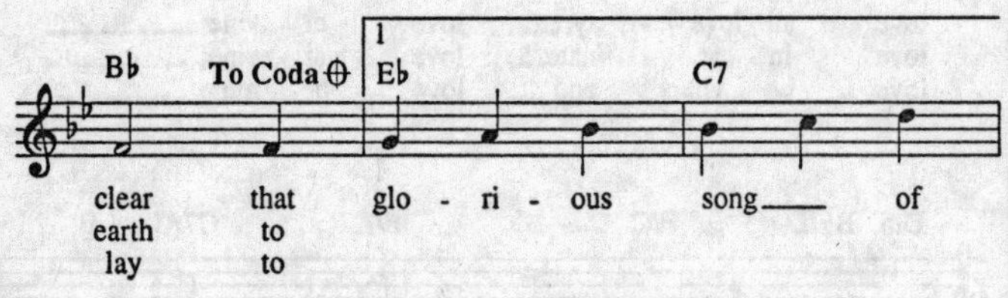
Bb
To Coda
1
Eb
C7
clear that glo - ri - ous song of
earth to
lay to

F
F7
2
Eb
Cm
old, From touch their

F7
Bb
harps
of
gold.
Peace

D7
Gm
D7
on
the
earth
good - will
to

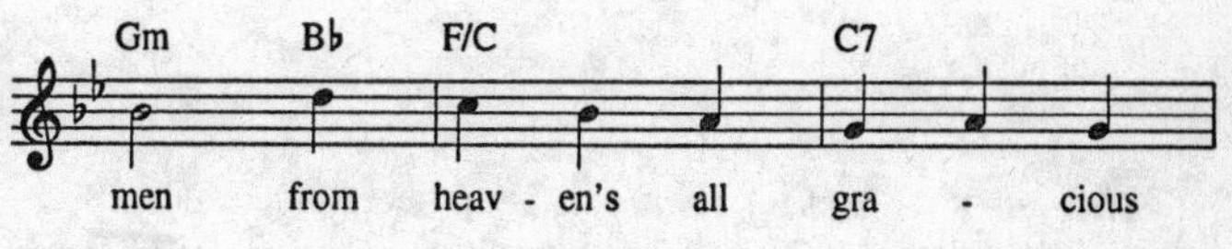
Gm
Bb
F/C
C7
men
from
heav - en's
all
gra - cious

F
F7
D.S. al Coda
King.
The

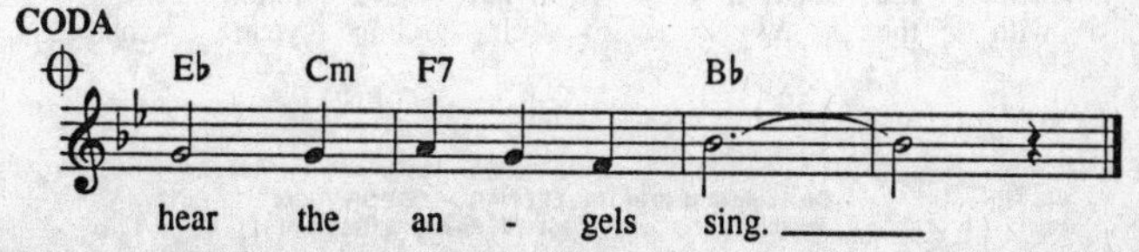
CODA
Eb
Cm
F7
Bb
hear
the
an - gels
sing.

# IT CAME UPON THE MIDNIGHT CLEAR

Words by EDMUND H. SEARS
Traditional English Melody
Adapted by ARTHUR SULLIVAN

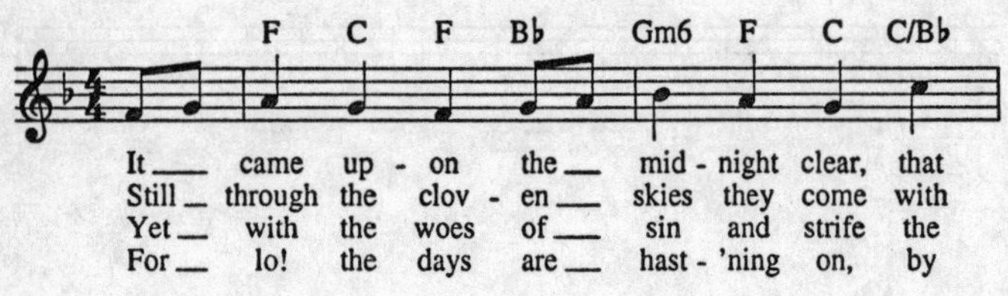
F C F Bb Gm6 F C C/Bb
It came up - on the mid - night clear, that
Still through the clov - en skies they come with
Yet with the woes of sin and strife the
For lo! the days are hast - 'ning on, by

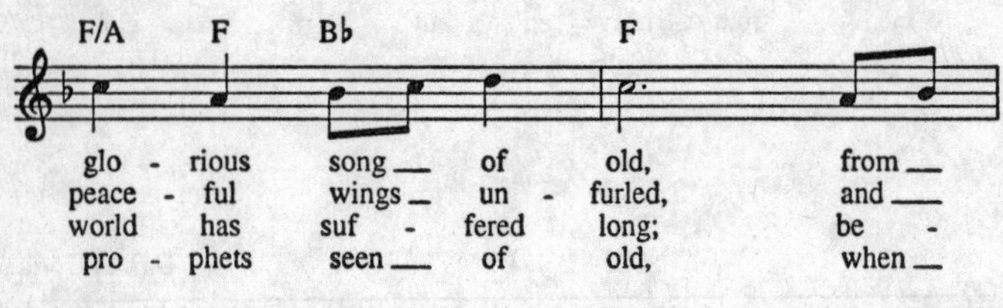
F/A F Bb F
glo - rious song of old, from
peace - ful wings un - furled, and
world has suf - fered long; be -
pro - phets seen of old, when

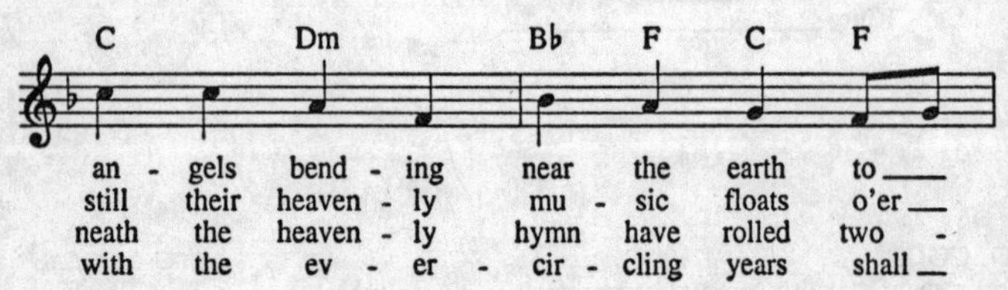
C Dm Bb F C F
an - gels bend - ing near the earth to
still their heaven - ly mu - sic floats o'er
neath the heaven - ly hymn have rolled two -
with the ev - er - cir - cling years shall

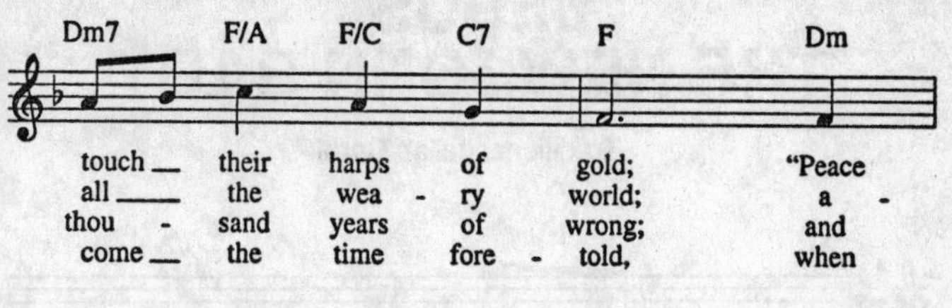
Dm7
F/A
F/C
C7
F
Dm
touch — their harps of gold; "Peace
all — the wea - ry world; a -
thou - sand years of wrong; and
come — the time fore - told, when

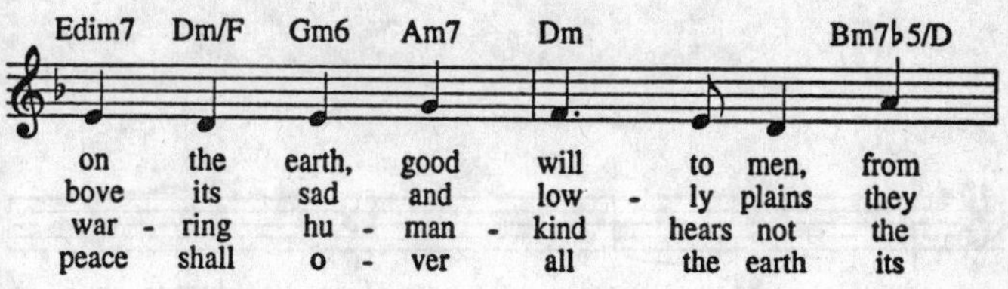
Edim7
Dm/F
Gm6
Am7
Dm
Bm7♭5/D
on the earth, good will to men, from
bove its sad and low - ly plains they
war - ring hu - man - kind hears not the
peace shall o - ver all the earth its

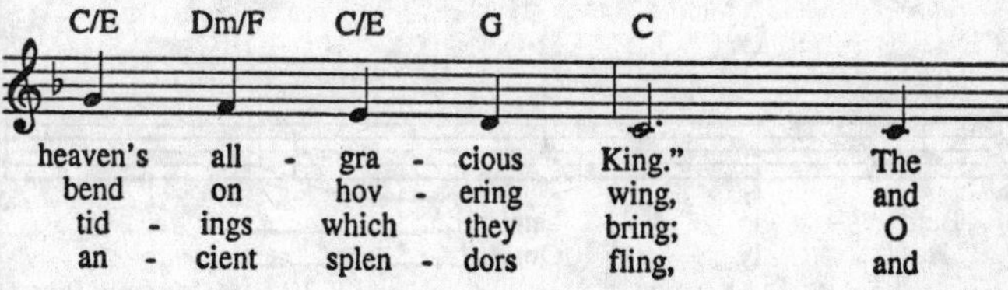
C/E
Dm/F
C/E
G
C
heaven's all - gra - cious King." The
bend on hov - ering wing, and
tid - ings which they bring; O
an - cient splen - dors fling, and

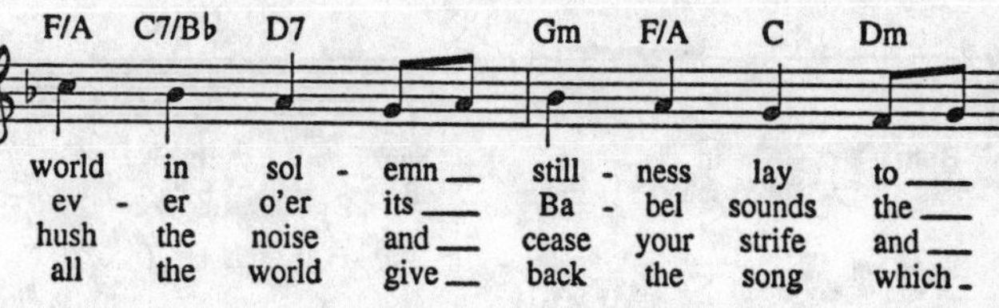
F/A
C7/B♭
D7
Gm
F/A
C
Dm
world in sol - emn — still - ness lay to —
ev - er o'er its — Ba - bel sounds the —
hush the noise and — cease your strife and —
all the world give — back the song which —

F/A
F
F/C
C7
F
hear — the an - gels sing.
bless - ed an - gels sing.
hear — the an - gels sing!
now — the an - gels sing.

# JESUS, THE NEWBORN BABY

Traditional Italian Carol

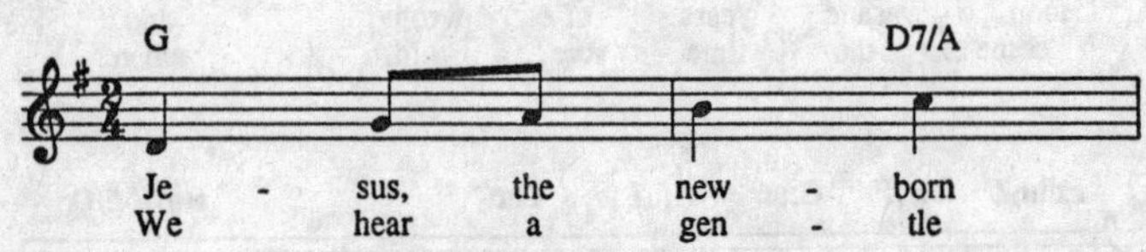
G
D7/A
Je - sus, the new - born
We hear a gen - tle

G
Ba - by. Lies here in
voice sing, Songs for the

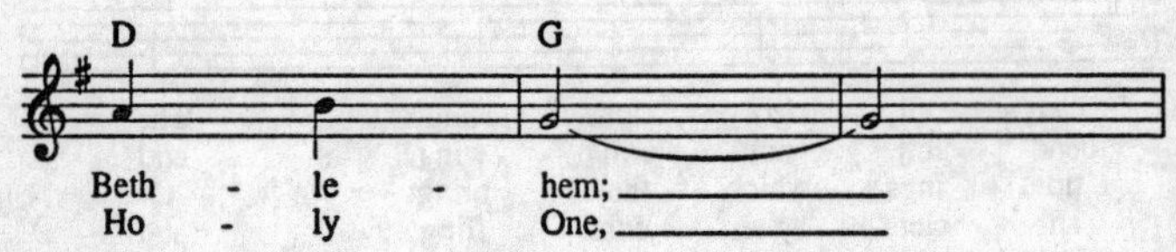
D
G
Beth - le - hem;
Ho - ly One,

D7/A
Born in a hum - ble
Jo - seph the Ba - by's

G
man - ger Is Heav - en's
fath - er Nes - tles Him

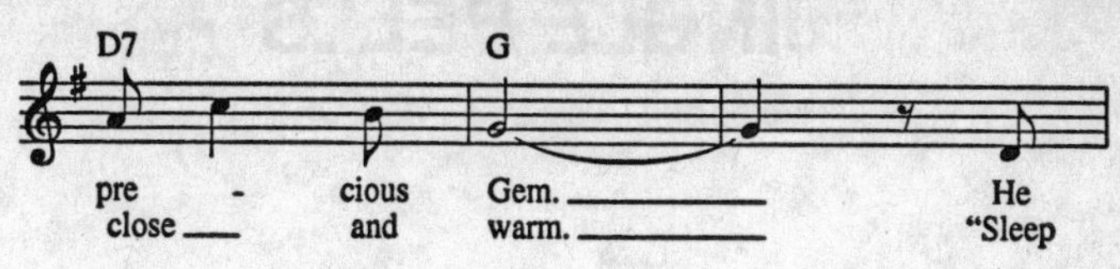
D7
G
pre - cious Gem.
He
close and warm.
"Sleep

is a pre - cious Gem,
Al -
sweet - ly my dear Son."
O

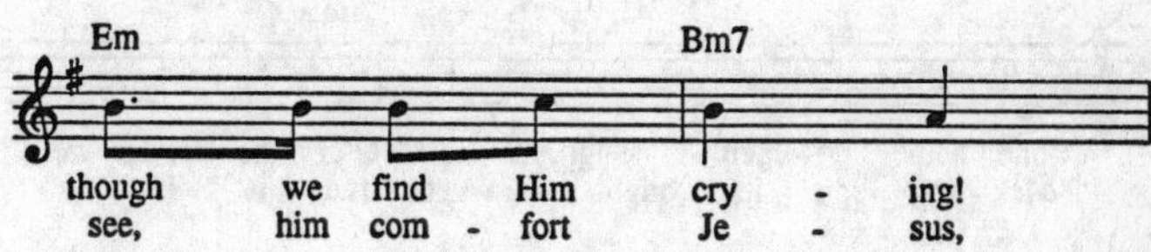
Em
Bm7
though we find Him cry - ing!
see, him com - fort Je - sus,

G
D7/A
In Ma - ry's arms He's
His ti - ny Ba - by

G
Am7
Am9
sigh - ing,
Je - sus, our
sooth - ing!
Glo - ry to

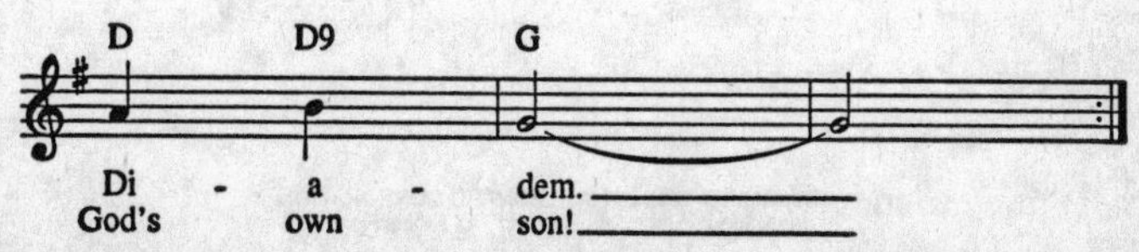
D
D9
G
Di - a - dem.
God's own son!

# JINGLE BELLS

Words and Music by J. PIERPONT

G
Dash - ing thru the snow, In a
Bells on bob - tail ring,

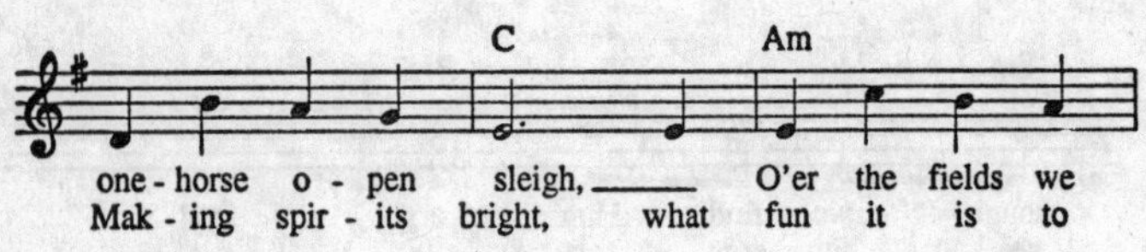
C
Am
one - horse o - pen sleigh, O'er the fields we
Mak - ing spir - its bright, what fun it is to

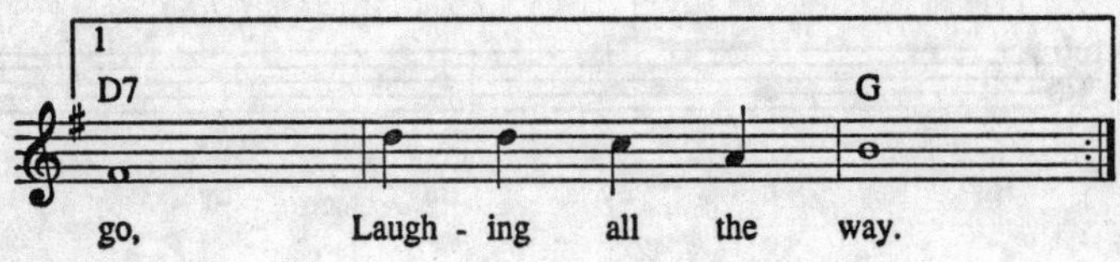
1
D7
G
go, Laugh - ing all the way.

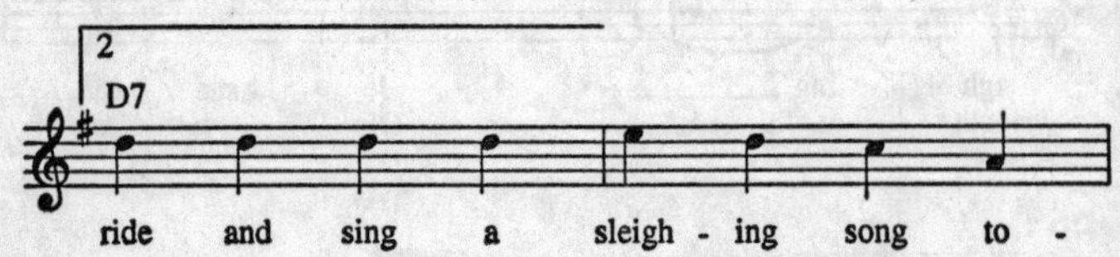
2
D7
ride and sing a sleigh - ing song to -

G
G
night.
Jin - gle bells,
jin - gle bells,

C
Jin - gle all the way!
Oh, what fun it

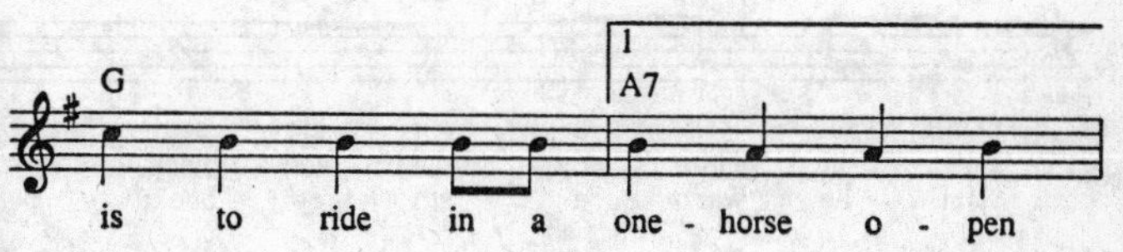
1
G
A7
is to ride in a one - horse o - pen

2
D
D7
D7
G
sleigh! Oh,
one - horse o - pen sleigh.

# JOLLY OLD ST. NICHOLAS

Traditional 19th Century American Carol

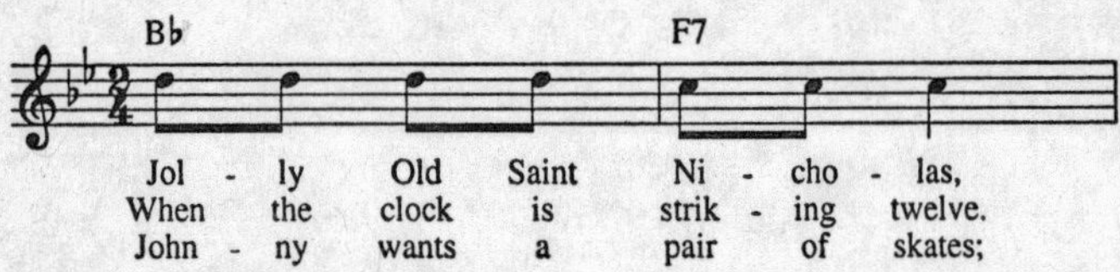
B♭
F7
Jol - ly Old Saint Ni - cho - las,
When the clock is strik - ing twelve.
John - ny wants a pair of skates;

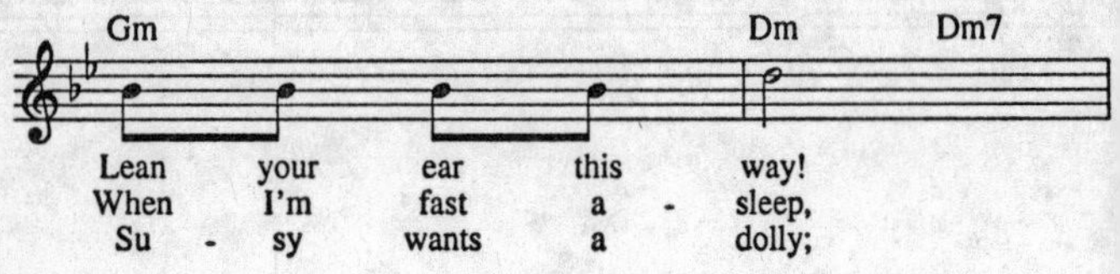
Gm
Dm
Dm7
Lean your ear this way!
When I'm fast a - sleep,
Su - sy wants a dolly;

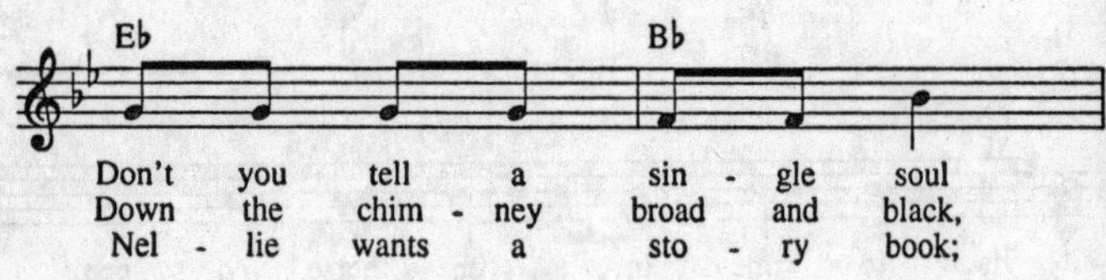
E♭
B♭
Don't you tell a sin - gle soul
Down the chim - ney broad and black,
Nel - lie wants a sto - ry book;

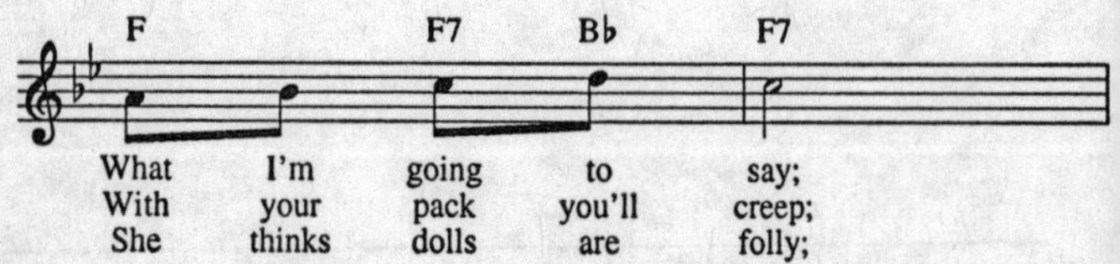
F
F7
B♭
F7
What I'm going to say;
With your pack you'll creep;
She thinks dolls are folly;

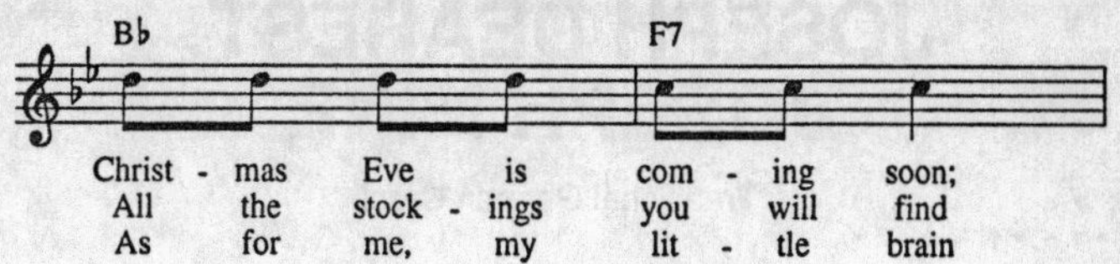
B♭
F7
Christ - mas Eve is com - ing soon;
All the stock - ings you will find
As for me, my lit - tle brain

Gm
Dm
Dm7
Now you dear old man,
Hang - ing in a row;
Is - n't ver - y bright;

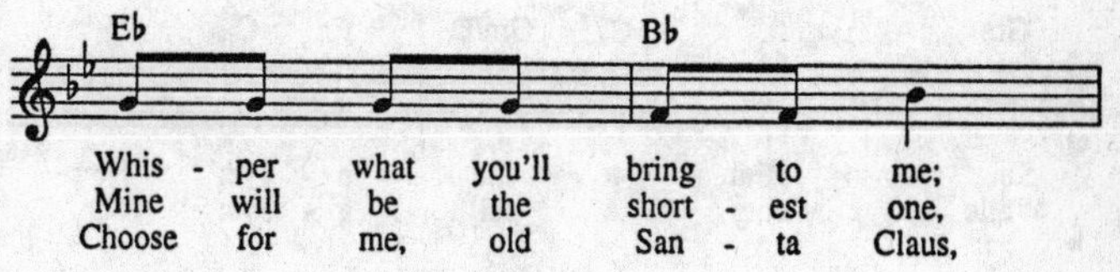
E♭
B♭
Whis - per what you'll bring to me;
Mine will be the short - est one,
Choose for me, old San - ta Claus,

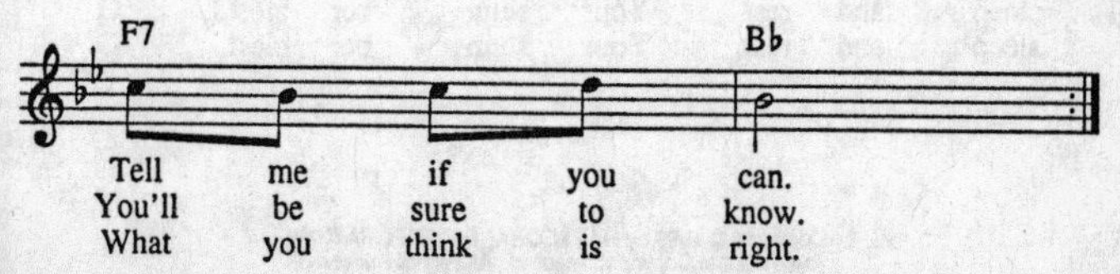
F7
B♭
Tell me if you can.
You'll be sure to know.
What you think is right.

# JOSEPH DEAREST, JOSEPH MINE

Traditional German Carol

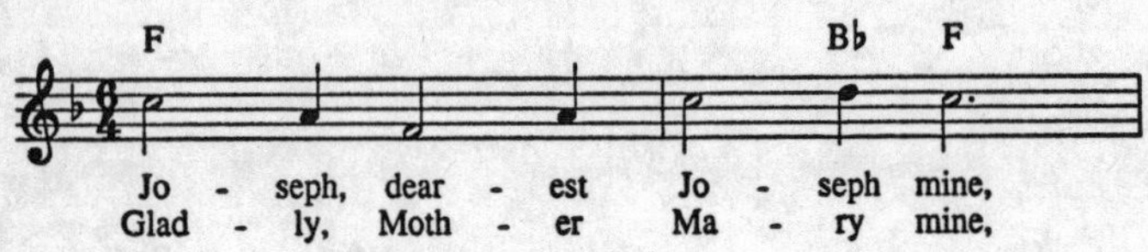
F
B♭
F
Jo - seph, dear - est Jo - seph mine,
Glad - ly, Moth - er Ma - ry mine,

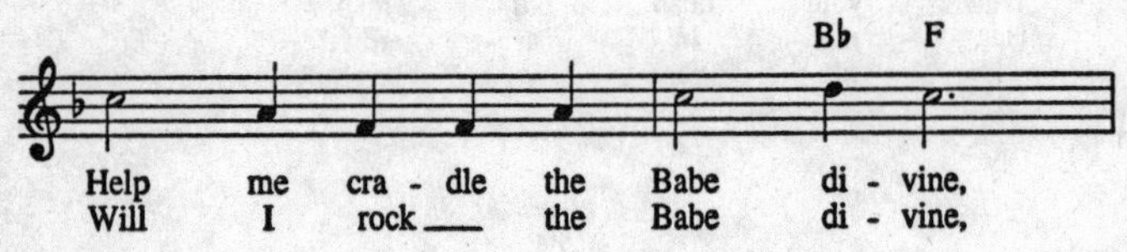
B♭
F
Help me cra - dle the Babe di - vine,
Will I rock ___ the Babe di - vine,

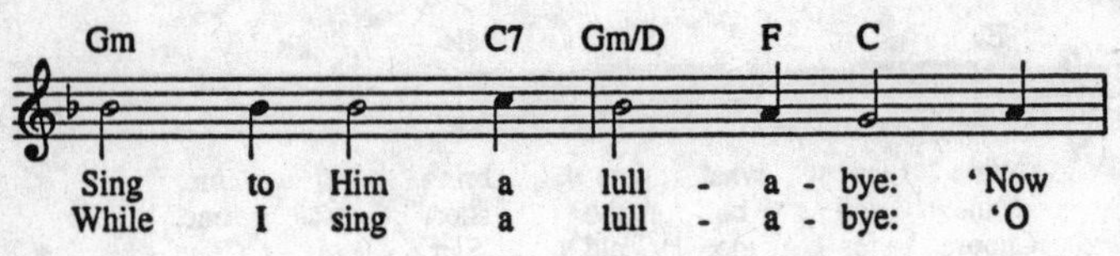
Gm
C7
Gm/D
F
C
Sing to Him a lull - a - bye: 'Now
While I sing a lull - a - bye: 'O

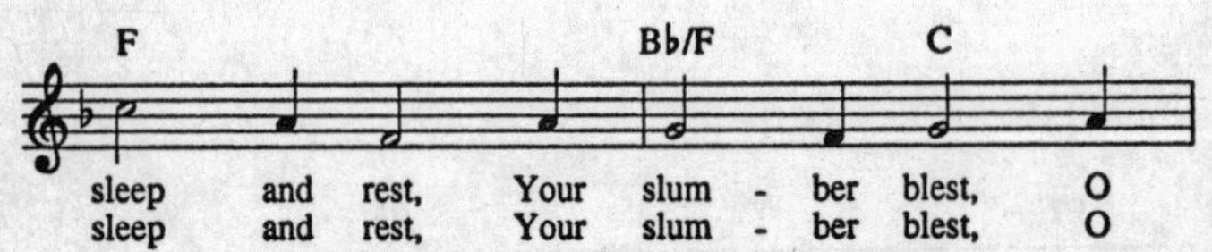
F
B♭/F
C
sleep and rest, Your slum - ber blest, O
sleep and rest, Your slum - ber blest, O

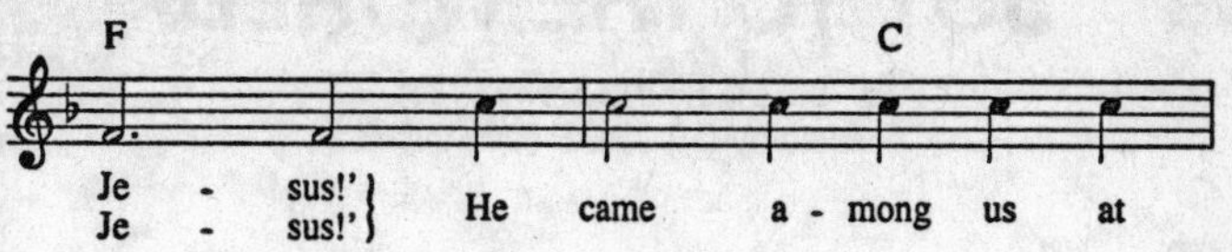
F
C
Je - sus!'
Je - sus!'
He came a - mong us at

Dm
B♭maj7
F/A
Dm
B♭maj7
F/A
Christ - mas time, At Christ - mas time in

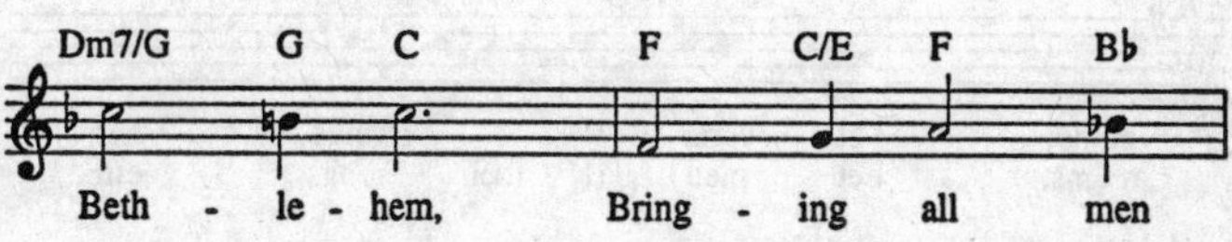
Dm7/G
G
C
F
C/E
F
B♭
Beth - le - hem, Bring - ing all men

C
C7
F
B♭/D
C
C7
F
far and wide Love's Di - a - dem.

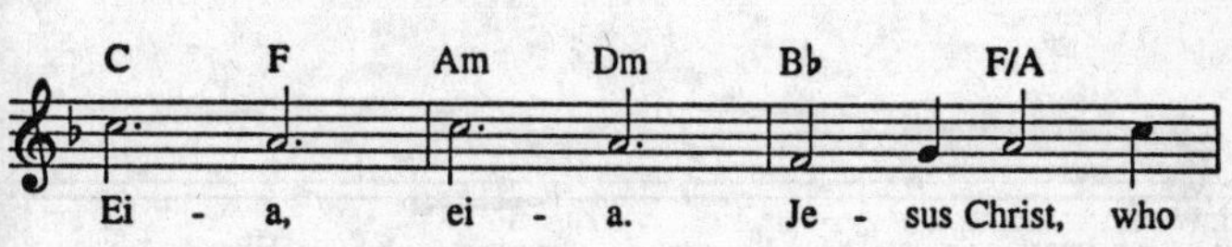
C
F
Am
Dm
B♭
F/A
Ei - a, ei - a. Je - sus Christ, who

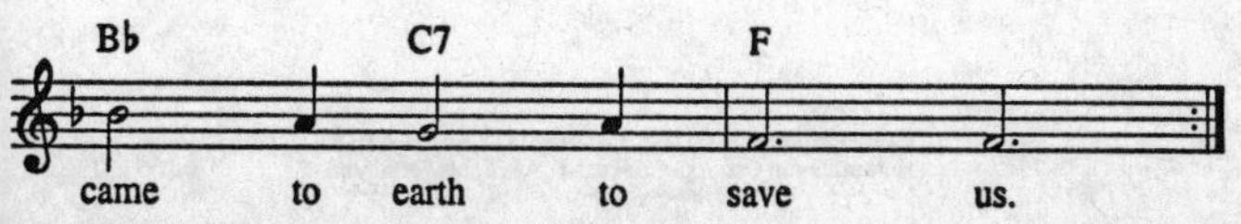
B♭
C7
F
came to earth to save us.

# JOY TO THE WORLD

Words by ISAAC WATTS
Music by GEORGE F. HANDEL

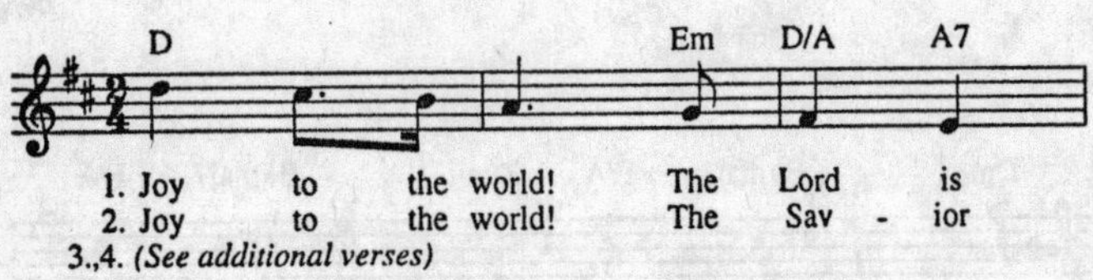
D
Em
D/A
A7
1. Joy to the world! The Lord is
2. Joy to the world! The Sav - ior
3.,4. (See additional verses)

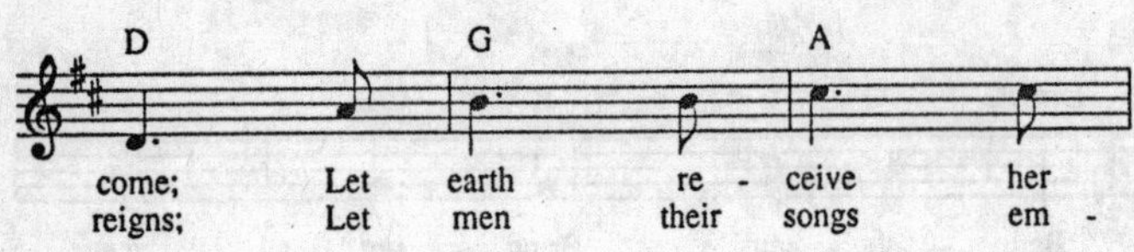
D
G
A
come; Let earth re - ceive her
reigns; Let men their songs em -

D
King; Let ev - 'ry
ploy; while fields and

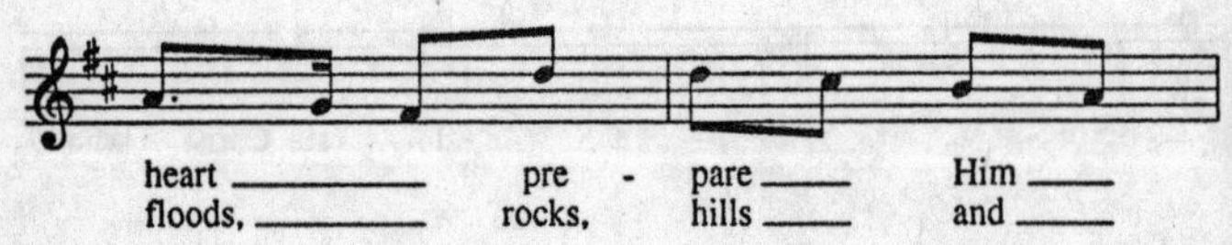
heart pre - pare Him
floods, rocks, hills and

room. And heav'n and na - ture
plains, Re - peat the sound - ing

A
sing. And heav'n and na - ture
joy. Re - peat the sound - ing

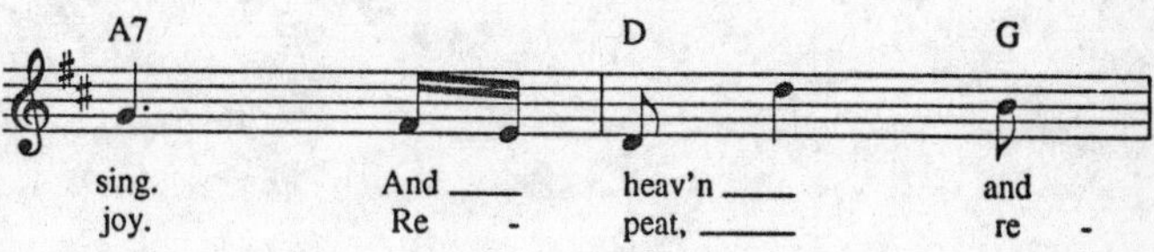
A7
D
G
sing. And heav'n and
joy. Re - peat, re -

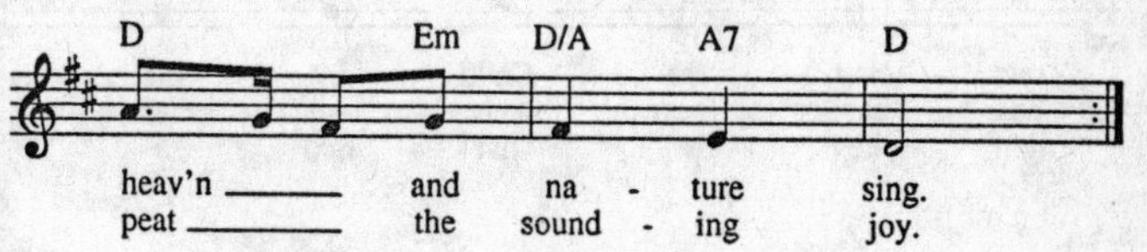
D
Em
D/A
A7
D
heav'n and na - ture sing.
peat the sound - ing joy.

*Additional Verses*

3. No more let sin and sorrow grow,
Nor thorns infest the ground;
He comes to make His blessings flow
Far as the curse is found,
Far as the curse is found,
Far as, far as the curse is found.

4. He rules the world with truth and grace,
And makes the nations prove
The glories of His righteousness,
And wonders of His love,
And wonders of His love,
And wonders, and wonders of His love.

# KING HEROD

Traditional Catalonian Carol

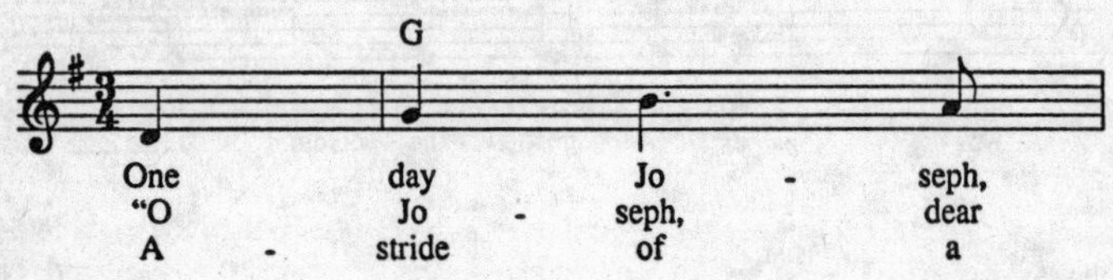
G
One day Jo - seph,
"O Jo - seph, dear
A - stride of a

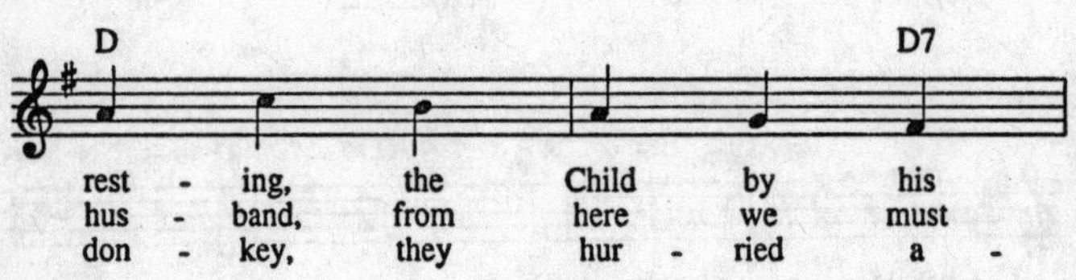
D
D7
rest - ing, the Child by his
hus - band, from here we must
don - key, they hur - ried a -

G
side, Heard shout - ing and
go, And where we are
long, Their path - way was

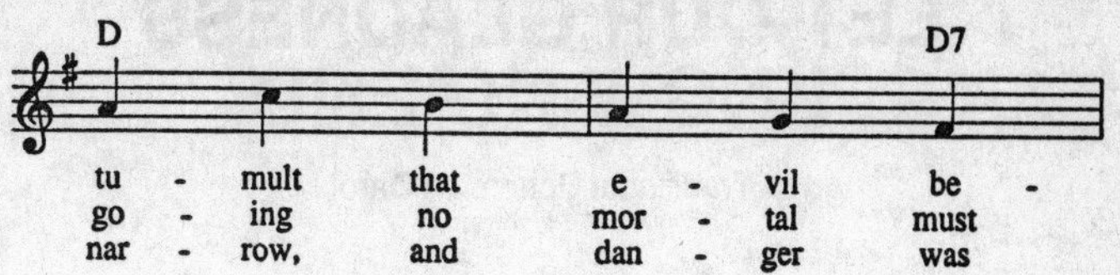
D
D7
tu - mult that e - vil be -
go - ing no mor - tal must
nar - row, and dan - ger was

G
tide: "The wretch - ed King
know. A - cross the hot
strong; God's an - gels, and

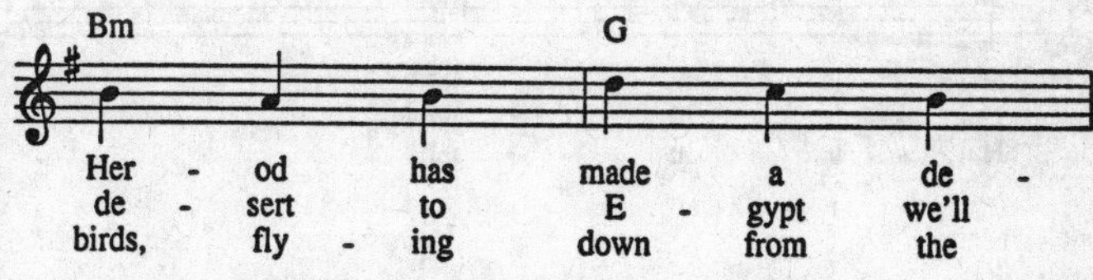
Bm
G
Her - od has made a de -
de - sert to E - gypt we'll
birds, fly - ing down from the

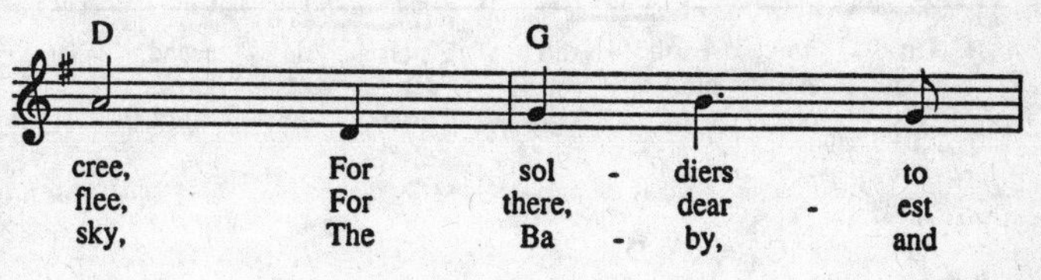
D
G
cree, For sol - diers to
flee, For there, dear - est
sky, The Ba - by, and

D
D7/G
G
D
G
kill ev - 'ry in - fant they see."
Je - sus pro - tect - ed will be."
Jo - seph, and Ma - ry did fly.

# LET OUR GLADNESS KNOW NO END

Traditional Bohemian Carol

G/B D/F# G C/E D G D
Let our glad - ness know no end,
See the love - l'est bloom - ing rose,
In - to flesh is made the word,
Am G C G
Hal - le - lu - jah!
Hal - le - lu - jah!
Hal - le - lu - jah!
G/B C D Bm C6
Un - to earth did Christ de - scend,
From the branch of Jes - se grows,
'Tis our re - fuge, Christ the Lord,
G C D G
Hal - le - lu - jah.
Hal - le - lu - jah.
Hal - le - lu - jah.

G
D/F♯
Em
C
Bm
Am
On this day God gave

G
Em
Am
B
Am
us.
Christ His Son to

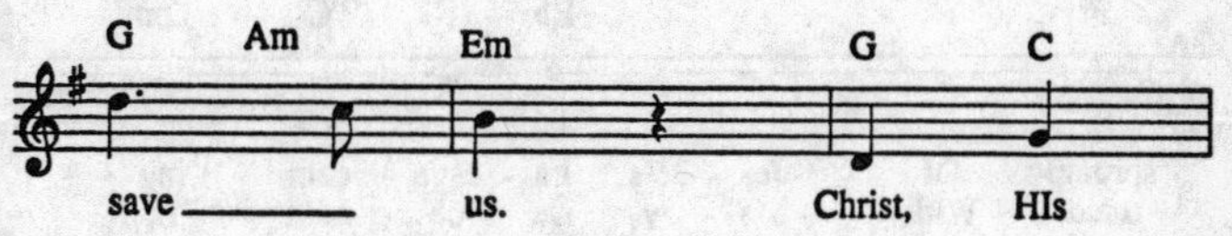
G
Am
Em
G
C
save
us.
Christ, HIs

G/B
C
D
Em
C
D7
G
Son, His Son to save us.

# LO, HOW A ROSE E'ER BLOOMING

from the ALTE CATHOLISCHE GEISTLICHE KIRCHENGESÄNG
15th Century German Tune

F
B♭
F
C
Dm
Lo, how a rose e'er bloom - ing
I - sa - iah 'twas fore - told it,

B♭
F
C
Dm
B♭
C
From ten - der stem hath
The Rose I have in

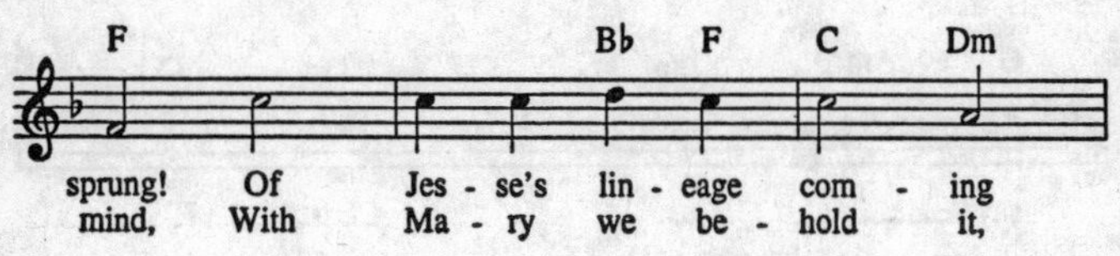
F
B♭
F
C
Dm
sprung! Of Jes - se's lin - eage com - ing
mind, With Ma - ry we be - hold it,

B♭
F
C
Dm
B♭
C
As men of old have
The Vir - gin Moth - er

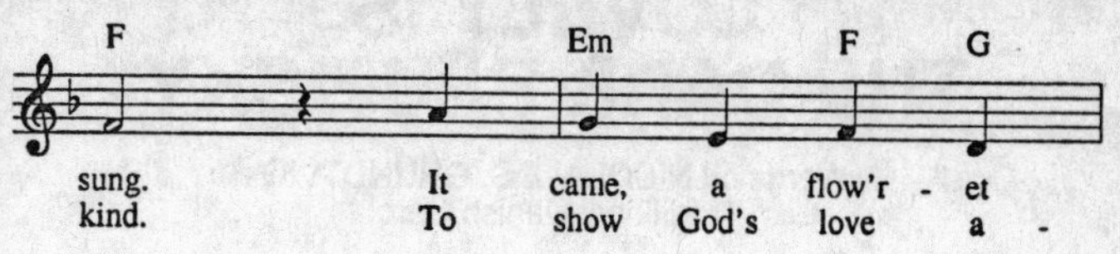
F
Em
F
G
sung. It came, a flow'r - et
kind. To show God's love a -

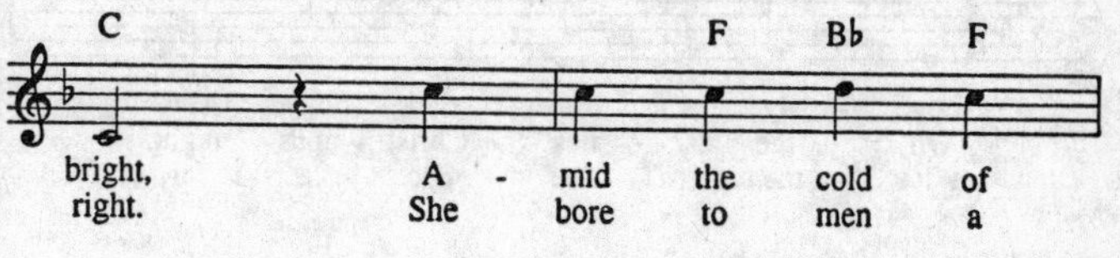
C
F
B♭
F
bright, A - mid the cold of
right. She bore to men a

C
D
Gm
Am
B♭
win - ter, When half
Sav - iour, When half

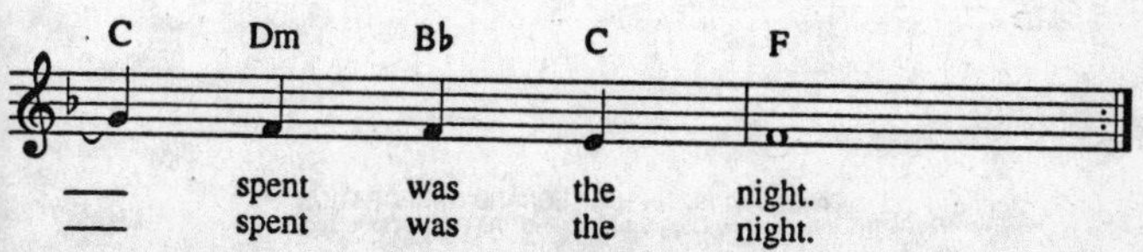
C
Dm
B♭
C
F
spent was the night.
spent was the night.

# LOVELY IS THE DARK BLUE SKY

Words by NICOLAI F.S. GRUNDTVIG
Traditional Danish Carol

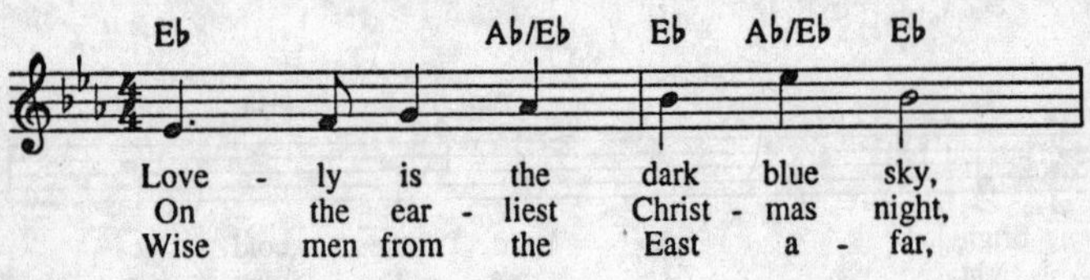
Eb
Ab/Eb
Eb
Ab/Eb
Eb
Love - ly is the dark blue sky,
On the ear - liest Christ - mas night,
Wise men from the East a - far,

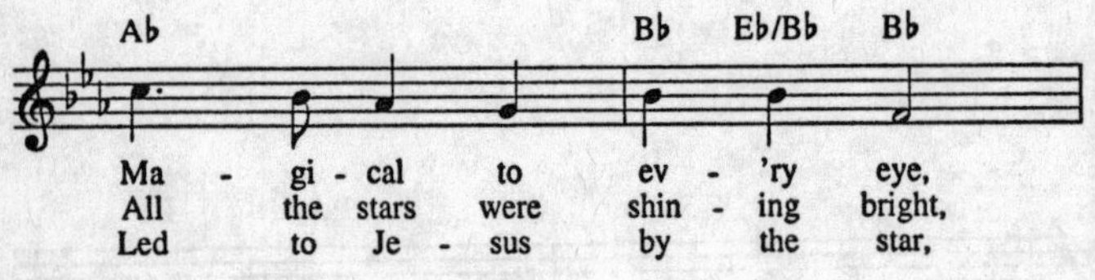
Ab
Bb
Eb/Bb
Bb
Ma - gi - cal to ev - 'ry eye,
All the stars were shin - ing bright,
Led to Je - sus by the star,

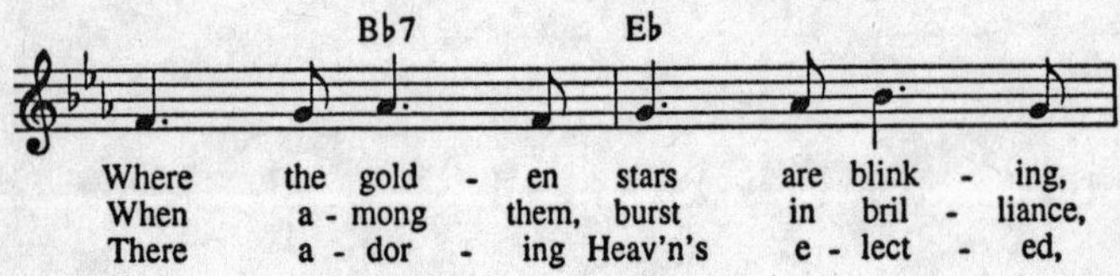
Bb7
Eb
Where the gold - en stars are blink - ing,
When a - mong them, burst in bril - liance,
There a - dor - ing Heav'n's e - lect - ed,

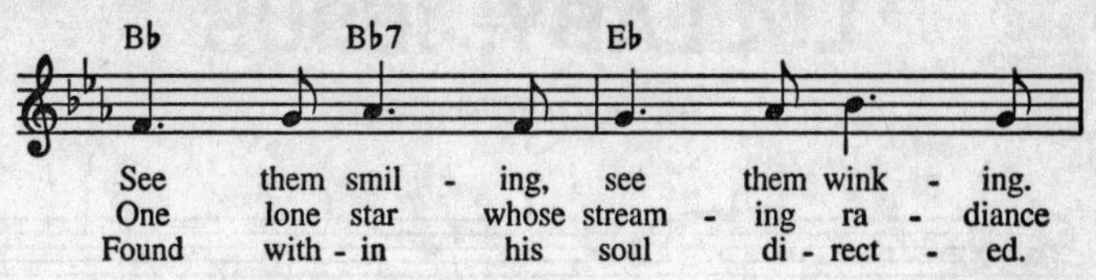
B♭ B♭7 E♭
See them smil - ing, see them wink - ing.
One lone star whose stream - ing ra - diance
Found with - in his soul di - rect - ed.

A♭/E♭ E♭ B♭7 E♭
Beck - 'ning us to Heav'n on high,
Far out - shown the sun's own light,
God's great Light and Love and Pow'r.

A♭/E♭ E♭ Fm B♭ E♭
Beck - 'ning us to Heav'n on high.
Far out - shown the sun's own light.
god's great Light and Love and Pow'r.

# LULLABY, JESUS

Traditional Polish Carol

F
C7/E
F
Lull - a - by, Je - sus, O
See how God's earth lies in
C
B♭/F
F
cease from your cry - ing,
sor - row and sad - ness;
C7/E
F
Here on Thy Moth - er's warm
Give us Thy bless - ing, O
C
C7
F
breast sweet - ly ly - ing.
bring Heav - en's glad - ness!
B♭/F
Lull - a - by, Je - sus, O
C7/E
B♭/F
F
sleep now, my pre - cious, Moth - er is
C7/E
F
C
C7
F
watch - ing with love none can meas - ure.

# MARY HAD A BABY

African-American Spiritual

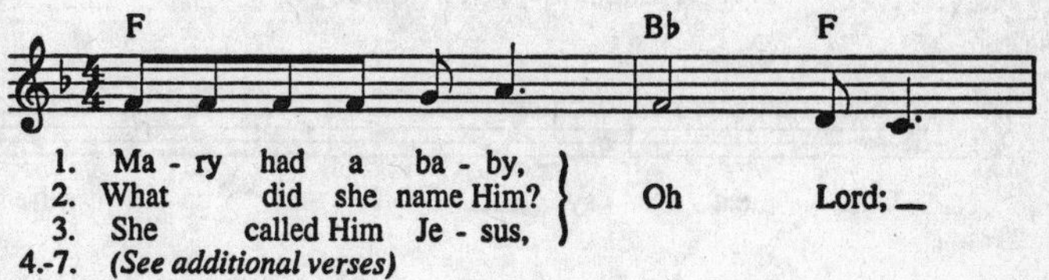
F
B♭
F
1. Ma - ry had a ba - by,
2. What did she name Him?
3. She called Him Je - sus,
4.-7. (See additional verses)
Oh Lord;

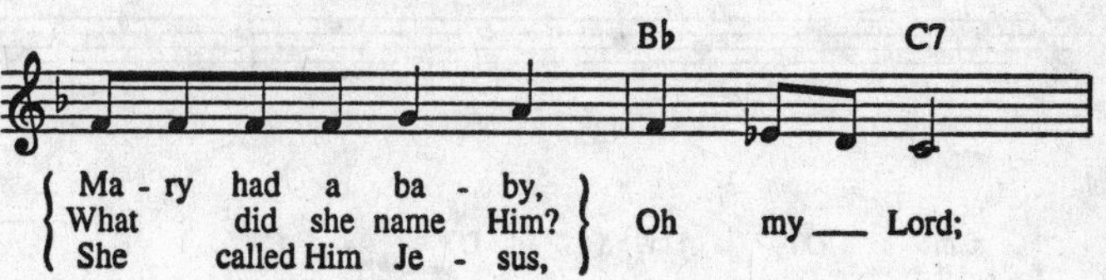
B♭
C7
Ma - ry had a ba - by,
What did she name Him?
She called Him Je - sus,
Oh my Lord;

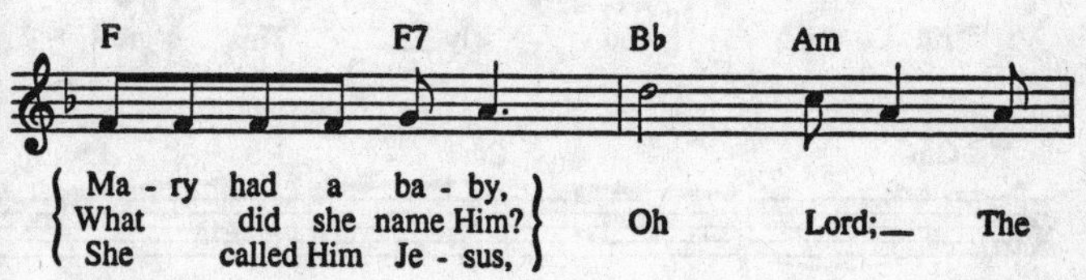
F
F7
B♭
Am
Ma - ry had a ba - by,
What did she name Him?
She called Him Je - sus,
Oh Lord; The

F
Dm
C7
F
peo - ple keep a - com - ing and the train done gone.

*Additional Verses*

4. Where was He born?
5. Born in a stable,
6. Where did they lay Him?
7. Laid Him in a manger,

# MARCH OF THE THREE KINGS

Words by M.L. HOHMAN
Traditional French Melody

Gm
This great day, I met up-on the
Cm Gm Cm D7+
way, The Kings of East as they came
Cm6 D7 Am7♭5 D7 Cm6 D7
rid - ing proud - ly This great
Gm Cm7
day, I met up - on the
B♭ Cm Gm Cm D7
way The Kings of East with all their
Cm7 D7 Gm Fine D7 Cm/E♭ D7
fine ar - ray. The gifts of

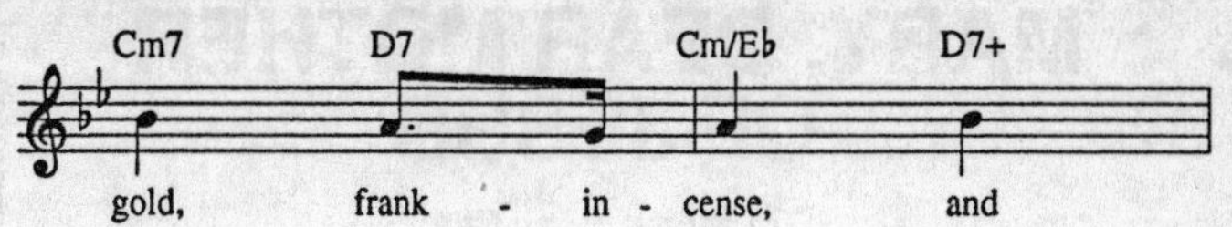
Cm7
D7
Cm/E♭
D7+
gold, frank - in - cense, and

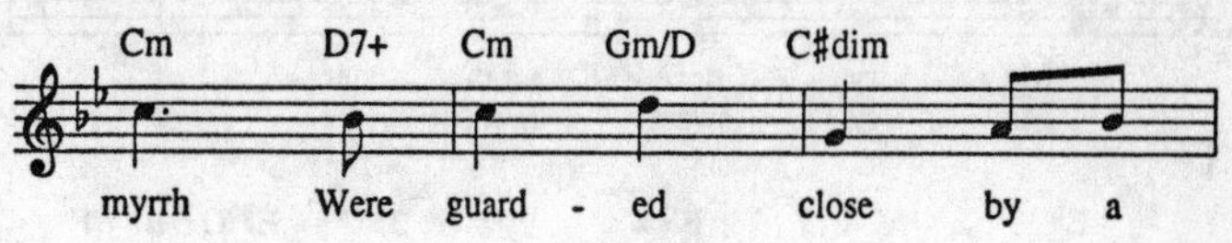
Cm
D7+
Cm
Gm/D
C♯dim
myrrh Were guard - ed close by a

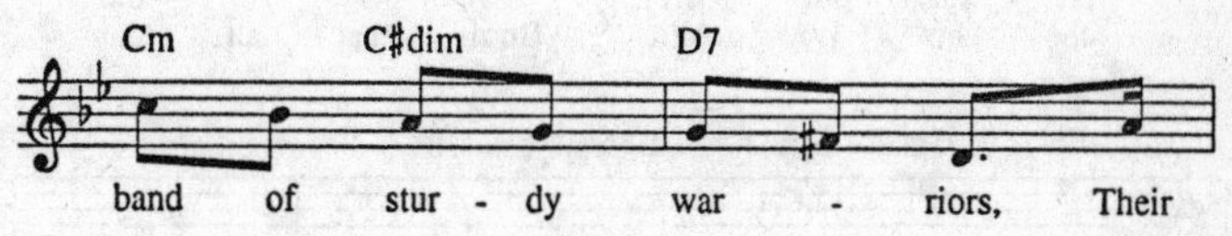
Cm
C♯dim
D7
band of stur - dy war - riors, Their

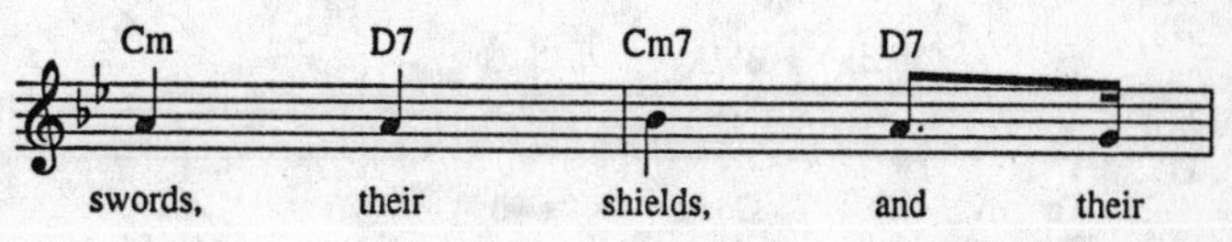
Cm
D7
Cm7
D7
swords, their shields, and their

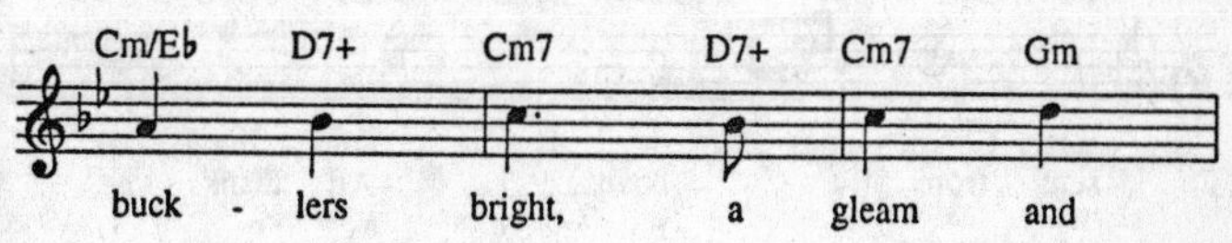
Cm/E♭
D7+
Cm7
D7+
Cm7
Gm
buck - lers bright, a gleam and

D.C. al Fine
Cm
D7
E♭6
Edim
F9sus
D7
Gm
spar - kling in the morn - ing light.

# MARY, DEAR MOTHER OF JESUS

Traditional Italian Carol

Eb
Fm7
Bb7
Ma - ry, dear moth - er of
Ma - ry, sweet moth - er of
Eb
Cm
Bb
Bb/Ab
Eb/G
Bb7/F
Je - sus, our Lord, We haste to the
the ho - ly child, Born that all man -
Eb
Cm
Gm/D
Eb6
F
Bb
crib with joy - ful ac - cord,
kind might be rec - on - cil'd,
Cm/Bb
Bb/Ab
Eb/G
To see God's own gift on
Thy in - fant son was God -
Ab
Eb/Bb
Bb
Eb
Ab/C
Eb/Bb
this Christ - mas day, Voic - ing our
sent from a - bove, All thanks be
Ab
Eb/G
Bb7/F
Ab6
Bbsus
Bb7
Eb
prais - es, The star lights our way.
to Him, For this gift of love.

# NOËL NOUVELET

Traditional French Carol

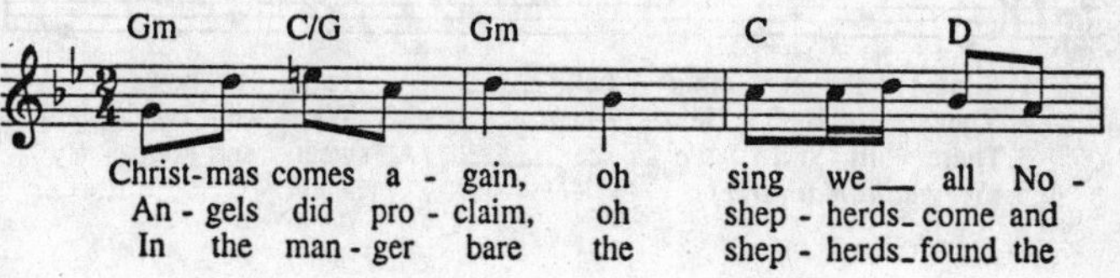
Gm C/G Gm C D
Christ-mas comes a - gain, oh sing we___ all No -
An - gels did pro - claim, oh shep - herds_come and
In the man - ger bare the shep - herds_found the

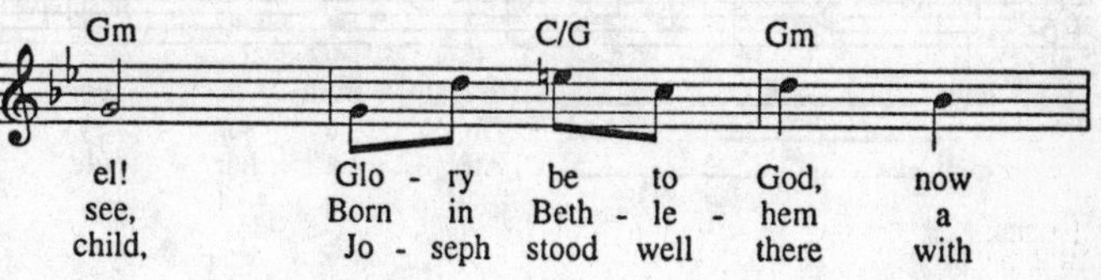
Gm C/G Gm
el! Glo - ry be to God, now
see, Born in Beth - le - hem a
child, Jo - seph stood well there with

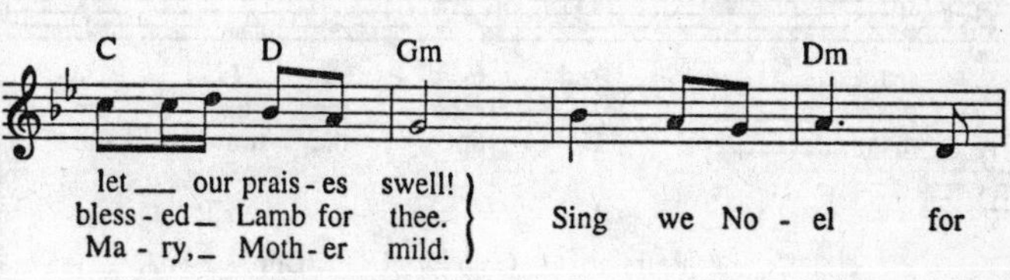
C D Gm Dm
let ___ our prais - es swell!
bless - ed_ Lamb for thee.
Ma - ry,_ Moth - er mild.
Sing we No - el for

Gm Dm Gm C/G
Christ the new - born King, No - el. Christ-mas comes a -

Gm C D Gm
gain, oh sing we___ all No - el.

# MASTERS IN THIS HALL

Traditional English

Dm
1. Mas - ters in this hall, Hear ye news to -
2. Then to Beth - 'lem town We went two and
3. There - in did we see A sweet and good - ly
4.,5. (See additional verses)
day Brought from o - ver
two, And in a sor - ry
may And a fair old
sea, And ev - er I you
place Heard the ox - en
man, Up - on the straw she
Refrain Gm6 Dm A7
pray.
low.
lay.
Now - ell! Now - ell! Now - ell!
Dm Gm6 Dm D7
Now - ell sing we clear! Holp - en

Gm
A7
Dm
B♭
are all folk on earth, Born

Dm
A7
Dm
Gm6
is God's Son so dear. Now - ell! Now - ell!

Dm
A7
Dm
Gm6
Now - ell! Now - ell sing we

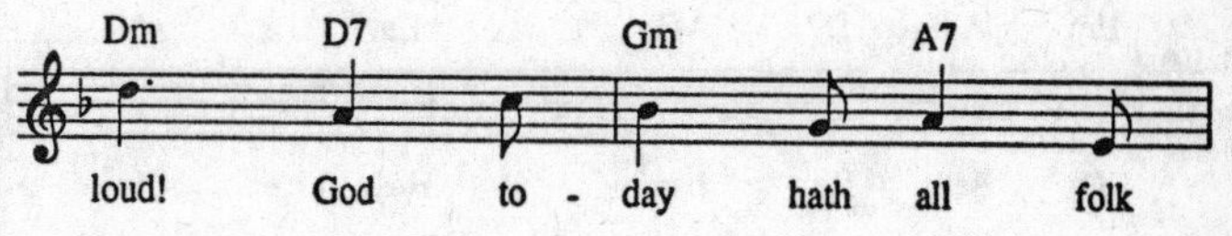
Dm
D7
Gm
A7
loud! God to - day hath all folk

Dm
B♭
Dm
A7
Dm
raised And cast a - down the proud.

*Additional Verses*

4. And a little child
On her arm had she,
'Wot ye who this is?'
Said the hinds to me.
*(Refrain)*

5. This is Christ the Lord,
Masters, be ye glad:
Christmas is come in,
And no folk should be sad.
*(Refrain)*

# O BETHLEHEM

Traditional Spanish

G Am D7 G D7
O Beth - le - hem, O'er you a

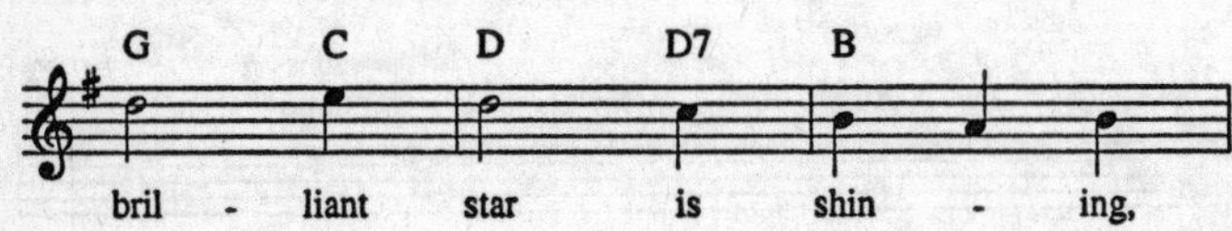
G C D D7 B
bril - liant star is shin - ing,

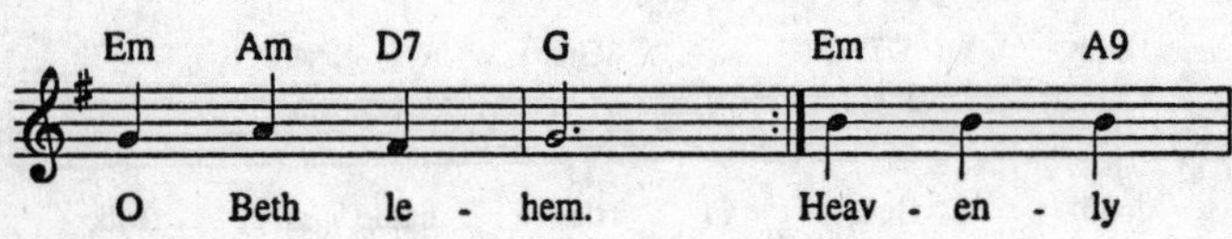
Em Am D7 G Em A9
O Beth le - hem. Heav - en - ly

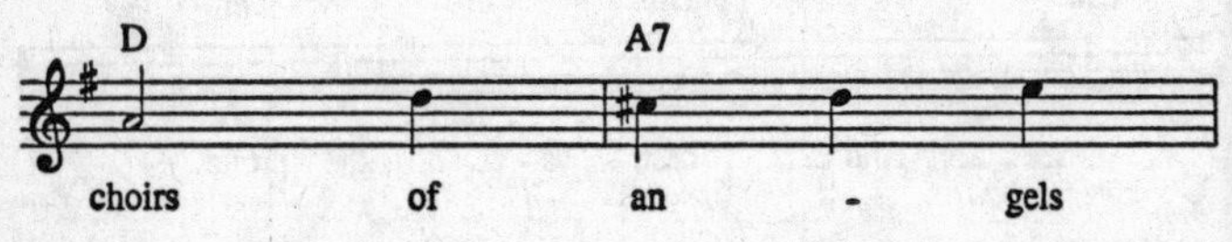
D A7
choirs of an - gels

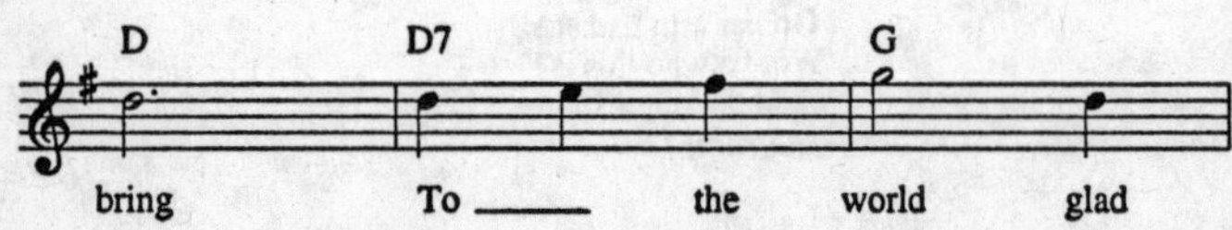
D D7 G
bring To the world glad

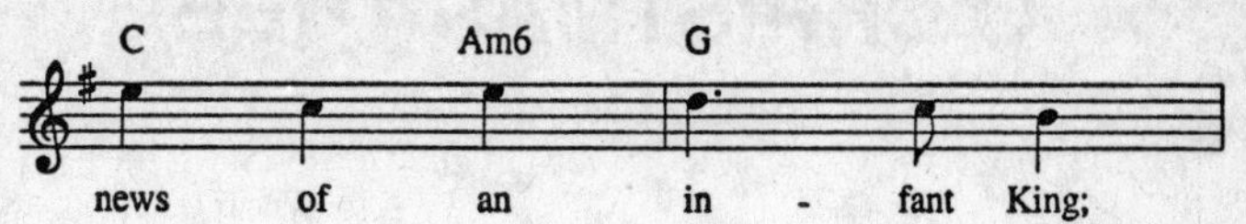
C
Am6
G
news of an in - fant King;

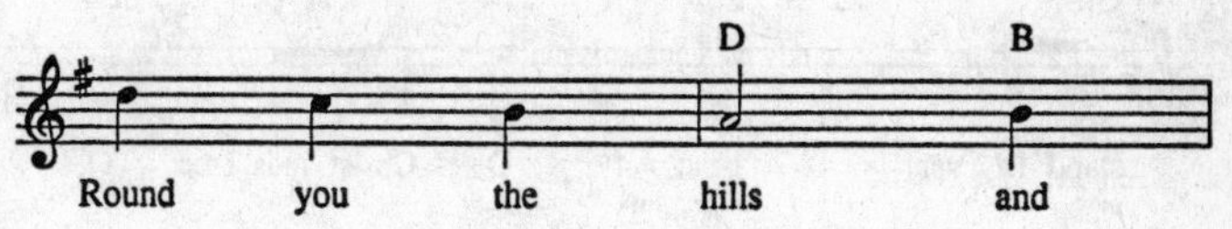
D
B
Round you the hills and

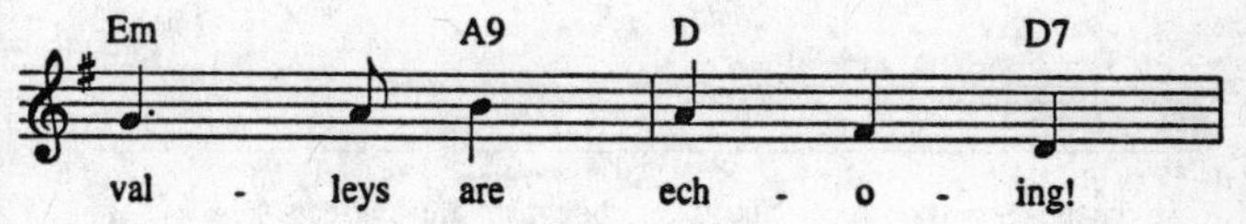
Em
A9
D
D7
val - leys are ech - o - ing!

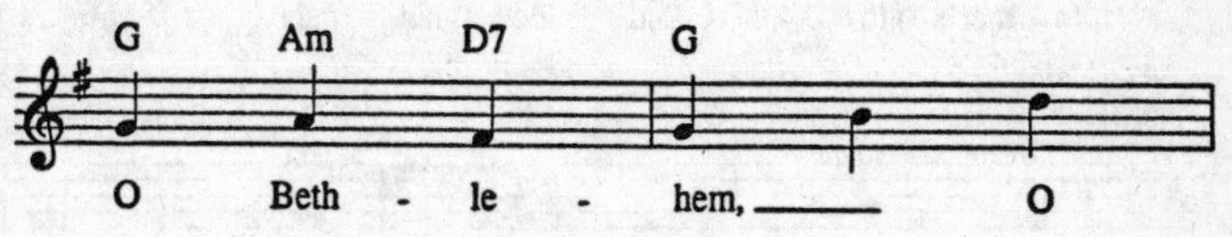
G
Am
D7
G
O Beth - le - hem, O

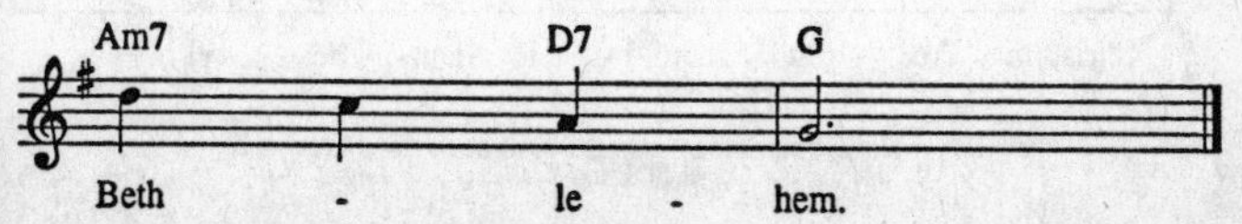
Am7
D7
G
Beth - le - hem.

# O CHRISTMAS TREE

Traditional German Carol

F C7 F Fmaj7
O Christ - mas Tree, O Christ - mas Tree, You
Gm7 C7 C7/F F C7
stand in ver - dant beau - ty! O Christ-mas Tree, O
F Fmaj7 F♯dim Gm7 C7
Christ - mas Tree, You stand in ver - dant
F F♯dim
beau - ty! Your boughs are green in
Gm7 C7
sum - mer's glow, And do not fade in
B♭/F F C7 F A7/E
win - ter's snow. O Christ - mas Tree O
Dm Gm C7 C7/F F
Christ-mas Tree, You stand in ver - dant beau - ty!

# O CHRISTMAS, YOU SEASON OF CHILDLIKE DELIGHTS

Words by GUSTAVA KIELLAND
Traditional Norwegian Carol

D
G/D
D
O Christ-mas you sea - son of Child-like de-light, We
O wise men who come from the lands of the East, We
In joy and thanks-giv - ing I hold out my hand, And
A7
D
all of-fer heart - i - est greet - ing; Our voic-es we raise in a
know of the Babe you are seek - ing; We pray we may join in your
ask that you give yours in to - ken, That we be u - ni - ted by
G/D
D
A7
song clear and bright; To bid you a thou - sand times
ho - ly quest, And fol - low the star bright-ly
this sa - cred band; God's love through the a - ges un -
D
wel - come.
gleam - ing.
bro - ken.
Our hands we will clap, clap, clap, As
A7
D
A7
hap - py as can be; So glad are we this
D
A7
Bm
D/A
G
D/A
A7
D
day to see, We swing a-round a cir - cle and curt - sey.

# O COME, ALL YE FAITHFUL

Words and Music by JOHN FRANCIS WADE
Latin Words translated by FREDERICK OAKELEY

G
D
A - des - te, fi - de - les,
O come all ye faith - ful,
Sing, choirs of an - gels,
Yea, Lord, we greet Thee,

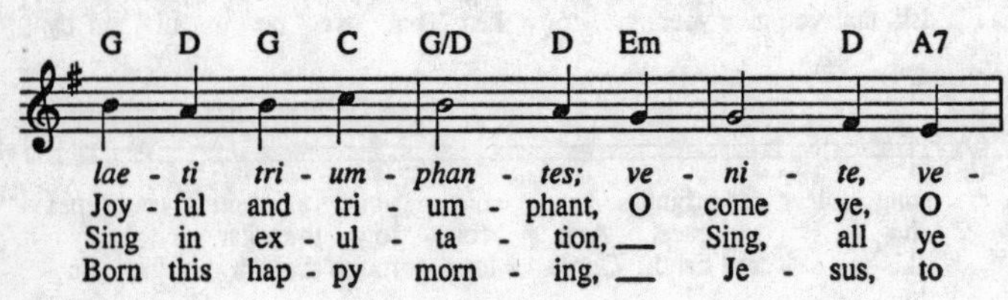
G D G C G/D D Em D A7
lae - ti tri - um - phan - tes; ve - ni - te, ve -
Joy - ful and tri - um - phant, O come ye, O
Sing in ex - ul - ta - tion, __ Sing, all ye
Born this hap - py morn - ing, __ Je - sus, to

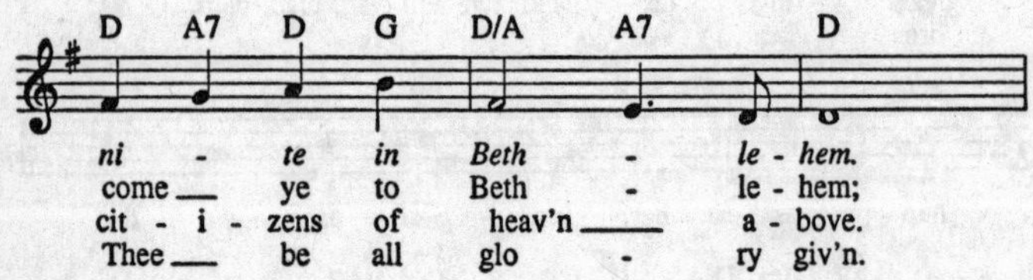
D A7 D G D/A A7 D
ni - te in Beth - le - hem.
come __ ye to Beth - le - hem;
cit - i - zens of heav'n __ a - bove.
Thee __ be all glo - ry giv'n.

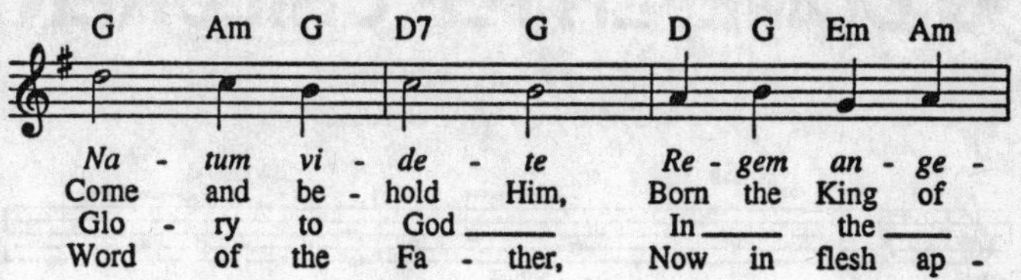
G Am G D7 G D G Em Am
Na - tum vi - de - te Re - gem an - ge -
Come and be - hold Him, Born the King of
Glo - ry to God In the
Word of the Fa - ther, Now in flesh ap -

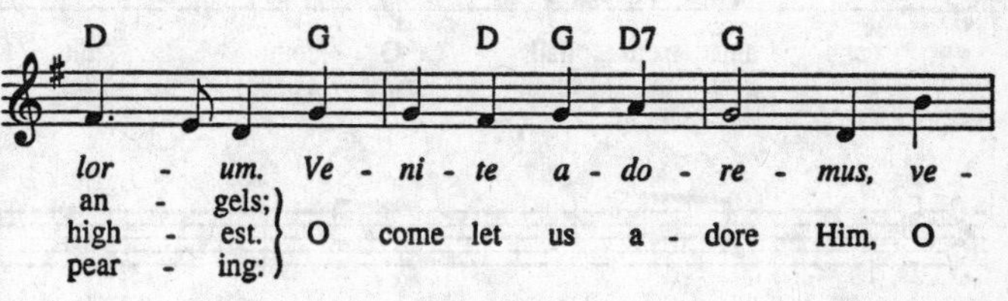
D G D G D7 G
lor - um. Ve - ni - te a - do - re - mus, ve -
an - gels;
high - est. O come let us a - dore Him, O
pear - ing:

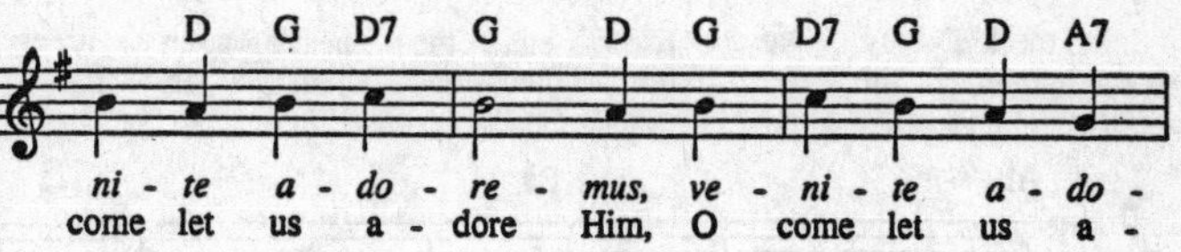
D G D7 G D G D7 G D A7
ni - te a - do - re - mus, ve - ni - te a - do -
come let us a - dore Him, O come let us a -

D D/C G/B C G/D D7 G
re - mus Do - mi - num.
dore Him, Christ the Lord.

# O COME, LITTLE CHILDREN

Words by C. von SCHMIDT
Music by J.P.A. SCHULZ

E♭
O come, lit - tle chil - dren, from
Now "Glo - ry to God!" sing the
B♭7 E♭
cot and from hall, O come to the
an - gels on high, And "Peace up - on
B♭7 E♭
man - ger in Beth - le - hem's stall. There
earth!" heav'n - ly voic - es re - ply. Then
B♭ B♭7 E♭
meek - ly He li - eth, the heav - en - ly
come lit - tle chil - dren, and join in the
A♭ B♭
Child, So poor and so
day That glad - dened the
E♭ B♭7 E♭
hum - ble, so sweet and so mild.
world on that first Christ - mas Day.

# O COME, O COME IMMANUEL

Traditional Melody
Words translated by JOHN M. NEALE and HENRY S. COFFIN

Em C D
O come, o come Im - man - u -
O come Thou Wis - dom from on
O come, De - sire of na - tions,
G D G C Am Bm
el, And ran - som cap - tive Is - ra -
high, And or - der all things far and
bind All peo - ple in one heart and
Em Am Em A
el, That mourns in lone - ly ex - ile
nigh; To us the path of know - ledge
mind; Bid en - vy, strife, and quar - rel's
D Em D Bm G C D
here Un - til the Son of God ap -
show, And cause us in her ways to
cease; Fill the whole world with heav - en's
G D Em Bm G C D
pear.
go.
peace.
Re - joice, re - joice! Im - man - u -
Em D G C Am Bm Em
el shall come to Thee, O Is - ra - el!

# O HOLY NIGHT

French Words by PLACIDE CAPPEAU
English Words by JOHN S. DWIGHT
Music by ADOLPHE ADAM

C
F
O ho - ly night! The stars are bright - ly
C
G7
shin - ing, it is the night of the dear Sav - iour's
C
birth. Long lay the
F
C
world in sin and er - ror pin - ing Till he ap -
Em
B7
Em
peared and the soul felt its worth. A
G7
C
thrill of hope the wea - ry world re-joic - es, For

G7 C

yon - der breaks a new and glo - rious morn,

Am Em

Fall on your knees! O

Dm Am

hear the an - gel voic - es! O

C G7 C C7 F

night di - vine! O

C G7 C

night when Christ was born, O

G7 C C7 F

night di - vine! O

C G7 C
night, O night di - vine!

# O LEAVE YOUR SHEEP

Traditional French Carol

F C7 F C F C F C7/G
O leave your sheep, ye shep-herds come a -
O see him there, so ti - ny and so
F/A C F C7 F C F C F C7/G
way, from your flocks come, your sheep and lambs will
weak, a lit - tle babe with - in a man - ger
F/A F C G7/B C F/A
stay. O stop your tears, Your
laid. From heav'n a - bove He
Dm C C7 F C F C F C7
souls with joy re - new. Come, hur - ry to a -
comes the earth to save As God's in - car - nate
F B♭ F B♭ F
dore the one, the one, the
Word. He is, he is Our
C7/G Gm Am/G Gm F/C C7 F
one who comes to com - fort you.
Lord and our faith - ful shep - herd.

# O SANCTISSIMA

Sicilian Carol

C F C G7 C F
Day of ho - li - ness, peace and
C G7 C G/B D/A G C/E
hap - pi - ness. Joy - ful, glo - ri - ous
G/D D7 G G7
Christ - mas day! An - gels tell the
C
sto - ry of this day of
Am Em/G F C/E
glo - ry. Praise Christ, our
F C/E F C/G G7 C
Sav - ior, born this Christ - mas day!

# O LITTLE TOWN OF BETHLEHEM

Words by PHILLIPS BROOKS
Music by LEWIS H. REDNER

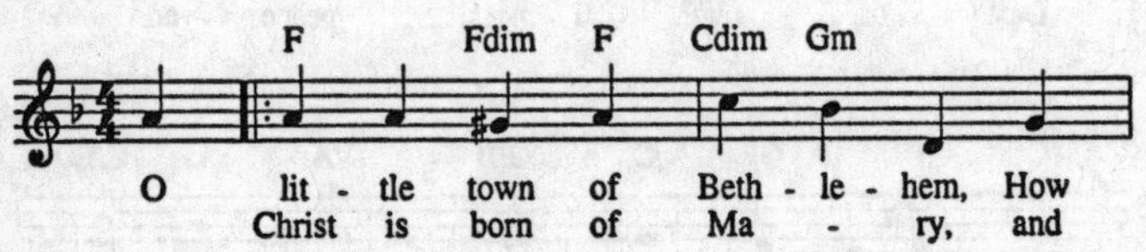
F
Fdim
F
Cdim
Gm
O
lit - tle
town
of
Beth - le - hem,
How
Christ
is
born
of
Ma - ry,
and

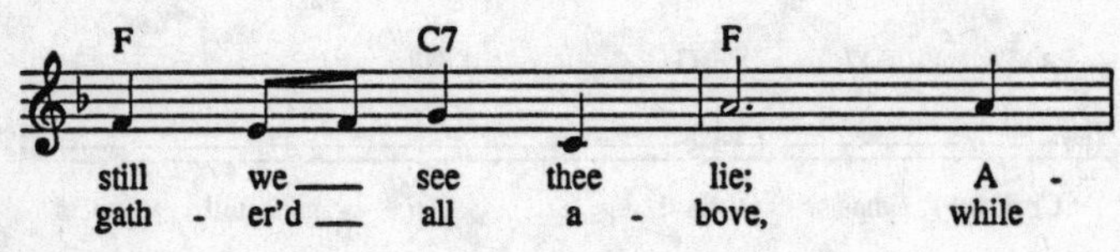
F
C7
F
still
we
see
thee
lie;
A -
gath - er'd
all
a - bove,
while

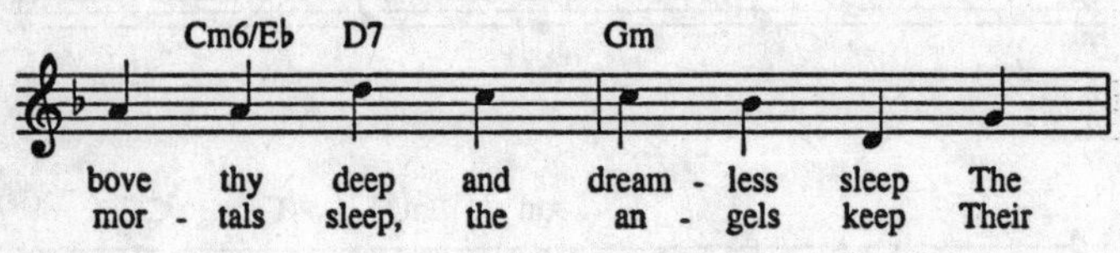
Cm6/Eb
D7
Gm
bove
thy
deep
and
dream - less
sleep
The
mor - tals
sleep,
the
an - gels
keep
Their

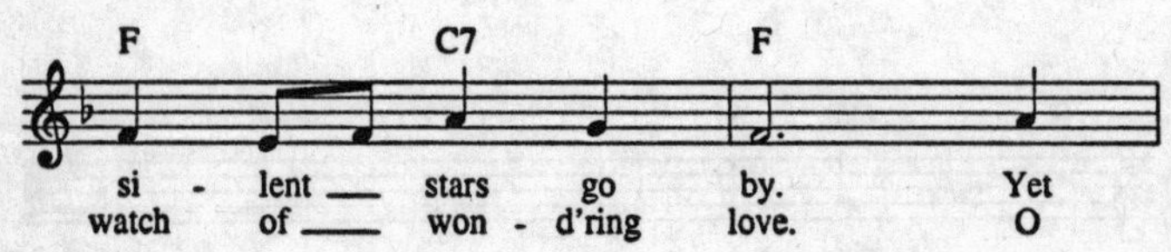
F
C7
F
si - lent
stars
go
by.
Yet
watch
of
won - d'ring
love.
O

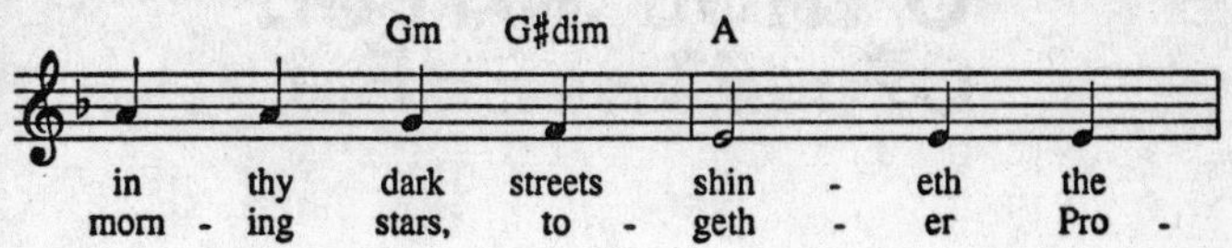
Gm G#dim A
in thy dark streets shin - eth the
morn - ing stars, to - geth - er Pro -

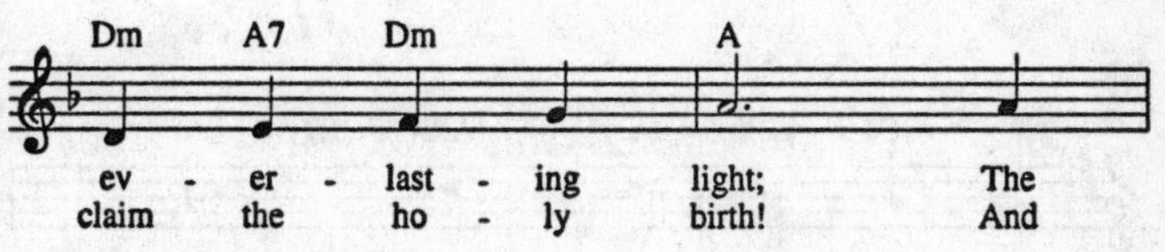
Dm A7 Dm A
ev - er - last - ing light; The
claim the ho - ly birth! And

F Fdim F Cdim Gm
hopes and fears of all the years are
prais - es sing to God the King, and

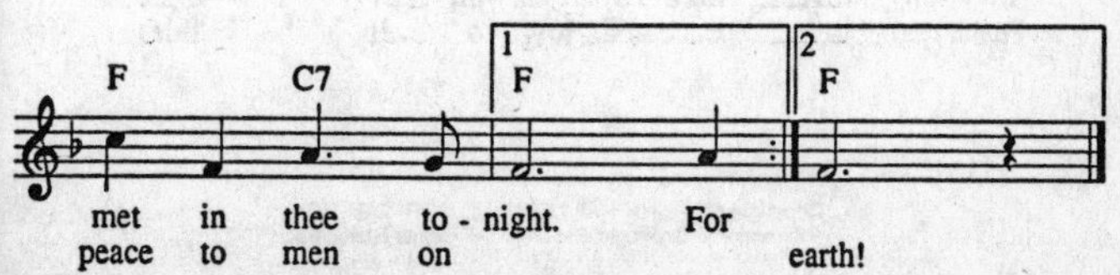
F C7 1 F 2 F
met in thee to - night. For
peace to men on earth!

# O THOU JOYFUL

Traditional German Carol

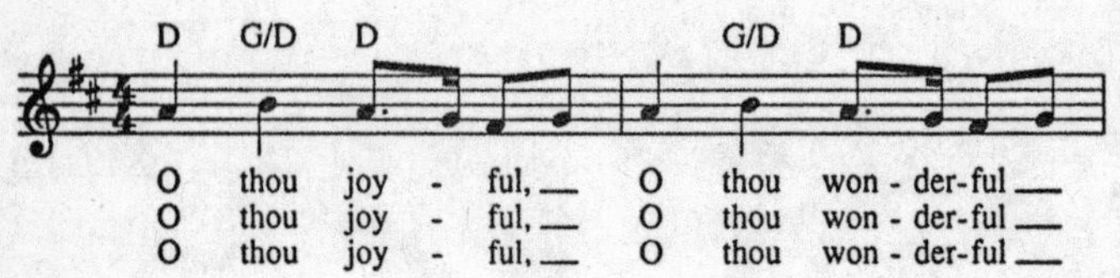
D G/D D G/D D
O thou joy - ful, O thou won - der-ful
O thou joy - ful, O thou won - der-ful
O thou joy - ful, O thou won - der-ful

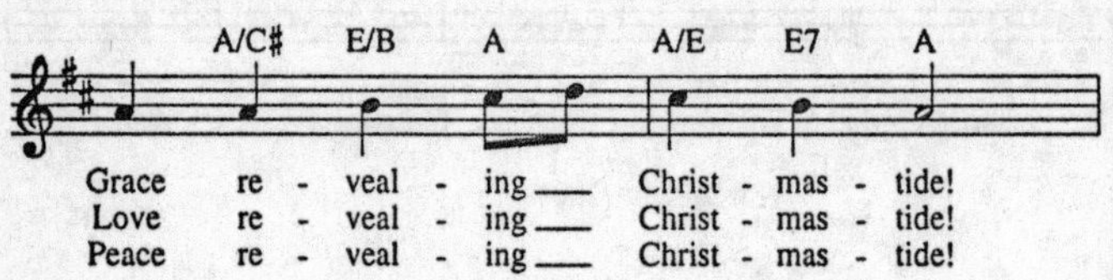
A/C# E/B A A/E E7 A
Grace re - veal - ing Christ - mas - tide!
Love re - veal - ing Christ - mas - tide!
Peace re - veal - ing Christ - mas - tide!

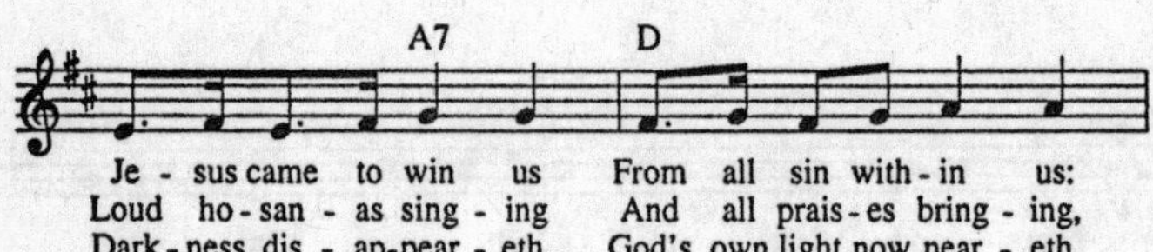
A7 D
Je - sus came to win us From all sin with - in us:
Loud ho - san - as sing - ing And all prais - es bring - ing,
Dark - ness dis - ap - pear - eth, God's own light now near - eth,

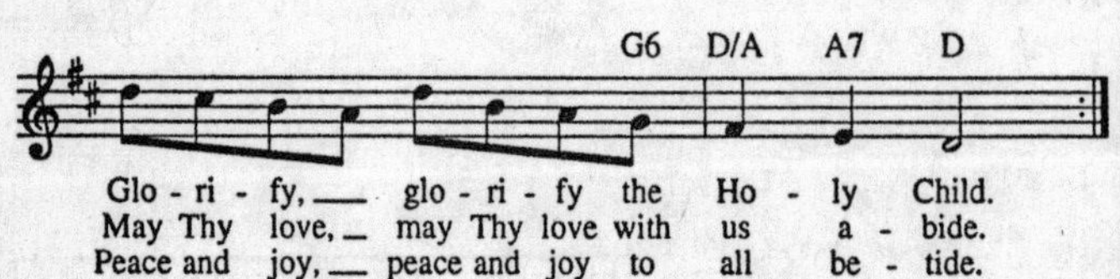
G6 D/A A7 D
Glo - ri - fy, glo - ri - fy the Ho - ly Child.
May Thy love, may Thy love with us a - bide.
Peace and joy, peace and joy to all be - tide.

# OH! DEAR JESUS

Traditional Italian Carol

C Am F C Dm G7 C
Thou cam - est from heav'n we are ___ told,
Thy pil - grim - age through star - ry ___ skies,
D/C G/B C G/D C/E D7 G
To keep God's prom - ise made of old,
We greet with ho - san - nas loud rise!
C Am F C Dm G7 C D/C G/B C G/D
His will was re - deem'd at Thy _ birth Thus we all wel-come
God's love made man - i - fest to ___ men, For God His on - ly
C/E D7 G C/E G/D C Am F G Am/G G
Thee to earth.
Son hath giv'n.
Oh! dear Je - sus, sweet an-gel - ic child, _
Am Dm/F E Am F Am D7 G C/E Em F A7/E
Oh! dear Je - sus, pre-cious Sav-ior mine, _ Oh! dear Je - sus,
D7 G G7/F C/E G/D C7 F F6/A G7 C
Oh! dear Je - sus, Keep my love, it is ev - er Thine.

# OH! INFANT JESUS

Traditional Italian Carol

G D G G/D D G
Oh! In - fant Je - sus, Thee I love;
Oh! Ho - ly In - fant, Thee I love;
D G G/D D G
Kin - dle a flame with - in my breast, Let Thy
Be kind to all who dwell on earth, Child of
D G D
spir - it di - vine dwell there - in So I
grace, to Thee I hum - bly pray While I
G D G D
will nev - er - more be dis - tress'd.
kneel and mar - vel at Your birth.
With
D7 G D C Am G
hearts that o - ver - flow with love, We
Am/C E/B Am B Em G/D D7 G
wor - ship Thee, King of Heav'n a - bove.

# OH! NIGHT AMONG THE THOUSANDS

Traditional Italian Carol

G/B D/A G D G/B A7/E D G/B
Oh! night a - mong the thou - sands, You
Oh! night a - mong the thou - sands, The
C6 A/C# G/D D7 G D G/B D/A G D
are a won-drous sight, Slow - ly the dark-ness
night when Christ was born, An - gels ac-claim your
G/B A7/E D G/B C6 A/C# G/D D7 G
fad - ed, A star shines high and bright. From
com - ing, The star gleams like the dawn. Now
C E7/B Am Dm7/A
whence comes this lu - mi - nous star? What
hear the heav - en - ly voic - es Ex -
G C/E G/B G D G G/B
is it the an-gels sing?
ult as they loud-ly sing:
It is the night of
D G A7/E G/D D7 G
thou - sands the birth - day of our King!

# ONCE IN ROYAL DAVID'S CITY

Words by C.F. ALEXANDER
Music by HENRY J. GAUNTLETT

F C F C C7 F Dm
1. Once in Roy - al Da - vid's_ Cit - y Stood a
2. He came down to earth_ from_ heav - en, Who is
3.,4. (See additional verses)

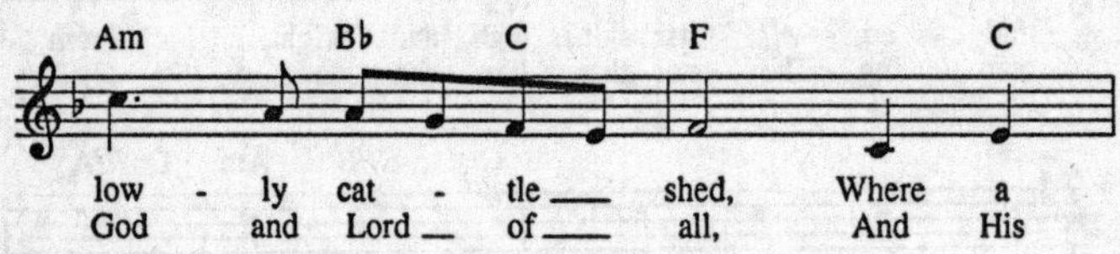
Am Bb C F C
low - ly cat - tle ___ shed, Where a
God and Lord __ of ___ all, And His

F C C7 F Dm
moth - er laid __ her __ Ba - by In a
shel - ter was __ a ___ sta - ble, And His

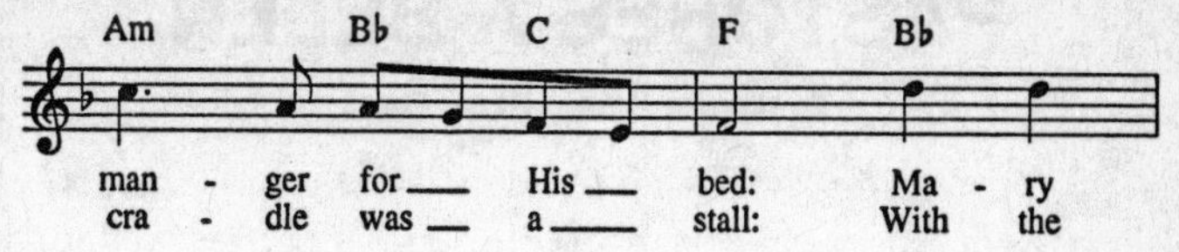
Am
Bb
C
F
Bb
man - ger for His bed: Ma - ry
cra - dle was a stall: With the

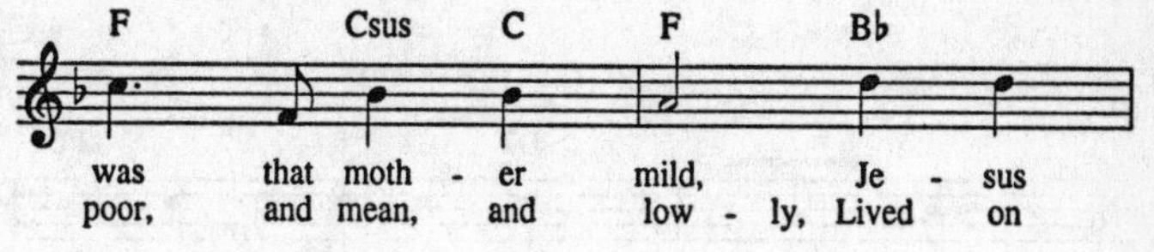
F
Csus
C
F
Bb
was that moth - er mild, Je - sus
poor, and mean, and low - ly, Lived on

F
Bb
C
F
Christ her lit - tle Child.
earth our Sav - ior ho - ly.

*Additional Verses*

3. Jesus is our childhood's pattern,
Day by day like us He grew;
He was little, weak and helpless,
Tears and smiles like us He knew:
And He feeleth for our sadness,
And He shareth in our gladness.

4. And our eyes at last shall see Him,
Through His own redeeming love;
For that Child so dear and gentle
Is our Lord in heav'n above:
And He leads His children on
To the place where He is gone.

# PASTORES A BELÉN

Traditional Puerto Rican Carol

G
The Lord on earth is here, ap -

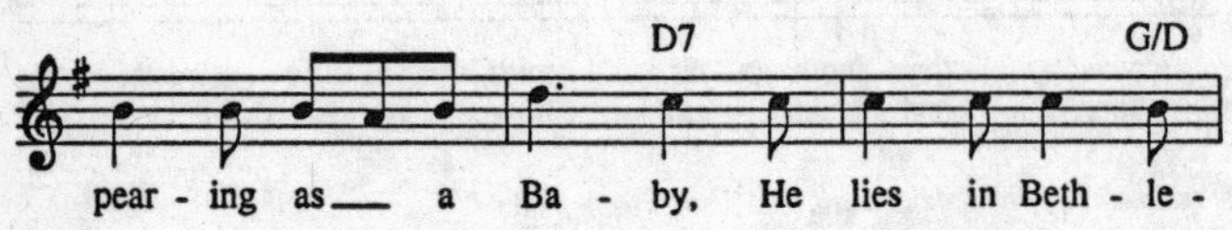
D7
G/D
pear - ing as a Ba - by, He lies in Beth - le -

D7
G/D
D7
C
G
hem, the bless - ed Son of Ma - ry. O

C/G
G
D
come, O come, O shep - herds, run to

G
C/G
G
see, The Ho - ly Child, That

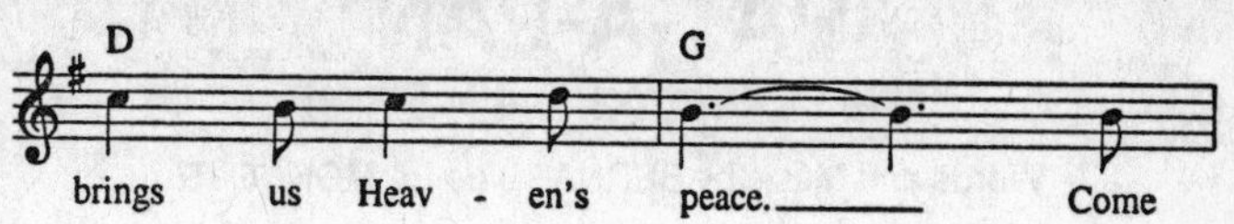
D
G
brings us Heav - en's peace.
Come

D
car - ry - ing some nuts and some hon - ey,

D7
G
Of - fer them to Je - sus to eat, Come car - ry - ing some

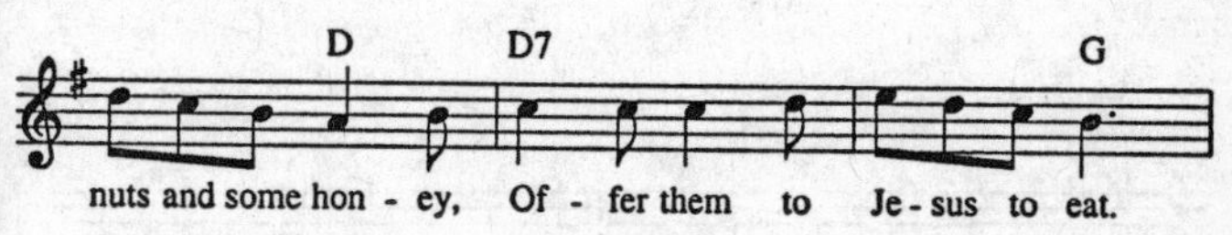
D
D7
G
nuts and some hon - ey, Of - fer them to Je - sus to eat.

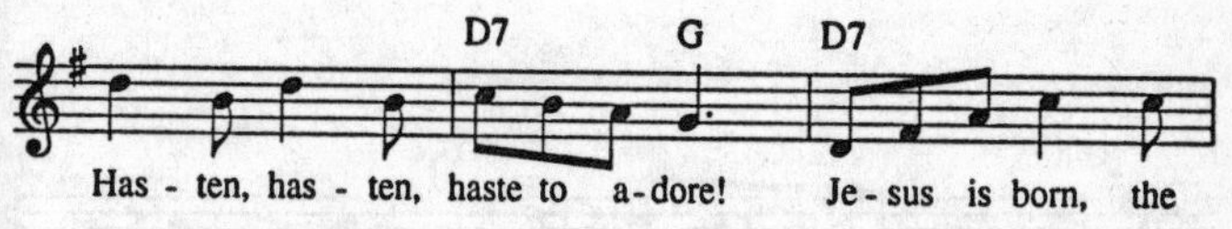
D7
G
D7
Has - ten, has - ten, haste to a - dore! Je - sus is born, the

G
D
G/D
D7
G
Son of our great Lord, Je - sus our King, for - ev - er-more.

# PAT-A-PAN

## (Willie, Take Your Little Drum)

Words and Music by BERNARD de LA MONNOYE

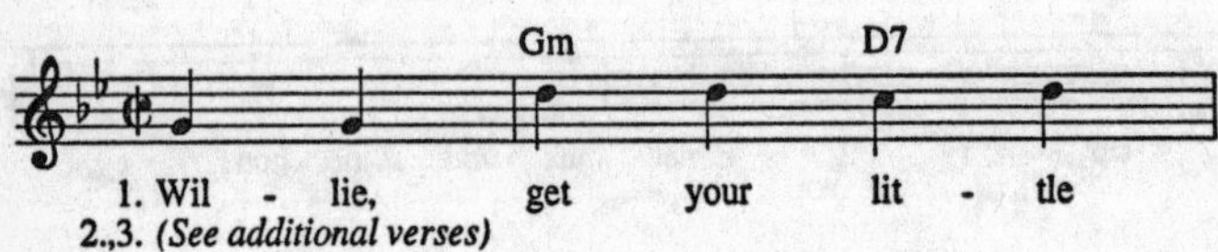
Gm
D7
1. Wil - lie, get your lit - tle
2.,3. (See additional verses)

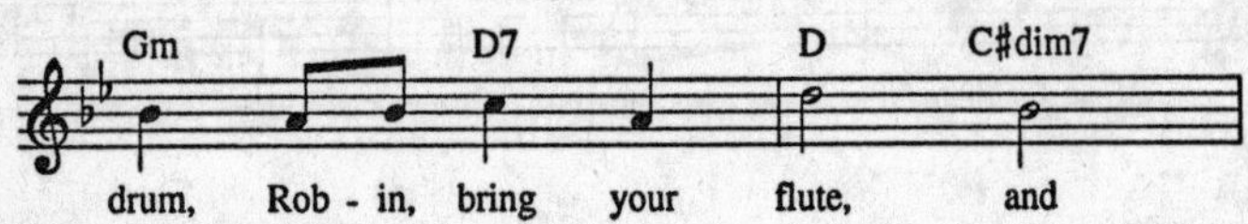
Gm
D7
D
C#dim7
drum, Rob - in, bring your flute, and

D
come. Aren't they fun to play up -

Gm
on? Tu - re - lu - re - lu, pat - a - pat - a -

D
pan; When you play your fife and

Gm Adim Gm D Gm
drum, How can an - y - one be glum?

*Additional Verses*

2. When the men of olden days
Gave the King of Kings their praise,
They had pipes to play upon.
Turelurelu, patapatapan.
And also the drums they'd play,
Full of joy, on Christmas Day.

3. God and man today become
Closely joined as flute and drum.
Let the joyous tune play on!
Turelurelu, patapatapan,
As the instruments you play,
We will sing, this Christmas Day.

# PRAY, GIVE US LODGING

Traditional Mexican Carol

Eb
1. Joseph: Pray give us lodg - ing dear,
2. Host: You can not stop here, I
3. Joseph: Please show us pit - y! Your
4. Host: You try my pa - tience! I'm
5.,6. (See additional verses)

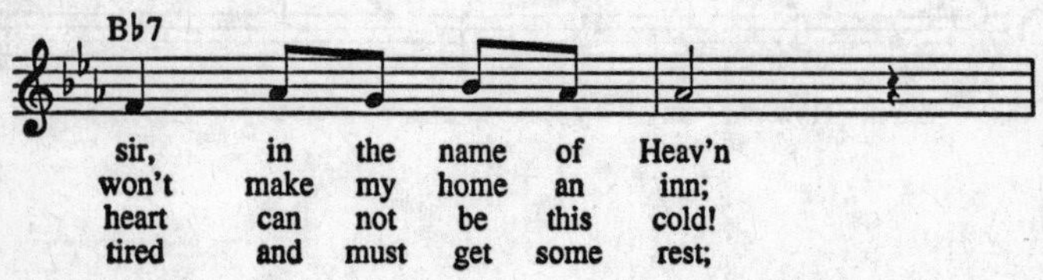
Bb7
sir, in the name of Heav'n
won't make my home an inn;
heart can not be this cold!
tired and must get some rest;

All day since morn - ing to
I do not trust you, your
Look at poor Ma - ry, so
I've told you kind - ly, but

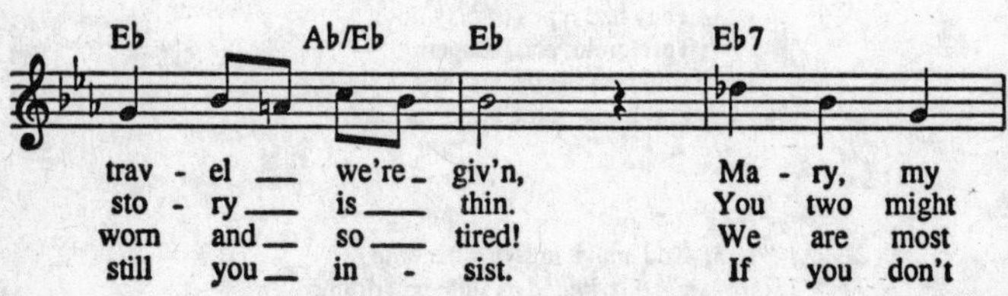
Eb
Ab/Eb
Eb
Eb7
trav - el we're giv'n, Ma - ry, my
sto - ry is thin. You two might
worn and so tired! We are most
still you in - sist. If you don't

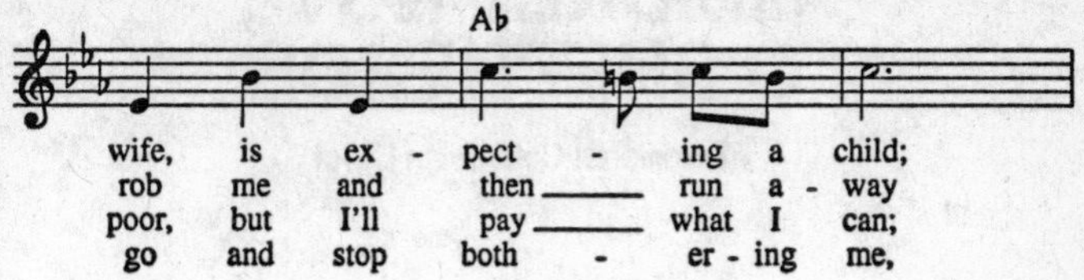
Ab
wife, is ex - pect - ing a child;
rob me and then ___ run a - way
poor, but I'll pay ___ what I can;
go and stop both - er - ing me,

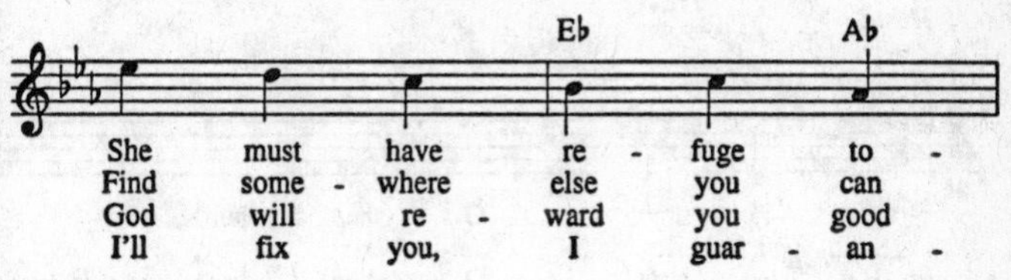
Eb
Ab
She must have re - fuge to -
Find some - where else you can
God will re - ward you good
I'll fix you, I guar - an -

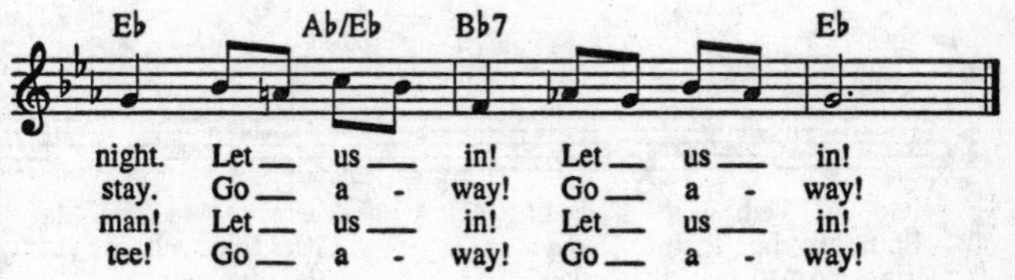
Eb
Ab/Eb
Bb7
Eb
night. Let ___ us ___ in! Let ___ us ___ in!
stay. Go ___ a - way! Go ___ a - way!
man! Let ___ us ___ in! Let ___ us ___ in!
tee! Go ___ a - way! Go ___ a - way!

*Additional Verses*

5. *Joseph:* Sir, I must tell you, my wife is the Queen of Heaven,
Chosen by God to deliver, his Son.
Jesus is coming to earth late this eve;
(O Heaven, make him believe!)
Let us in! Let us in!

6. *Host:* Joseph, dear Joseph! O how could I be so blind?
Not to know you and the Virgin so fine!
Enter, blest trav'lers, my house is your own;
Praise be to God on His throne!
Please come in! Please come in!

# QUICKLY NOW, O SHEPHERDS

Traditional Colombian Carol

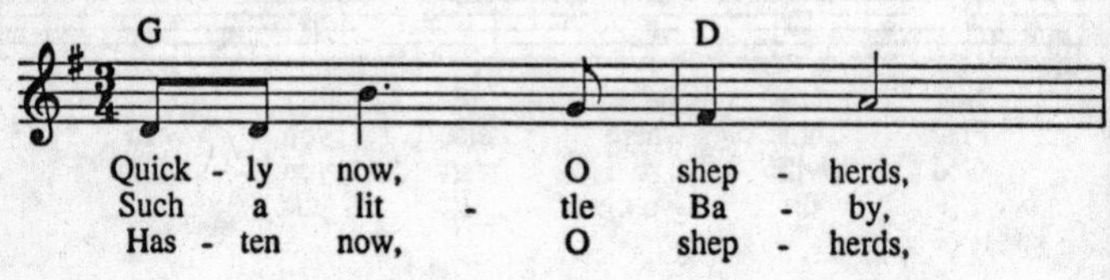
G
D
Quick - ly now, O shep - herds,
Such a lit - tle Ba - by,
Has - ten now, O shep - herds,

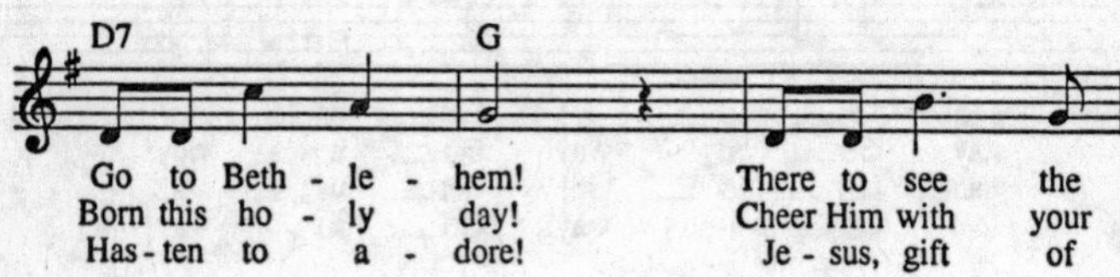
D7
G
Go to Beth - le - hem! There to see the
Born this ho - ly day! Cheer Him with your
Has - ten to a - dore! Je - sus, gift of

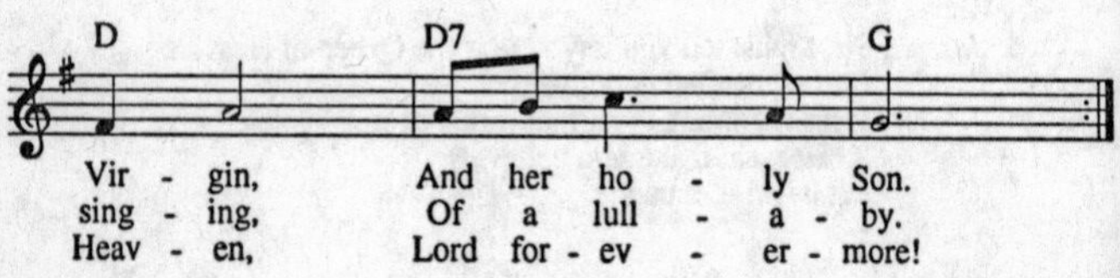
D
D7
G
Vir - gin, And her ho - ly Son.
sing - ing, Of a lull - a - by.
Heav - en, Lord for - ev - er - more!

# REJOICE AND BE MERRY

Gallery Carol

G D G D G D7
Re - joice and be mer - ry in
G D7 G D G C G C
songs and in mirth! O praise our Re -
G Am7 G C D7
deem - er, all mor - tals on
G D7 G D7 G D7
earth! For this is the birth - day of
E7 Am D7 Em Bm C
Je - sus our King, Who brought us sal -
D Em7 D7 G C D7 G
va - tion His prais - es we'll sing!

# RING OUT, YE WILD AND MERRY BELLS

Words and Music by
C. MAITLAND

C G7/D C/E G7/D
Ring out, ye wild and mer - ry bells, ring
Ring out, ye sil - v'ry bells, ring out ring
C G7 C
out ___ the old ___ old sto - ry That
out ___ your ex - ul - ta - tion That
C G7/D C/E G7/D
first was told by an - gel tongues from
God with man is re - con - ciled. Go
G/B Am/C D7 G
out the realms of Glo - ry.
tell it to the na - tions.
Em
Peace on earth was their sweet song,
There - fore let us all to - day,
D7 G7
Glo - ry in the high - est!
Glo - ry in the High - est!

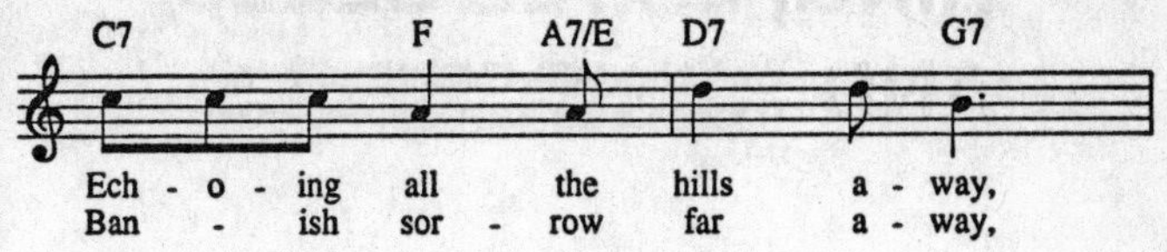
C7
F
A7/E
D7
G7
Ech - o - ing all the hills a - way,
Ban - ish sor - row far a - way,

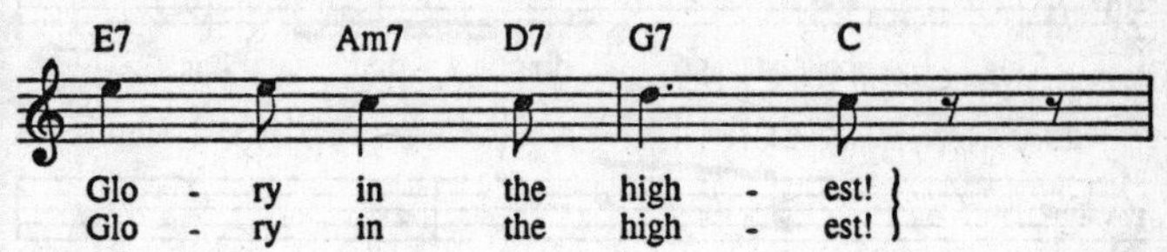
E7
Am7
D7
G7
C
Glo - ry in the high - est!
Glo - ry in the high - est!

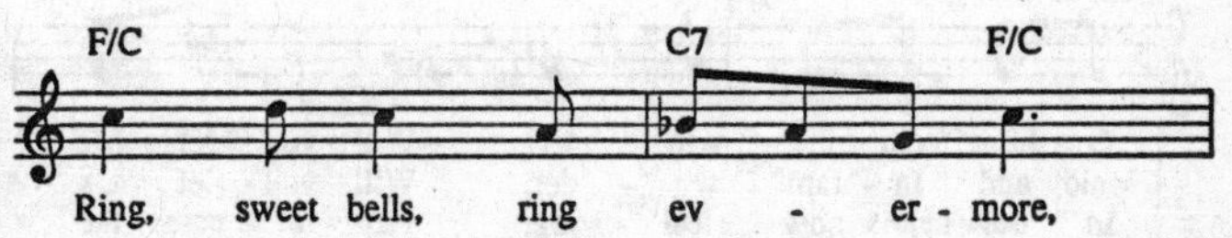
F/C
C7
F/C
Ring, sweet bells, ring ev - er - more,

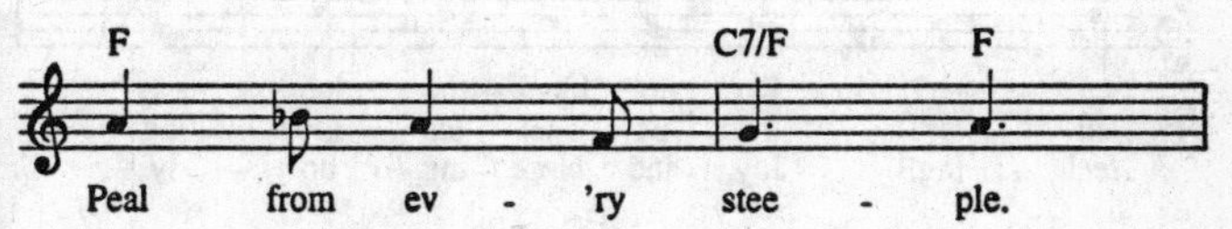
F
C7/F
F
Peal from ev - 'ry stee - ple.

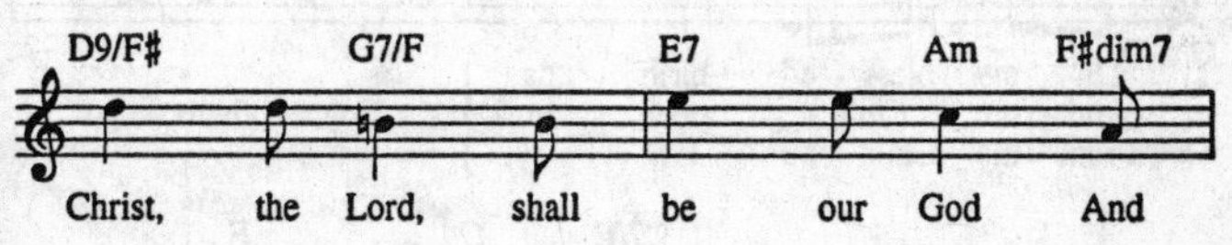
D9/F#
G7/F
E7
Am
F#dim7
Christ, the Lord, shall be our God And

C
Am
G7
C
we shall be His peo - ple!

# RING, LITTLE BELLS

Words by KARL ENSLIN
Traditional German Carol

F Bb F
Ring, bells, go ding - a - ling - a - ling,
C7/E C F
Ring, lit - tle bells!
C Dm/C F/C C C7/E C
O how cold the win - ter! Will you let Me
Maid and In - fant ten - der, Will you let Us
In our hearts now steal - ing, Hap - pi - ness the
C7/F F G7 C/G
en - ter? Do not block the door - way
en - ter? To us shel - ter giv - ing
feel - ing, Joy and bless - ing ho - ly
F G7 Dm/C C F Bb
On my bless - ed birth - day!
And the Child prais - ing?
From the Child so low - ly,
Ring, bells, go
F C7/E C F
ding - a - ling - a - ling. Ring, lit - tle bells!

# ROCKING

Traditional Czech Carol

F G7/F G C
Ba - by Je - sus, gen - tly sleep,
Ma - ry's pre - cious ba - by sleep,
Gsus G C B♭/D C7/E F Dm
do not stir; We will bring a
gen - tly sleep, Sleep in com - fort,
B♭6 C F B♭ F C F/C C
coat of fur.
slum - ber deep.
We will rock you, rock you, rock you,
F B♭ F Gm/B♭ B♭maj7 C F
Gen - tly slum - ber as we rock you,
See the fur to
We will praise you
G7/F G C B♭ C7/E F Dm B♭6 C F
keep you warm, Snug - ly fits your ti - ny form.
all we can, Dar - ling, dar - ling lit - tle man.

# RISE UP, SHEPHERD, AND FOLLOW

African-American Spiritual

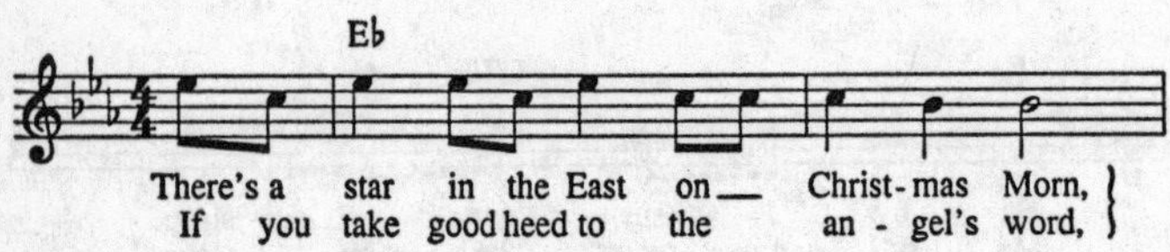
E♭
There's a star in the East on Christ-mas Morn,
If you take good heed to the an - gel's word,

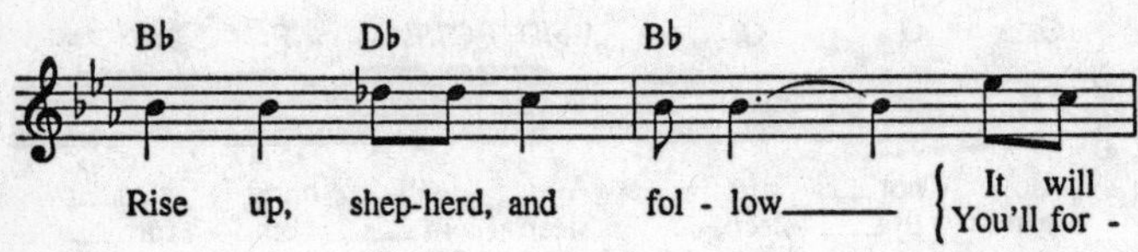
B♭ D♭ B♭
Rise up, shep-herd, and fol - low
It will
You'll for -

E♭ G Cm
lead to the place where the Sav - ior's born;
get your flock, you'll for - get your herd;

Fm A♭ E♭
Rise up, shep-herd, and fol - low.

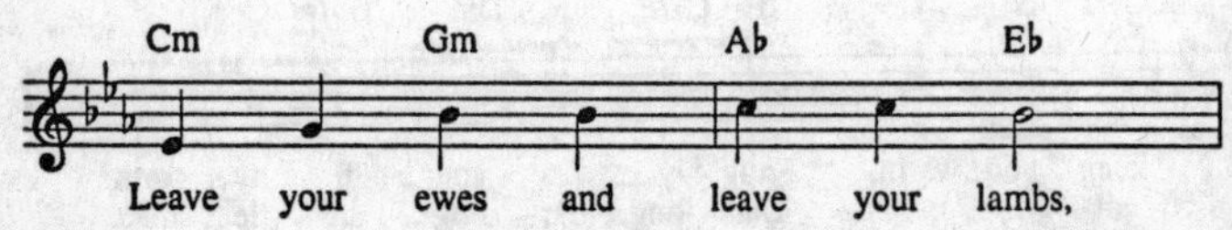
Cm Gm A♭ E♭
Leave your ewes and leave your lambs,

Bb C#dim7 Bb7
Rise up, shep-herd, and fol - low,

Cm Gm Ab Eb F9 Fm Ab
Leave your sheep and leave your rams, Rise up, shep -herd, and

Eb Bb+ Bb7
fol - low. Fol - low, fol - low,

Bbm6 Bb+ Eb
Rise up, shep-herd, and fol-low, fol-low the star of

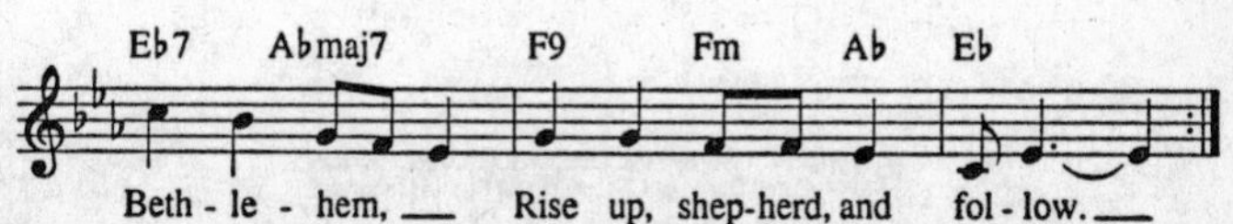
Eb7 Abmaj7 F9 Fm Ab Eb
Beth - le - hem, Rise up, shep-herd, and fol - low.

# SHEPHERD! SHAKE OFF YOUR DROWSY SLEEP

Traditional French Carol

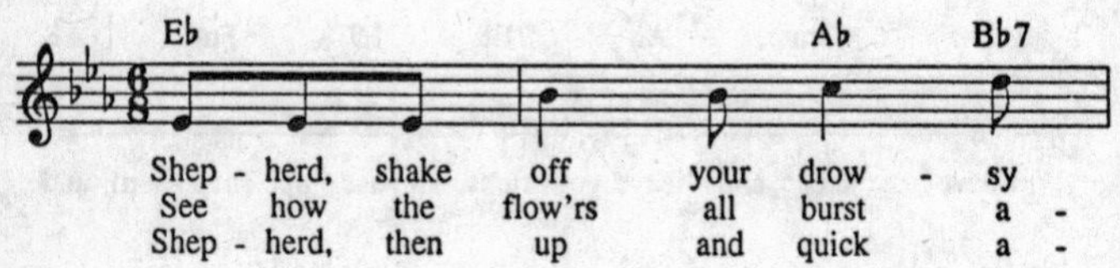
E♭
A♭
B♭7
Shep - herd, shake off your drow - sy
See how the flow'rs all burst a -
Shep - herd, then up and quick a -

E♭
B♭/F
F
sleep, Rise and leave your sil - ly
new, Think - ing snow is sum - mer
way! Seek the Babe ere break of

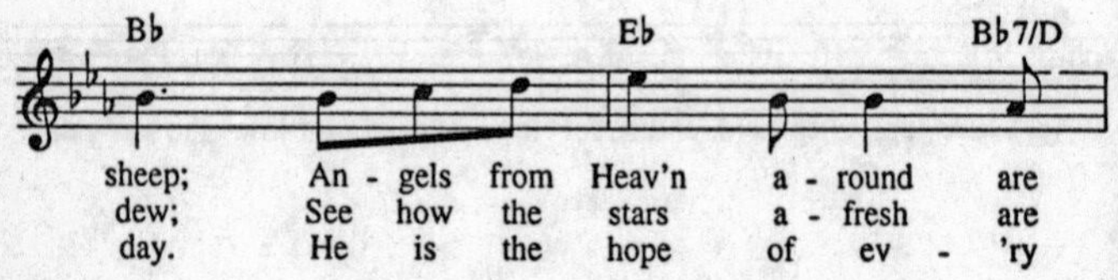
B♭
E♭
B♭7/D
sheep; An - gels from Heav'n a - round are
dew; See how the stars a - fresh are
day. He is the hope of ev - 'ry

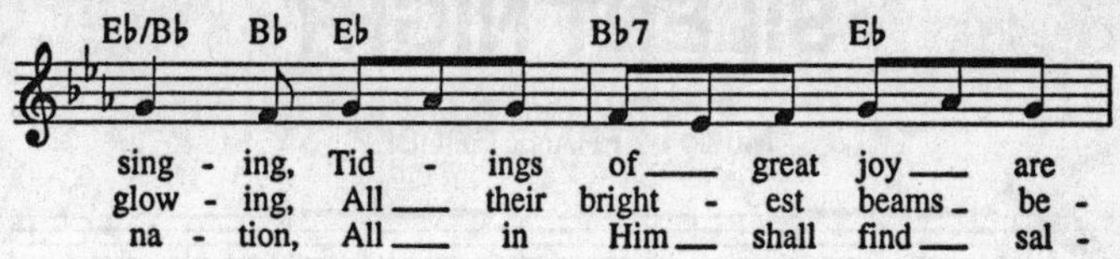
Eb/Bb Bb Eb Bb7 Eb
sing - ing, Tid - ings of great joy are
glow - ing, All their bright - est beams be -
na - tion, All in Him shall find sal -

Bb7 Eb Bb
bring - ing.
stow - ing.
va - tion.
Shep - herd! The

Eb Cm Bb7/D
cho - rus come and swell! Sing No -

Fm Cm Ab Bb7 Eb
el, O sing No - el!

# SILENT NIGHT

Words by JOSEPH MOHR
Music by FRANZ GRUBER

C
Si - lent night! Ho - ly night!
Si - lent night! Ho - ly night!
Si - lent night! Ho - ly night!
G7
C
All is calm, all is bright.
Shep - herds quake at the sight!
Son of God, love's pure light
F
C
Round yon vir - gin moth - er and Child!
Glo - ries stream from Heav - en a - far.
Ra - diant beams from Thy ho - ly face.
F
C
Ho - ly In - fant, so ten - der and mild,
Heav - 'nly hosts sing Al - le - lu - ia,
With the dawn of re - deem - ing grace,
G7
C
Sleep in heav - en - ly peace.
Christ the Sa - vior, is born!
Je - sus, Lord, at Thy birth.
G7
C
Sleep in heav - en - ly peace.
Christ the Sa - vior is born.
Je - sus, Lord, at Thy birth.

# SING WE NOW OF CHRISTMAS

Traditional

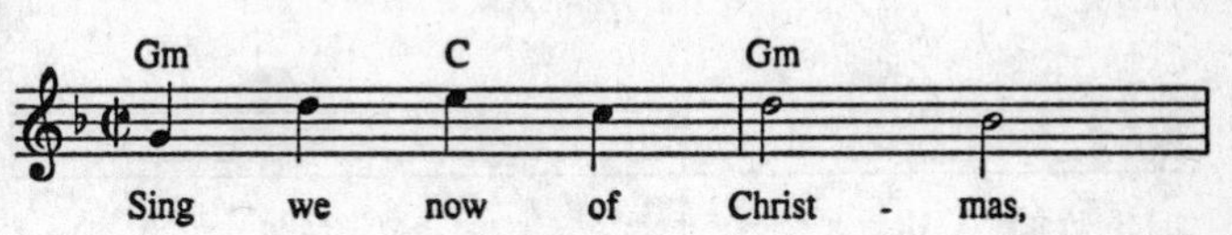
Gm
C
Gm
Sing we now of Christ - mas,

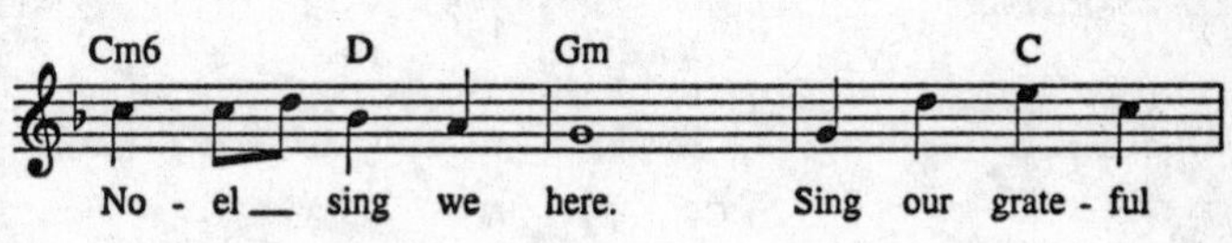
Cm6
D
Gm
C
No - el sing we here. Sing our grate - ful

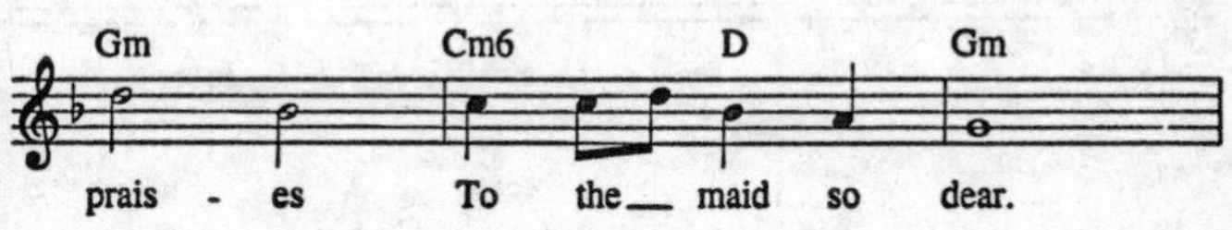
Gm
Cm6
D
Gm
prais - es To the maid so dear.

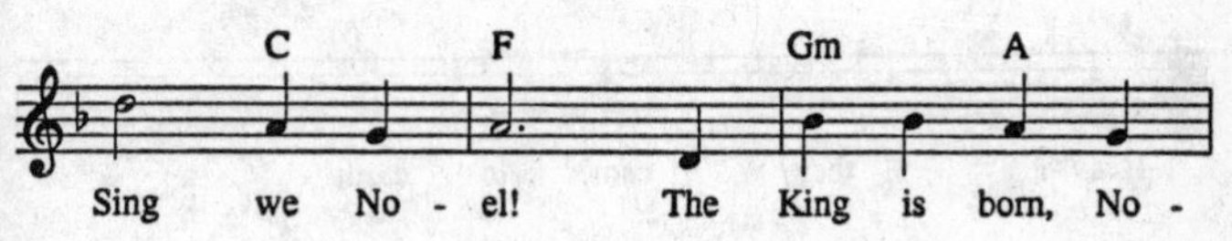
C
F
Gm
A
Sing we No - el! The King is born, No -

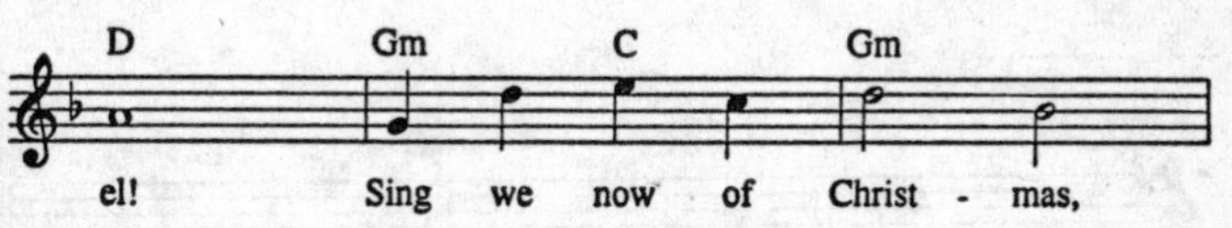
D
Gm
C
Gm
el! Sing we now of Christ - mas,

Cm6
D
Gm
Sing we here No - el.

# THE SIMPLE BIRTH

Traditional Flemish Carol

G
1. From Heav'n there came to earth a
2.-5. (See additional verses)

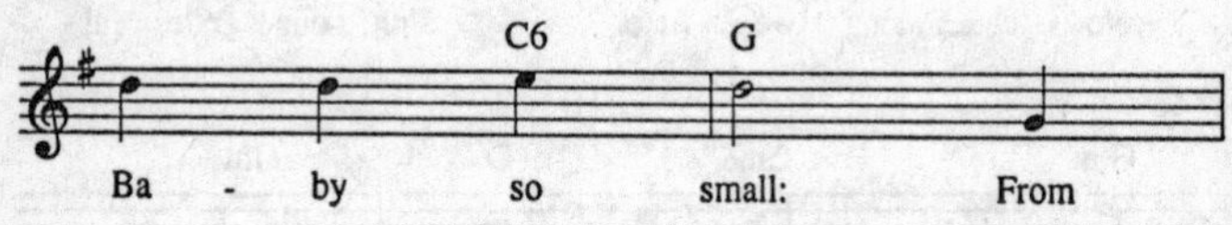
C6 G
Ba - by so small: From

Heav'n there came to earth a

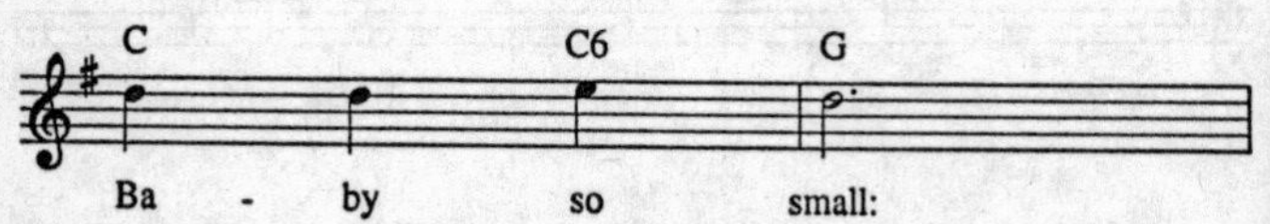
C C6 G
Ba - by so small:

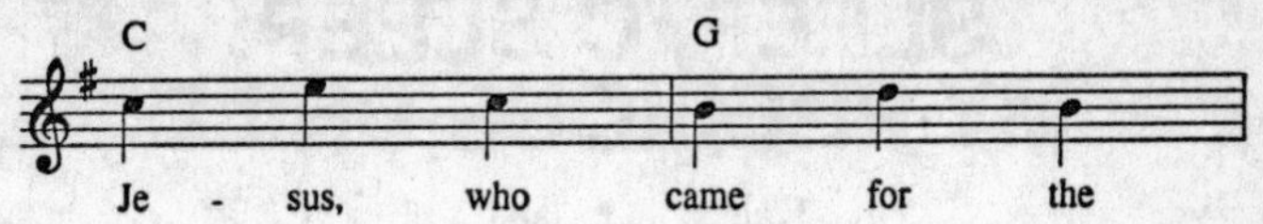
C
G
Je - sus, who came for the

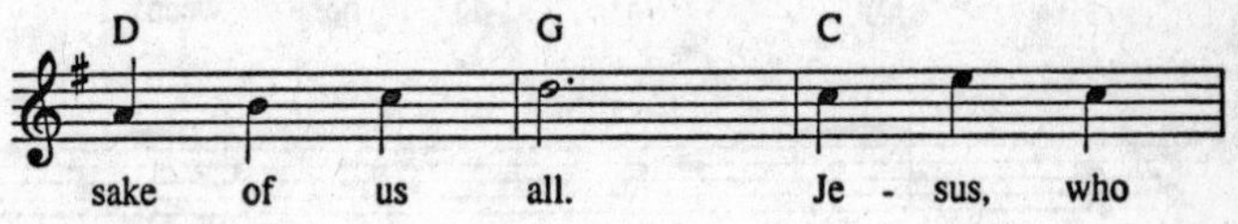
D
G
C
sake of us all. Je - sus, who

G
D7
G
came for the sake of us all.

*Additional Verses*

2. Beneath His tiny head no pillow but hay;
   God's richest treasures in rude manger lay.

3. His eyes of blackest jet were sparkling with light,
   Rosy cheeks bloomed on His face fair and bright.

4. And from His lovely mouth, the laughter did swell,
   When He saw Mary, whom He loved so well.

5. He came to weary earth, so dark and so drear,
   To wish to mankind a blessed New Year.

# SLEEP, O SLEEP, MY PRECIOUS CHILD

Traditional Italian Carol

F
C7/F
F
B♭maj7
F
Sleep, o sleep, my pre - cious Child,
O my dar - ling, do not weep!
C
F
King di - vine, King di -
Sweet - ly sleep, Sweet - ly
C
F
B♭
vine. Close Your eyes and sweet - ly
sleep, Close Your eyes my Son, my
C
Dm
Gm/B♭
C7
F
slum - ber, King di - vine,
dear one. Sweet - ly sleep,
Gm/B♭
C7
F
C7/F
F
King di - vine. Close Your eyes and
sweet - ly sleep. Close Your eyes, my
B♭/F
F/C
C7
F
sweet - ly slum - ber.
Son, My dear one.

(♪ = ♪)
C7
F
Fa la la la, Fa la la la la,

C7
F
Fa la la la, Fa la la la,

Gm/B♭
Fa ______ la, ______

C7
F
B♭
Fa ______ la, ______ Fa ______

Gm/B♭
C7
F
la, ______ Fa ______ la.

# THE SLEEP OF THE INFANT JESUS

Traditional French Carol

Em
B7/D#
Em
Here, 'mid the ass and
Here, 'mid the rose and
Here, 'mid the shep - herds'
B
Em
B7/D#
Em
ox - en mild, Sleep,
lil - y bright, Sleep,
glad de - light, Sleep,
G/D
C
B
sleep, sleep, thou ti - ny Child.
sleep, sleep, thou ti - ny Child.
sleep, sleep, thou ti - ny Child.
Em
Am/E
D
G
G/B
Thou - sand che - ru - bim, thou - sand ser - a -
C
D/C
C
D/C
phim Guard - ing o'er the
Em/B
Am
B7
Em
bed of the great Lord of love.

# STILL, STILL, STILL

Salzburg Melody, c.1819
Traditional Austrian Text

D
Bm
Still, still, still, To
Sleep, sleep, sleep, While
Em
A7
D
sleep is now His will. On
we Thy vi - gil keep. And
A7
D
Ma - ry's breast He rests in slum - ber,
an - gels come from Heav - en sing - ing,
A7
D
While we pray in end - less num - ber,
Songs of ju - bi - la - tion bring - ing,
Bm
Still, Still, Still, To
Sleep, sleep, sleep, While
Em
A7
D
sleep is now His will.
we Thy vi - gil keep.

# THE SNOW LAY ON THE GROUND

Traditional Irish Carol

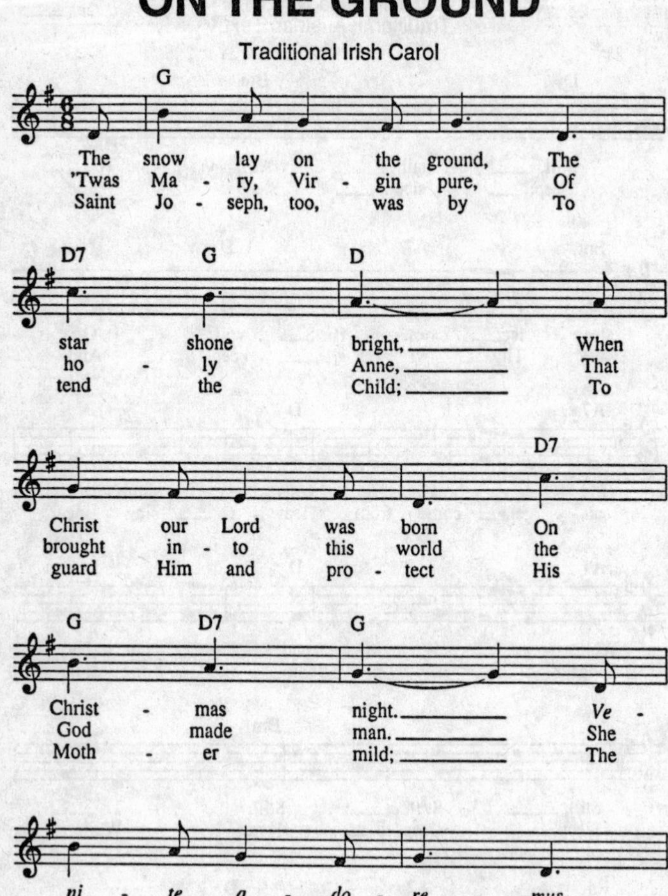
G
The snow lay on the ground, The
'Twas Ma - ry, Vir - gin pure, Of
Saint Jo - seph, too, was by To
D7 G D
star shone bright, When
ho - ly Anne, That
tend the Child; To
D7
Christ our Lord was born On
brought in - to this world the
guard Him and pro - tect His
G D7 G
Christ - mas night. Ve -
God made man. She
Moth - er mild; The
ni - te a - do - re - mus
laid Him in a stall At
an - gels hov - ered round, And

D7
G
D
Do - mi - num; Ve -
Beth - le - hem, The
sang this song: Ve -
D7
ni - te a - do - re - mus
ass and ox - en share the
ni - te a - do - re - mus
G
D7
G
Do - mi - num.
roof with them.
Do - mi - num.
Ve -
ni - te a - do - re - mus
Am
E
Am
Do - mi - num, Ve -
D7
ni - te a - do - re - mus
G
D7
G
Do - mi - num.

# THE SON OF MARY

Traditional Catalonian Carol

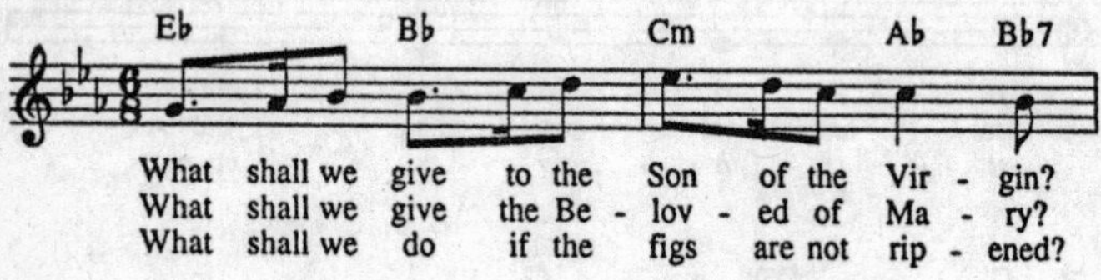
Eb Bb Cm Ab Bb7
What shall we give to the Son of the Vir - gin?
What shall we give the Be - lov - ed of Ma - ry?
What shall we do if the figs are not rip - ened?

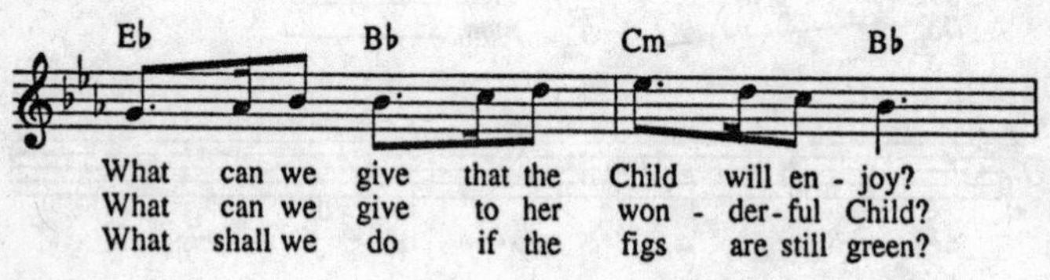
Eb Bb Cm Bb
What can we give that the Child will en - joy?
What can we give to her won - der-ful Child?
What shall we do if the figs are still green?

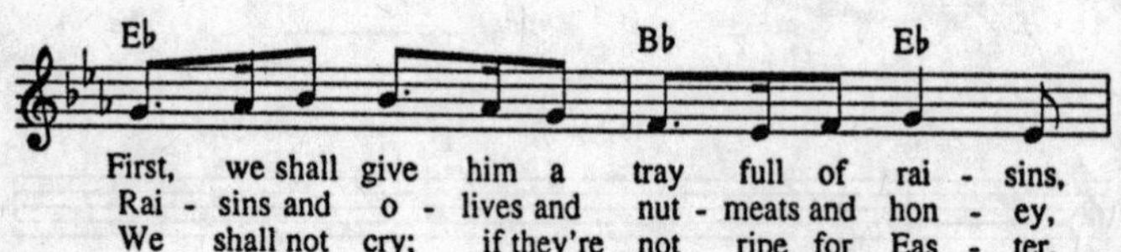
Eb Bb Eb
First, we shall give him a tray full of rai - sins,
Rai - sins and o - lives and nut - meats and hon - ey,
We shall not cry; if they're not ripe for Eas - ter,

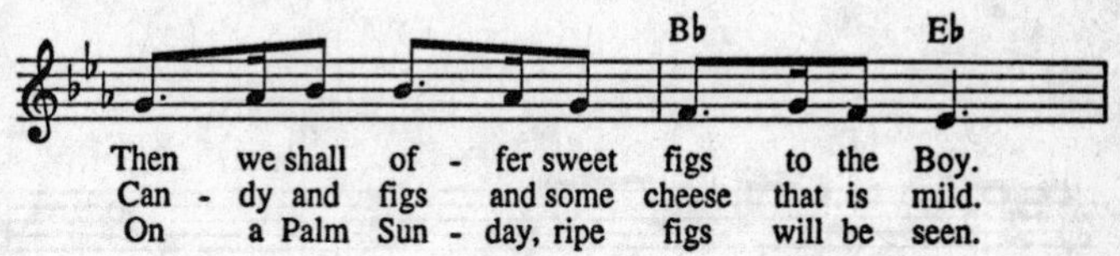
B♭
E♭
Then we shall of - fer sweet figs to the Boy.
Can - dy and figs and some cheese that is mild.
On a Palm Sun - day, ripe figs will be seen.

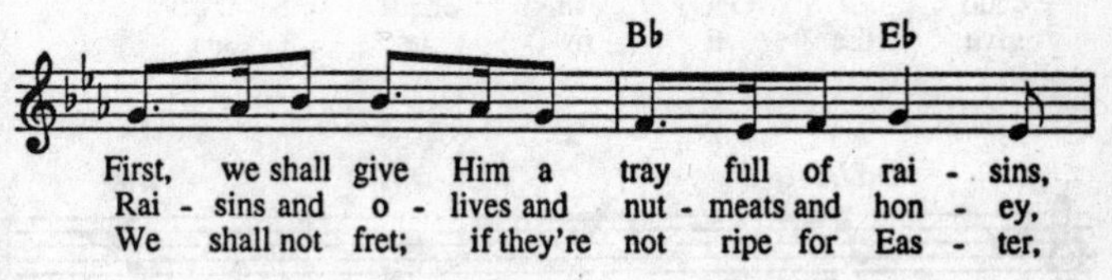
B♭
E♭
First, we shall give Him a tray full of rai - sins,
Rai - sins and o - lives and nut - meats and hon - ey,
We shall not fret; if they're not ripe for Eas - ter,

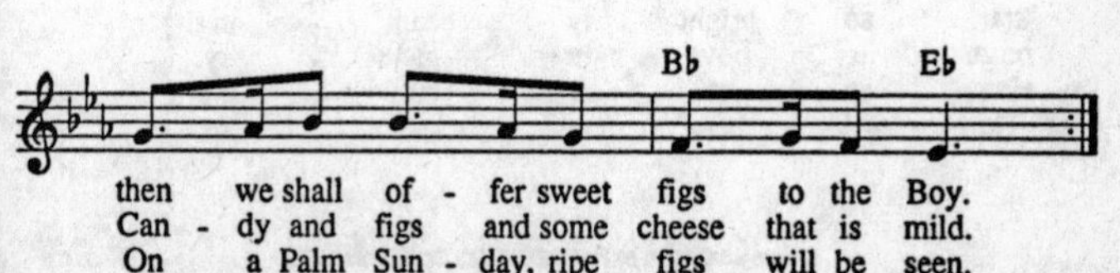
B♭
E♭
then we shall of - fer sweet figs to the Boy.
Can - dy and figs and some cheese that is mild.
On a Palm Sun - day, ripe figs will be seen.

# SONG OF THE WISE MEN

Traditional Puerto Rican Carol

Dm
A7/C#
From a far - off home the
Glow - ing gold I bring the
Frank - in - cense I bring the
Bit - ter myrrh have I to
Dm
A7/C#
Sav - ior we come seek - ing,
new - born Child so ho - ly,
child of God's own choos - ing,
give the ti - ny Je - sus,
Dm/A
A
Dm
Us - ing as our guide the
To - ken of His pow'r to
To - ken of our praise to
To - ken of the pain that
A
A7
Dm
star, so bright - ly beam - ing.
reign a - bove in glo - ry.
Heav - en ev - er ris - ing.
He will bear to save us.

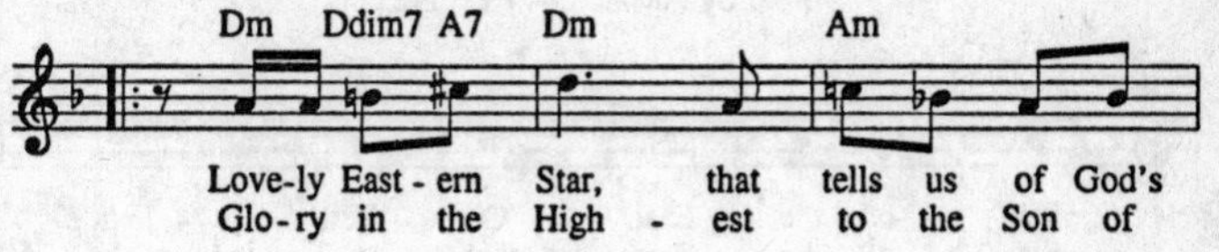
Dm Ddim7 A7 Dm Am
Love-ly East-ern Star, that tells us of God's
Glo-ry in the High - est to the Son of

Dm/A A Dm/A A7
great love, Heav-en won-drous light O
Heav - en And up-on the earth be

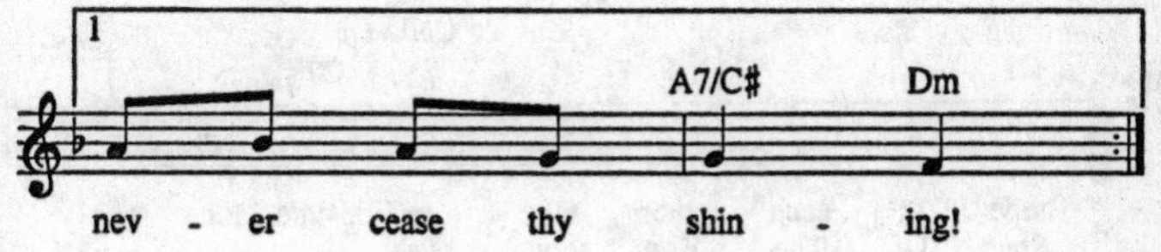
1
A7/C# Dm
nev - er cease thy shin - ing!

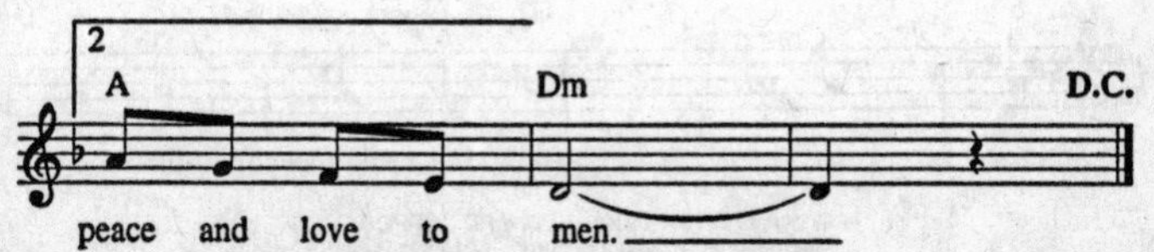
2
A Dm D.C.
peace and love to men.

# STAR OF THE EAST

Words by GEORGE COOPER
Music by AMANDA KENNEDY

F
Bb
Star of the East, Oh Beth - le - hem's
Star of the East, thou hope of the
F
star, Guid - ing us on to
soul. While 'round us here the
C7
F
heav - en a - far! Sor - row and
dark bil - lows roll, Lead us from
Bb
F
grief are lull'd by thy light, Thou
sin to glo - ry a - far, Thou
To Coda
C7
F
C7
hope of each mor - tal, in death's lone - ly
Star Of The East, thou sweet
F
Bb
night! Fear - less and tran - quil, we
F
C7
look up to thee! Know - ing thou beam'st thro' e -

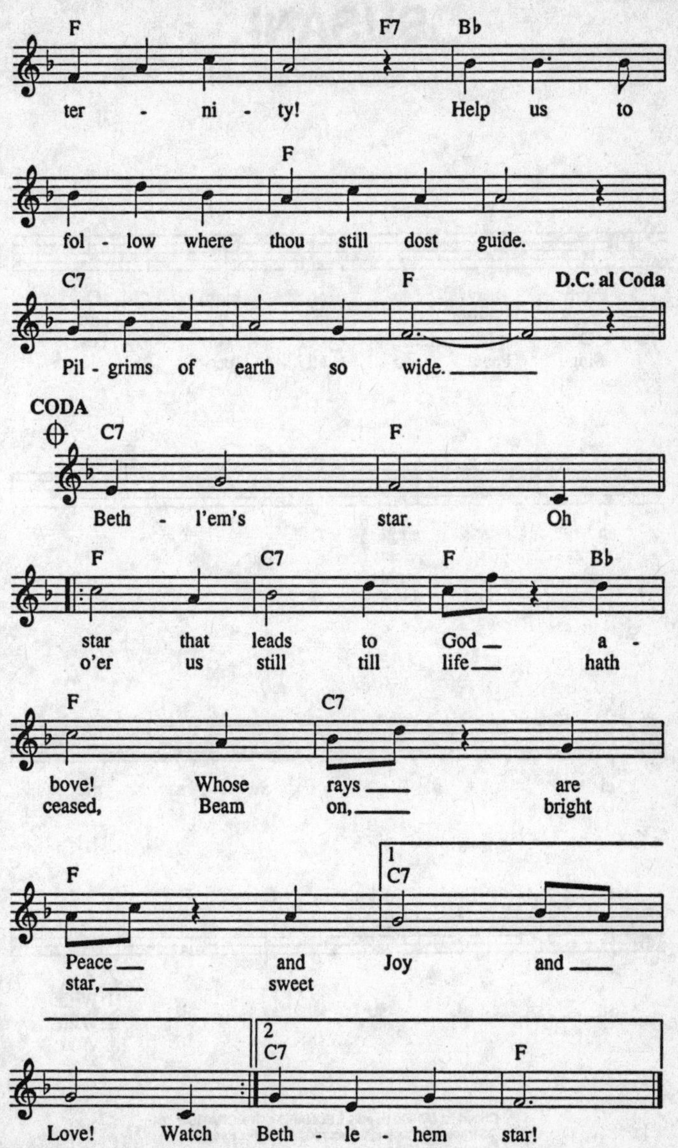
F
F7
B♭
ter - ni - ty!
Help us to
F
fol - low where thou still dost guide.
C7
F
D.C. al Coda
Pil - grims of earth so wide.
CODA
C7
F
Beth - l'em's star.
Oh
F
C7
F
B♭
star that leads to God a -
o'er us still till life hath
F
C7
bove! Whose rays are
ceased, Beam on, bright
F
1
C7
Peace and Joy and
star, sweet
Love! Watch
2
C7
F
Beth - le - hem star!

# SUSANI

14th Century German Carol

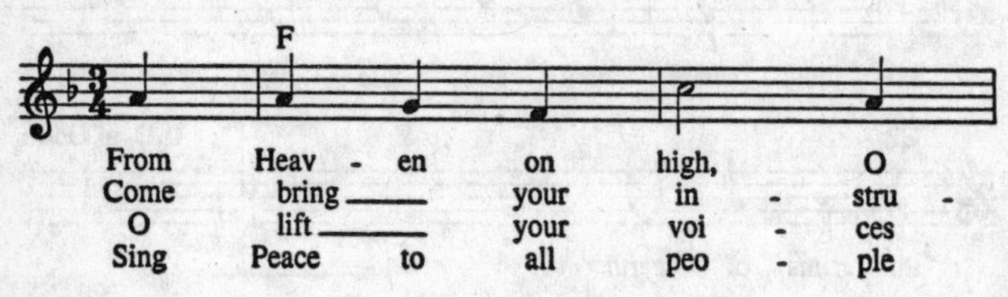
F
From Heav - en on high, O
Come bring your in - stru -
O lift your voi - ces
Sing Peace to all peo - ple

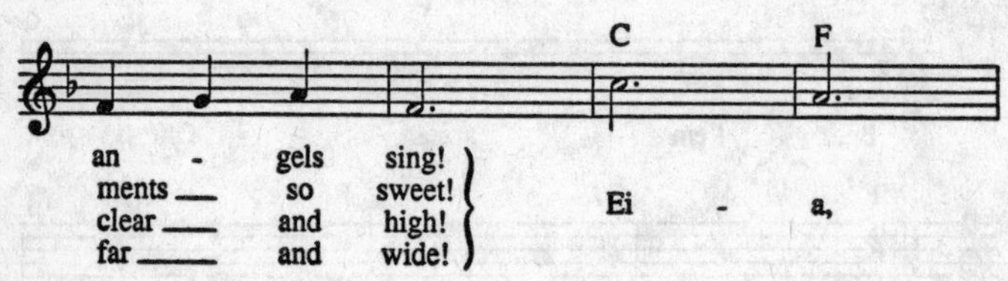
C F
an - gels sing!
ments so sweet!
clear and high!
far and wide!
Ei - a,

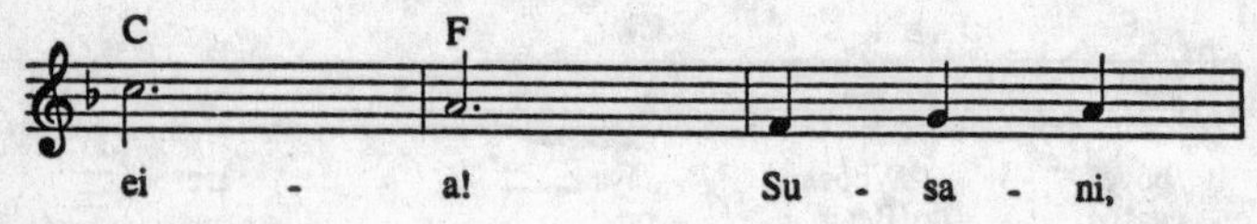
C F
ei - a! Su - sa - ni,

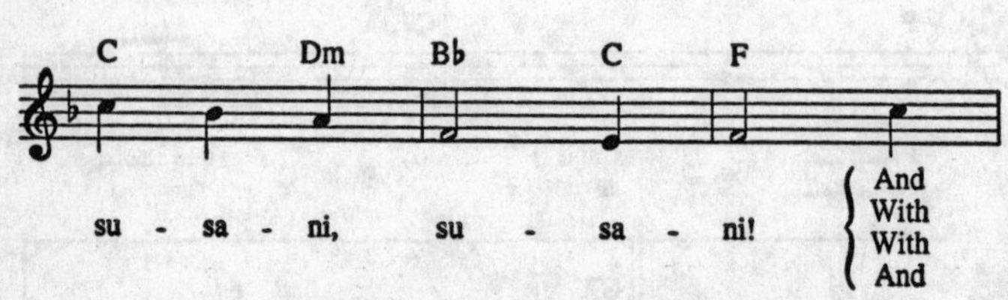
C Dm B♭ C F
su - sa - ni, su - sa - ni!
And
With
With
And

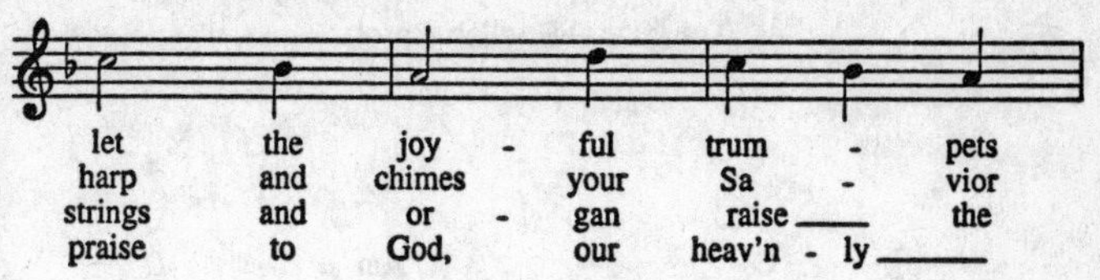
let the joy - ful trum - pets
harp and chimes your Sa - vior
strings and or - gan raise the
praise to God, our heav'n - ly

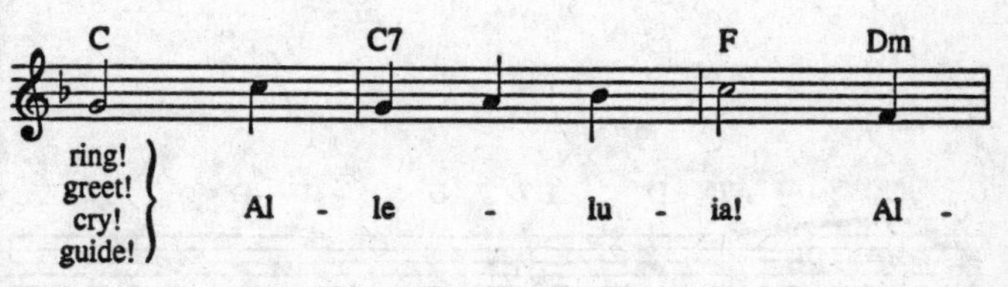
C
C7
F
Dm
ring!
greet!
cry!
guide!
Al - le - lu - ia! Al -

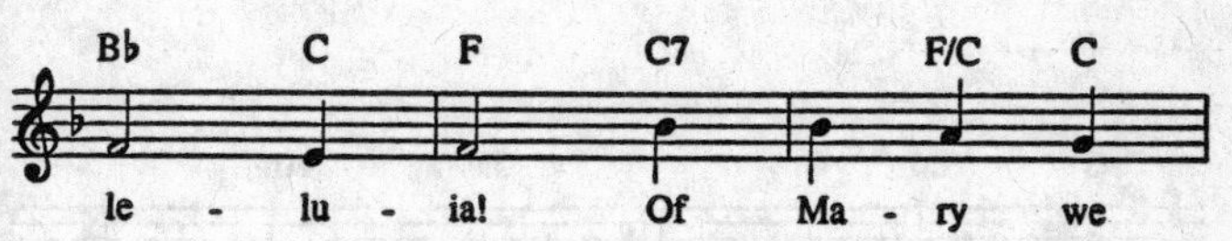
B♭
C
F
C7
F/C
C
le - lu - ia! Of Ma - ry we

F
F/E
Dm
C7
F
sing, and Christ, her Son.

# SUSSEX CAROL

Traditional English Carol

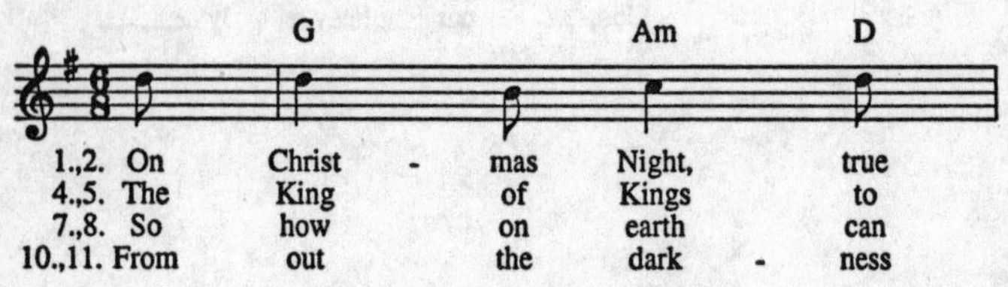
G Am D
1.,2. On Christ - mas Night, true
4.,5. The King of Kings to
7.,8. So how on earth can
10.,11. From out the dark - ness

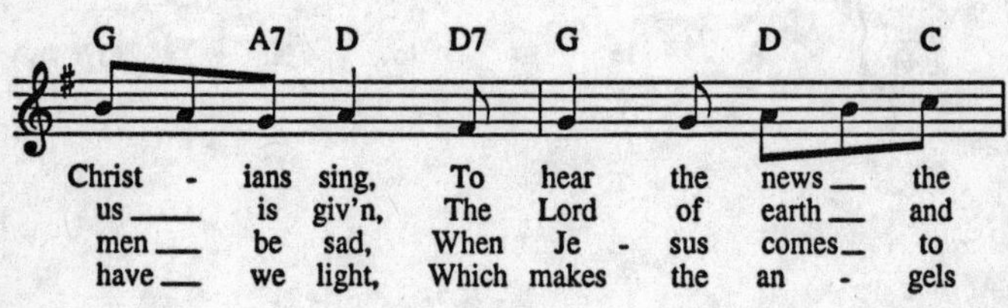
G A7 D D7 G D C
Christ - ians sing, To hear the news __ the
us __ is giv'n, The Lord of earth __ and
men __ be sad, When Je - sus comes __ to
have __ we light, Which makes the an - gels

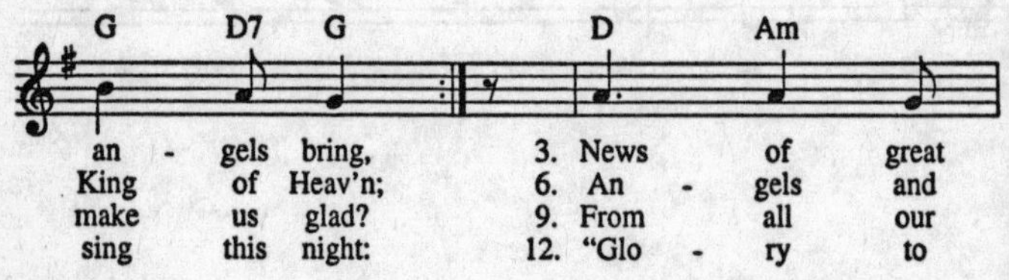
G D7 G D Am
an - gels bring, 3. News of great
King of Heav'n; 6. An - gels and
make us glad? 9. From all our
sing this night: 12. "Glo - ry to

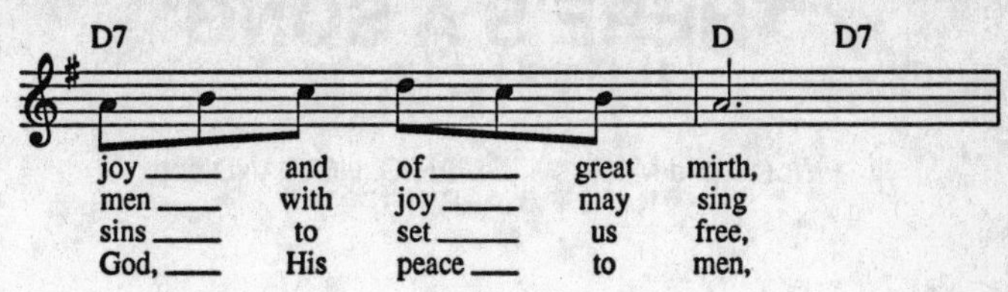
D7
D
D7
joy ___ and of ___ great mirth,
men ___ with joy ___ may sing
sins ___ to set ___ us free,
God, ___ His peace ___ to men,

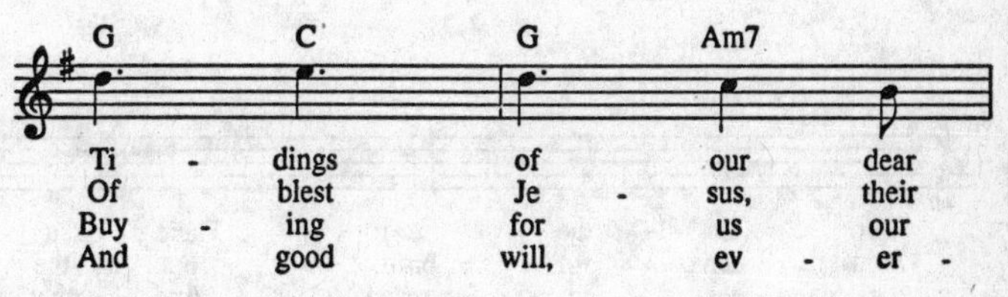
G
C
G
Am7
Ti - dings of our dear
Of blest Je - sus, their
Buy - ing for us our
And good will, ev - er -

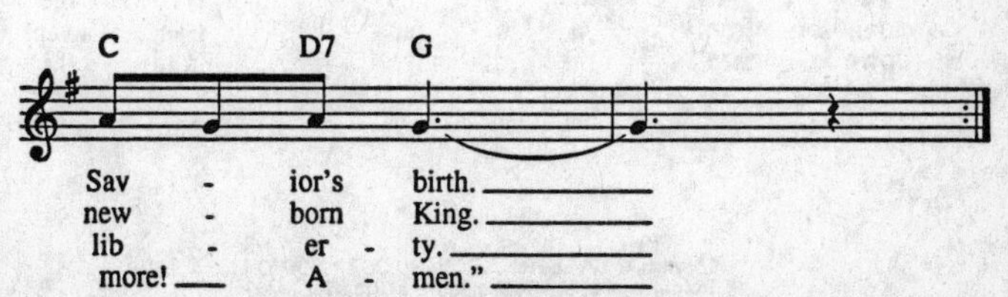
C
D7
G
Sav - ior's birth. ___
new - born King. ___
lib - er - ty. ___
more! ___ A - men." ___

# THERE'S A SONG IN THE AIR

Words and Music by JOSIAH G. HOLLAND and KARL P. HARRINGTON

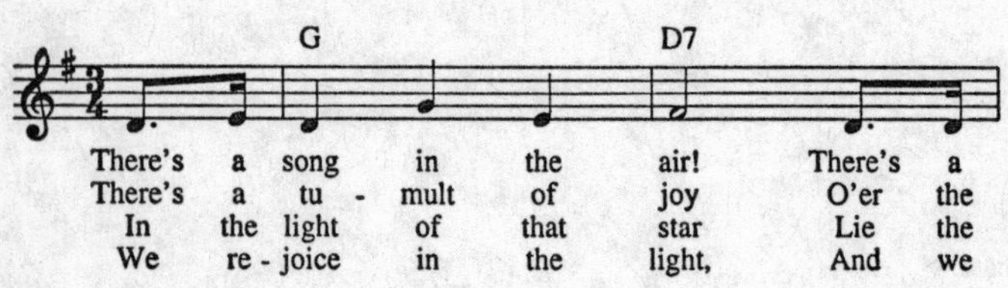
G
D7
There's a song in the air! There's a
There's a tu - mult of joy O'er the
In the light of that star Lie the
We re - joice in the light, And we

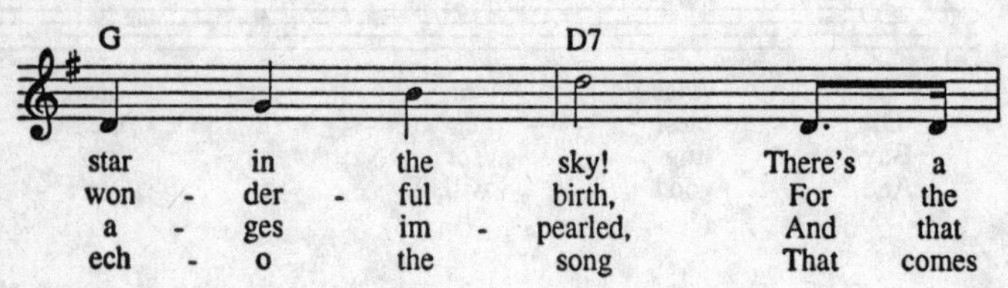
G
D7
star in the sky! There's a
won - der - ful birth, For the
a - ges im - pearled, And that
ech - o the song That comes

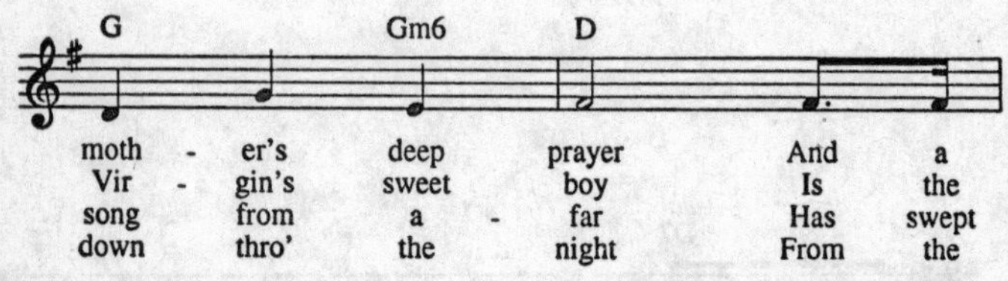
G
Gm6
D
moth - er's deep prayer And a
Vir - gin's sweet boy Is the
song from a - far Has swept
down thro' the night From the

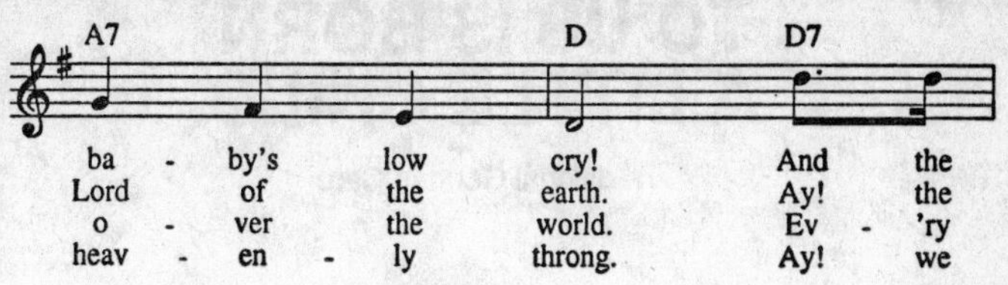
A7
D
D7
ba - by's low cry! And the
Lord of the earth. Ay! the
o - ver the world. Ev - 'ry
heav - en - ly throng. Ay! we

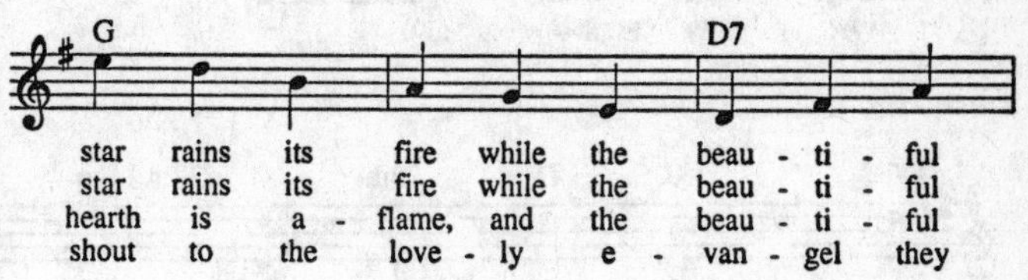
G
D7
star rains its fire while the beau - ti - ful
star rains its fire while the beau - ti - ful
hearth is a - flame, and the beau - ti - ful
shout to the love - ly e - van - gel they

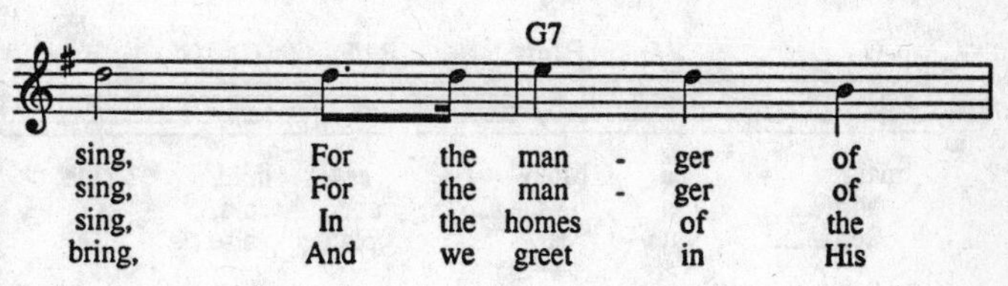
G7
sing, For the man - ger of
sing, For the man - ger of
sing, In the homes of the
bring, And we greet in His

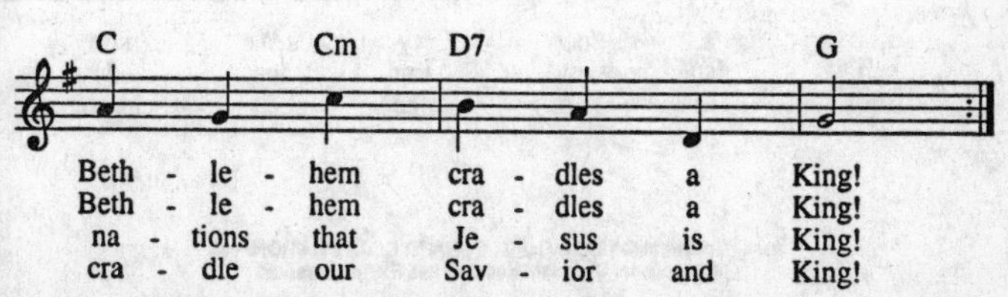
C
Cm
D7
G
Beth - le - hem cra - dles a King!
Beth - le - hem cra - dles a King!
na - tions that Je - sus is King!
cra - dle our Sav - ior and King!

# TO US IS BORN A LITTLE CHILD

Traditional German Carol

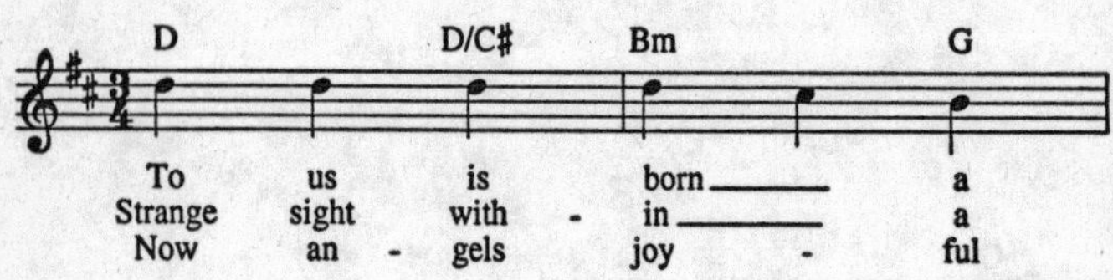
D
D/C♯
Bm
G
To us is born a
Strange sight with - in a
Now an - gels joy - ful

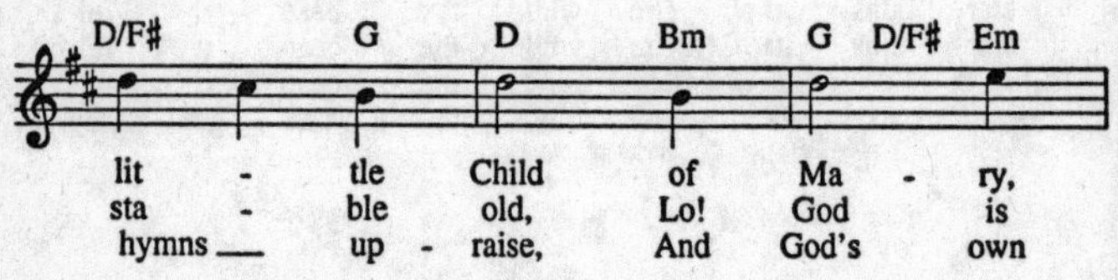
D/F♯
G
D
Bm
G
D/F♯
Em
lit - tle Child of Ma - ry,
sta - ble old, Lo! God is
hymns up - raise, And God's own

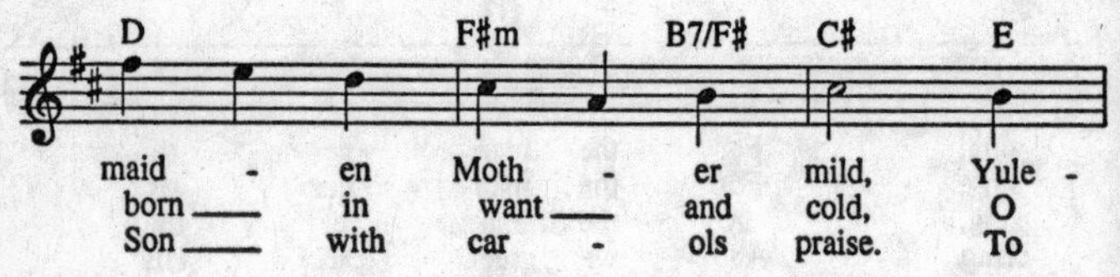
D
F♯m
B7/F♯
C♯
E
maid - en Moth - er mild, Yule -
born in want and cold, O
Son with car - ols praise. To

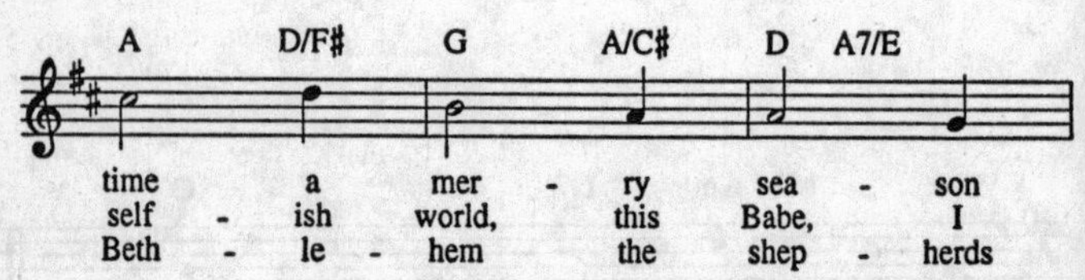
A
D/F♯
G
A/C♯
D
A7/E
time a mer - ry sea - son
self - ish world, this Babe, I
Beth - le - hem the shep - herds

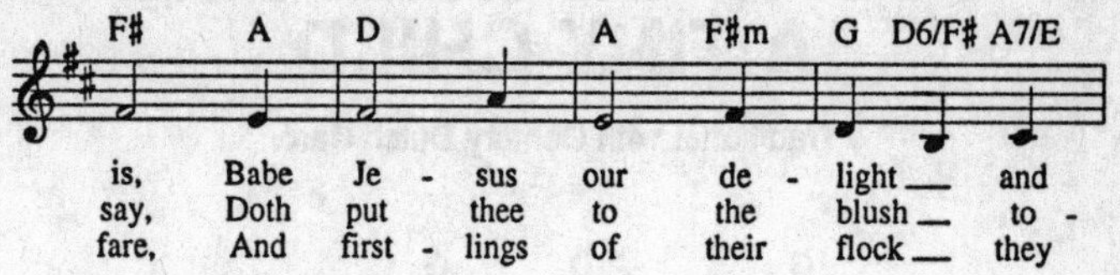
F# A D A F#m G D6/F# A7/E
is, Babe Je - sus our de - light ___ and
say, Doth put thee to the blush ___ to -
fare, And first - lings of their flock ___ they

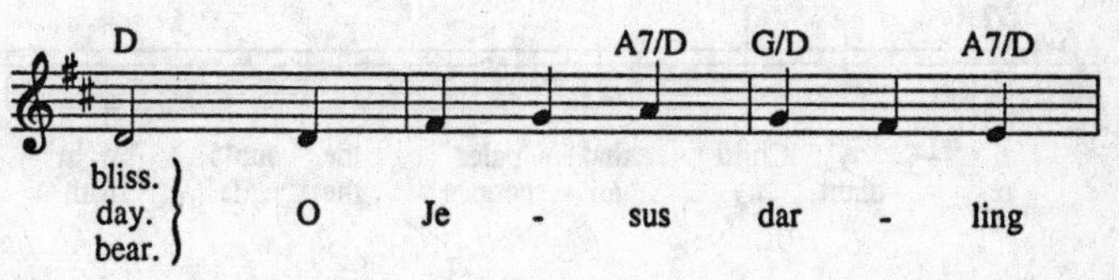
D A7/D G/D A7/D
bliss.
day.
bear.
O Je - sus dar - ling

D D7 G/D D
of ___ my heart, ___ How rich in

A G F#m G A D
mer - cy, Babe, ___ Thou art.

# TODAY WE WELCOME A TINY CHILD

Traditional 14th Century Dutch Carol

G D G C
To - day we wel - come a
The stars that fill ___ the
D7 G
ti - ny Child that pales the sun's bright
ra - diant sky an - nounce the gift from
D G D Am G
shin - ing; Our hope and joy, this
Heav - en, While Ma - ry a - dores her
D Bm G
In - fant mild, whom
Ho - ly Child, that
C G/D D G
an - gels' songs are pro - claim - ing.
God the Fa - ther has giv - en.

# THE TWELVE DAYS OF CHRISTMAS

Traditional English Carol

F
Dm
B♭
C7
F
On the first day of Christ-mas, my true love gave to me: A

B♭
Dm
C7
F
par - tridge in a pear tree. 2. On the

F
Dm
B♭
C7
F
sec - ond day of Christ - mas, my true love gave to me:
third day of Christ - mas, my true love gave to me:
fourth day of Christ - mas, my true love gave to me:

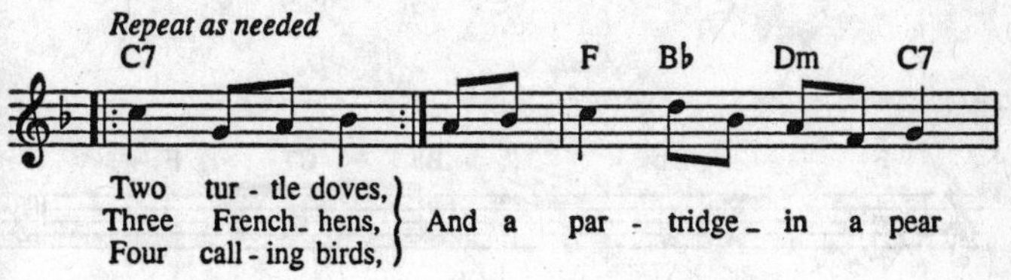
Repeat as needed
C7
F
B♭
Dm
C7
Two tur - tle doves,
Three French hens,
Four call - ing birds,
And a par - tridge in a pear

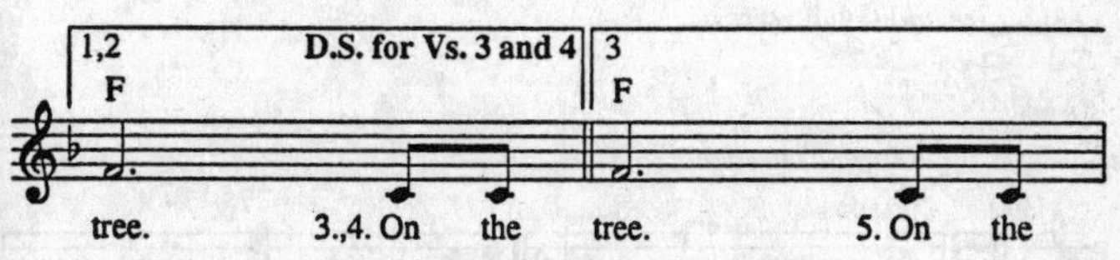
1,2
F
D.S. for Vs. 3 and 4
3
F
tree. 3.,4. On the tree. 5. On the

Dm
B♭
C7
F
fifth day of Christ - mas, my true love gave to me:

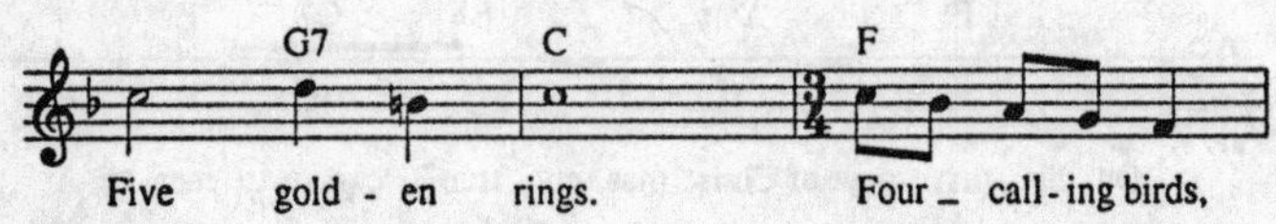
G7
C
F
Five gold - en rings. Four _ call - ing birds,

B♭
G7
C
Three French hens, Two _ tur - tle doves, And a

F
B♭
Dm
C7
F
par - tridge _ in a pear tree. 6. On the

F
Dm
B♭
C7
F
sixth day of Christ - mas, my true love gave to me:
7.-12. (See additional verses)

Repeat as needed
C7
F
G7
Six geese a - lay-ing Five gold - en

C
F
B♭
rings!
Four _ call - ing birds,
Three French hens,

G7
C
F
B♭
Dm
C7
Two _ tur - tle doves,
And a
par - tridge _ in a pear

F
D.S.S. for Vs. 7-12
F
Fine
tree.
On the
tree.

*Additional Verses*

7. On the seventh day of Christmas my true love gave to me:
   Seven swans a-swimming.

8. ... Eight maids a-milking

9. ... Nine ladies dancing

10. ... Ten lords a-leaping

11. ... 'Leven pipers piping.

12. ... Twelve drummers drumming

# TOURO-LOURO-LOURO

Traditional French Lyrics
Music by NICOLAS SABOLY

G
C
Tou - ro - lou - ro - lou - ro, cocks are
Tou - ro - lou - ro - lou - ro, cold winds
Tou - ro - lou - ro - lou - ro, what good
G
Em
C
D7
crow - ing, Long be - fore the morn - ing
howl - ing, Make my bod - y numb with
for - tune, I have found the Ho - ly
G
C
light, High a - bove, the stars are
cold, But I can - not yet be
Child! There up - on the straw, the
G
Em
C
D7
shin - ing, O'er the Ho - ly Land to -
stop - ping, For the day is grow - ing
hand - some Ba - by looks at me and
G
D
G
night. "Will you go there?" "No, I can - not!" "Go with me
old. "Please let me rest." "No rest for you." "I must find
smiles! "Good day to you!" (He's laugh - ing now!) "Good day to

D G D G D
there?" "No, I can - not." O Wil - liam, O Wil -
rest." "No rest for you." O farm - er, O farm -
you!" (Jo - seph's so proud!) O Ma - ry, O Ma -
G C D7
liam, If I nev - er should re -
er, Give me shel - ter for the
ry, May your name be ev - er
G C/E G/D D
turn, Say a psalm to give me bless -
night, In the hay - loft I'd be sleep -
blessed, For the Child that Heav - en sent
G Em D G
ing! Still, I must go, Yea,
ing. Shel - ter, I do pray, Just,
thee! Saint Jo - seph too, Bless -
Em D7 G D
I must go; Though the jour - ney will be
for this day; For I'm near to freez - ing
ings un - to you! For the love - ly Child so
G D7 G D7 G
long, Still I must go, Yea, I must go.
now. Don't let me die! Don't let me die!
dear, That we all love, That we all love.

# 'TWAS THE NIGHT BEFORE CHRISTMAS

Words by CLEMENT CLARK MOORE
Music by F. HENRI KLICKMAN

C A7 Dm7 G7
1.'Twas the night be-fore Christ-mas, when all through the house, Not a
2.-7.(See additional verses)
Dm7 G7 C
crea-ture was stir - ring, not e - ven a mouse; The
A7♭5 G
stock-ings were hung by the chim-ney with care, In
D7 G7
hopes that Saint Nich - o - las soon would be there, The
C A7 Dm7 G7
chil-dren were nest - led all snug in their beds, While
Dm7 G7 C C7
vis-ions of sug - ar plums danced through their heads; And
F Adim C Gm6 A7
ma - ma in her 'ker - chief and I in my cap, Had just
D7 G7 C
set - tled our brains for a long win - ter's nap.

*Additional Verses*

2. When out on the lawn there arose such a clatter;
I sprang from my bed to see what was the matter.
Away to the window I flew like a flash,
Tore open the shutters and threw up the sash.
The moon, on the breast of the new-fallen snow,
Gave a lustre of midday to objects below;
When what to my wondering eyes should appear
But a miniature sleigh and eight tiny reindeer.

3. With a little old driver; so lively and quick,
I knew in a moment it must be St. Nick.
More rapid than eagles his coursers they came,
And he whistled, and shouted, and called them by name;
"Now, Dasher! now, Dancer! now, Prancer! now, Vixen
On, Comet! on, Cupid! on Donder and Blitzen!
To the top of the porch, to the top of the wall!
Now dash away, dash away, dash away all!"

4. As dry leaves that before the wild hurricane fly,
When they meet with an obstacle, mount to the sky,
So up to the house-top the coursers they flew,
With the sleigh full of toys, and St. Nicholas, too.
And then in a twinkling I heard on the roof
The prancing and pawing of each little hoof.
As I drew in my head, and was turning around,
Down the chimney St Nicholas came with a bound.

5. He was dressed all in fur from his head to his foot,
And his clothes were all tarnished with ashes and soot;
A bundle of toys he had flung on his back,
And he looked like a peddler just opening his pack.
His eyes how they twinkled! his dimples how merry!
His cheeks were like roses, his nose like a cherry,
His droll little mouth was drawn up like a bow,
And the beard of his chin was as white as the snow.

6. The stump of a pipe he held tight in his teeth,
And the smoke, it encircled his head like a wreath.
He had a broad face, and a round little belly
That shook, when he laughed, like a bowl full of jelly.
He was chubby and plump - a right jolly old elf-
And I laughed when I saw him, in spite of myself.
A wink of his eye, and a twist of his head,
Soon gave me to know I had nothing to dread.

7. He spake not a word, but went straight to his work,
And filled all the stockings; then turned with a jerk,
And laying his finger aside of his nose,
And giving a nod, up the chimney he rose.
He sprang to his sleigh, to his team gave a whistle,
And away they all flew like the down of a thistle;
But I heard him exclaim, ere he drove out of sight -
"Happy Christmas to all, and all a Good-night!"

# UP ON THE HOUSETOP

Words and Music by B.R. HANDY

Eb
Up on the house - top rein - deer pause,
First comes the stock - ing of lit - tle Nell;
Next comes the stock - ing of lit - tle Will;
Ab Eb Bb7 Eb
Out jumps good old San - ta Claus; Down thro' the chim - ney with
Oh, dear San - ta, fill it well; Give her a dol - lie that
Oh, just see what a glor - ious fill! Here is a ham - mer and
Ab Eb
lots of toys, All for the lit - tle ones,
laughs and cries, One that will o - pen and
lots of tacks, Al - so a ball and a
Bb7 Eb Ab Eb
Christ - mas joys.
shut her eyes.
whip that cracks.
Ho, ho, ho! who would - n't go!
Bb7 Eb
Ho, ho, ho! who would - n't go!
Eb7 Ab
Up on the House - top, click, click, click.
Eb Bb7 Eb
Down thro' the chim - ney with good Saint Nick.

# WASSAIL, WASSAIL

Old English Air

F
Was - sail, Was - sail all
The was - s'ling bowl with a
Come but - ler bring us a
C7 F
o - ver the town! Our
toast with - in, Come,
bowl of your best, And
C/E F Dm C
bread it is white and our ale it is brown; Our
fill it up now un - to the brim. Come,
we hope your soul in heav - en shall rest. But
F C7 A7/E Dm Gm/B♭
bowl is made of the ma - ple tree, So
fill it up that we may all see, With the
if you bring us a bowl too small, Then
A Gm Dm Gm/B♭ C7 F
here my good fel - low, I'll drink to thee.
was - sail - ing bowl, I'll drink to thee.
down shall go but - ler and bowl and all.

# A VIRGIN UNSPOTTED

Traditional English Carol

D A D
A Vir - gin un - spot - ted, the
Then God sent an an - gel from
Then pres - ent - ly af - ter, the
To teach us hu - mil - i - ty
A7 D
proph - et fore - told, Should
Heav - en so high, To
shep - herds did spy Vast
all this was done, And
A D
bring forth a Sav - ior, which
cer - tain poor shep - herds in
num - bers of an - gels to
learn we from thence haugh - ty
A7 D
we now be - hold; To
fields where they lie, And
stand in the sky; They
pride for to shun; A
A7 D A7 A9
be our Re - deem - er from
bade them no long - er in
joy - ful - ly talk - ed and
man - ger His cra - dle who

D Bm E A
death, hell, and sin, Which
sor - row to stay, Be -
sweet - ly did sing: "To
came from a - bove, The
D A D
Ad - am's trans - gres - sion had
cause that our Sav - ior was
God be all glo - ry, our
great God of mer - cy, of
A7 D
wrap - ped us in.
born on this day.
heav - en - ly King."
peace and of love.
Aye, and
A7 D Em7 A A9
there - fore be mer - ry, set
D Bm E7 A D
sor - row a - side, Christ
A7 D
Je - sus, our Sav - ior, was
A7 D
born on this tide.

# WASSAIL SONG

Traditional English Carol

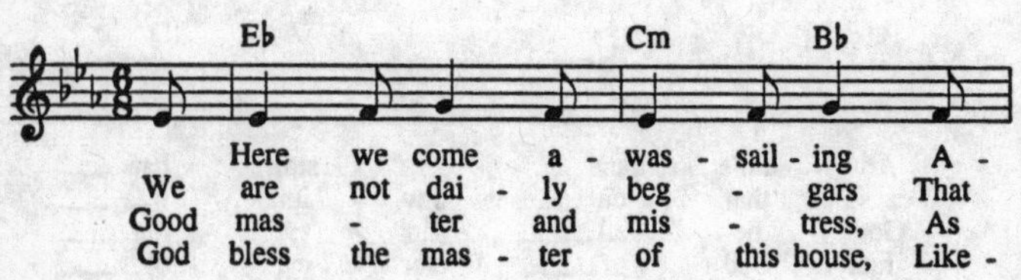
Eb Cm Bb
Here we come a - was - sail - ing A -
We are not dai - ly beg - gars That
Good mas - ter and mis - tress, As
God bless the mas - ter of this house, Like -

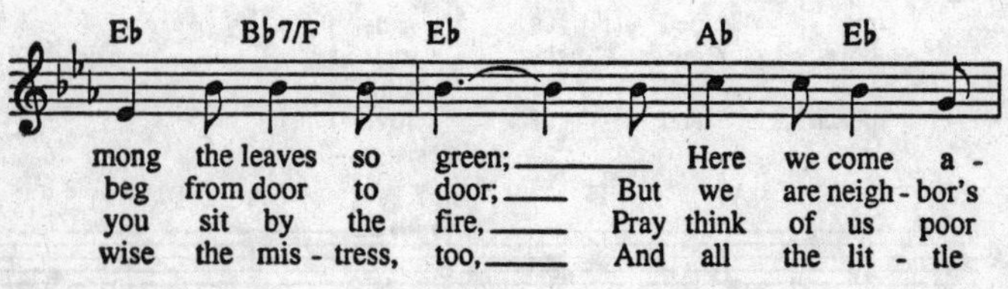
Eb Bb7/F Eb Ab Eb
mong the leaves so green; Here we come a -
beg from door to door; But we are neigh - bor's
you sit by the fire, Pray think of us poor
wise the mis - tress, too, And all the lit - tle

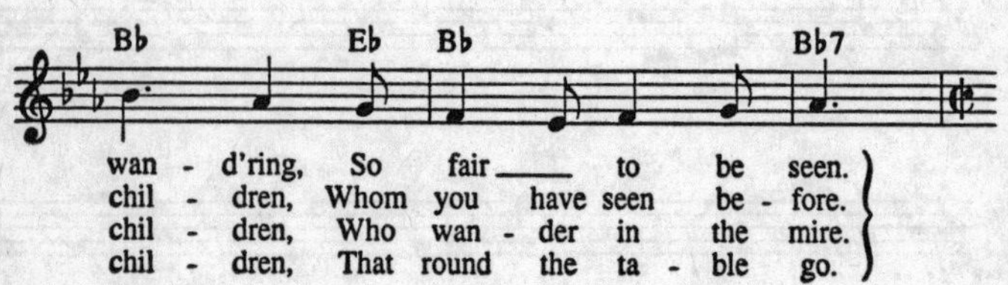
Bb Eb Bb Bb7
wan - d'ring, So fair to be seen.
chil - dren, Whom you have seen be - fore.
chil - dren, Who wan - der in the mire.
chil - dren, That round the ta - ble go.

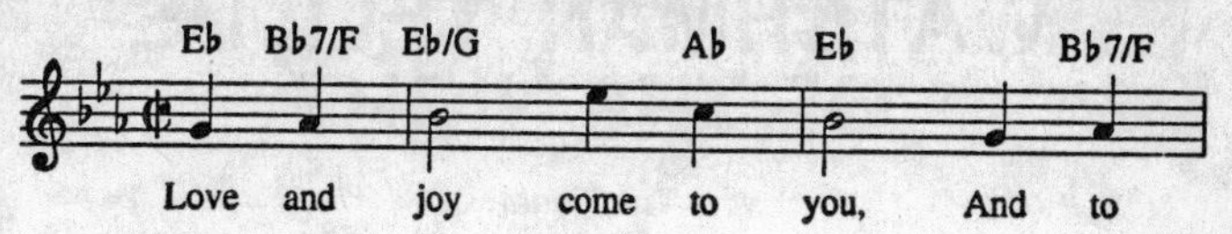
Eb Bb7/F Eb/G Ab Eb Bb7/F
Love and joy come to you, And to

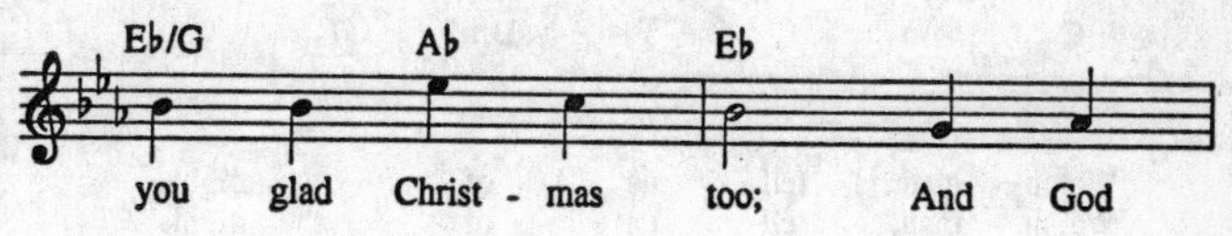
Eb/G Ab Eb
you glad Christ - mas too; And God

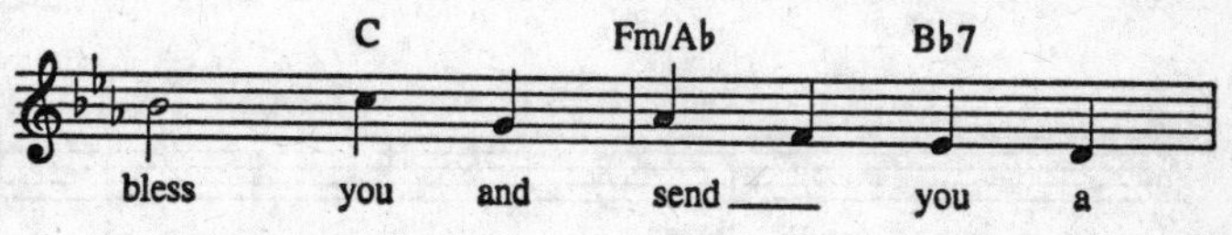
C Fm/Ab Bb7
bless you and send ___ you a

Eb Bb7
hap - py New Year, And God

Eb C Fm/Ab Eb/Bb Bb7 Eb
send you a hap - py New ___ Year.

# WATCHMAN, TELL US OF THE NIGHT

Traditional

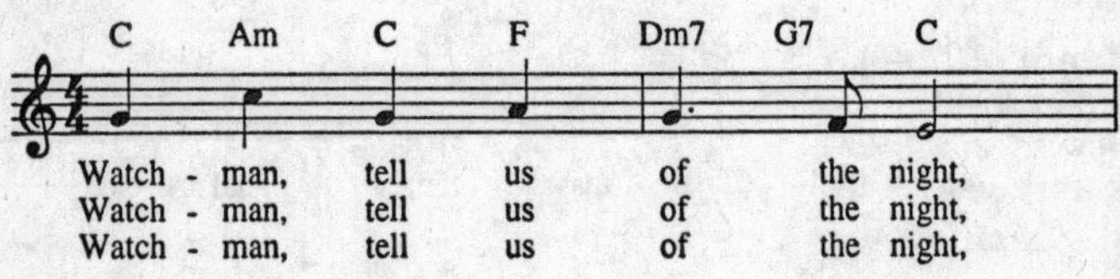
C Am C F Dm7 G7 C
Watch - man, tell us of the night,
Watch - man, tell us of the night,
Watch - man, tell us of the night,

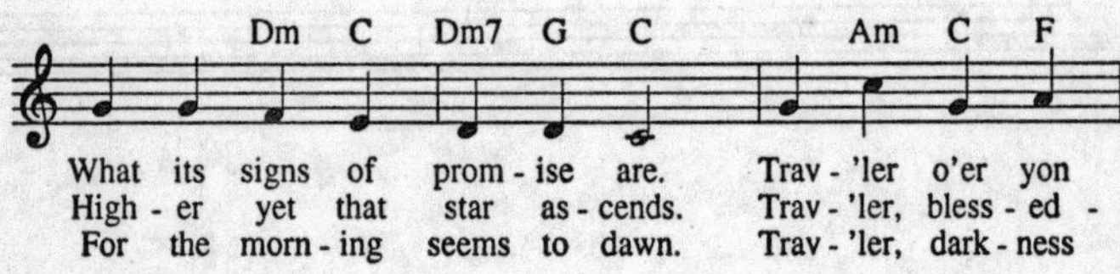
Dm C Dm7 G C Am C F
What its signs of prom - ise are. Trav - 'ler o'er yon
High - er yet that star as - cends. Trav - 'ler, bless - ed -
For the morn - ing seems to dawn. Trav - 'ler, dark - ness

Dm7 G7 C Dm C
moun - tain's height, See that glo - ry
ness and light, peace and truth, its
takes its flight; Doubt and ter - ror

Dm7 G7 C G C Em
beam - ing star. Watch - man, does ___ its
course por - tends. Watch - man, will ___ its
are with - drawn. Watch - man, let ___ thy

Am7 D7 G Dm Am
beau - teous ray Aught of joy or
beams a - lone Gild the spot that
wan - derings cease; Hie thee to thy

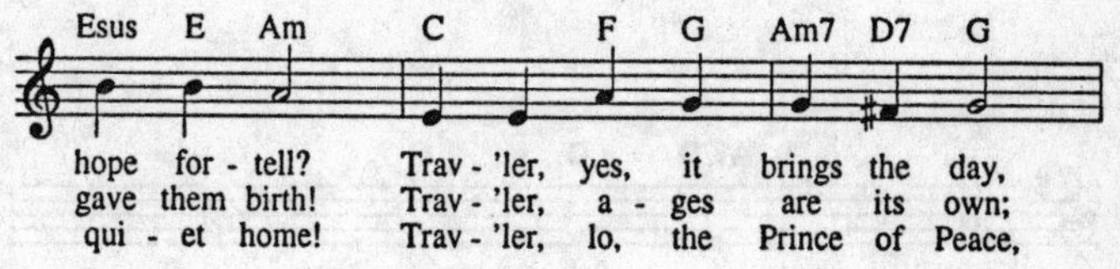
Esus E Am C F G Am7 D7 G
hope for - tell? Trav - 'ler, yes, it brings the day,
gave them birth! Trav - 'ler, a - ges are its own;
qui - et home! Trav - 'ler, lo, the Prince of Peace,

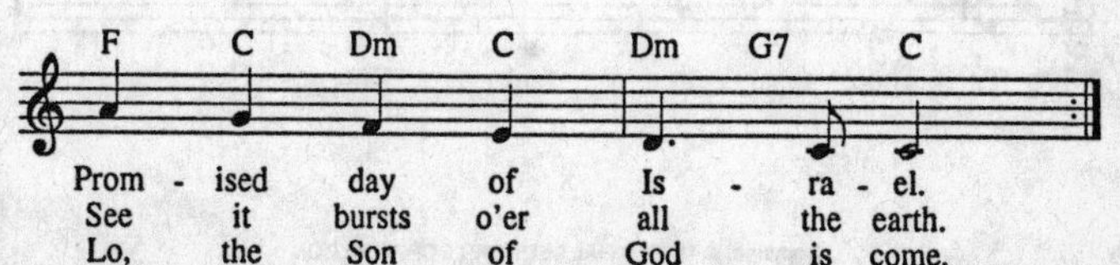
F C Dm C Dm G7 C
Prom - ised day of Is - ra - el.
See it bursts o'er all the earth.
Lo, the Son of God is come.

# WE ARE SINGING

Traditional Venezuelan Folk Carol

Refrain

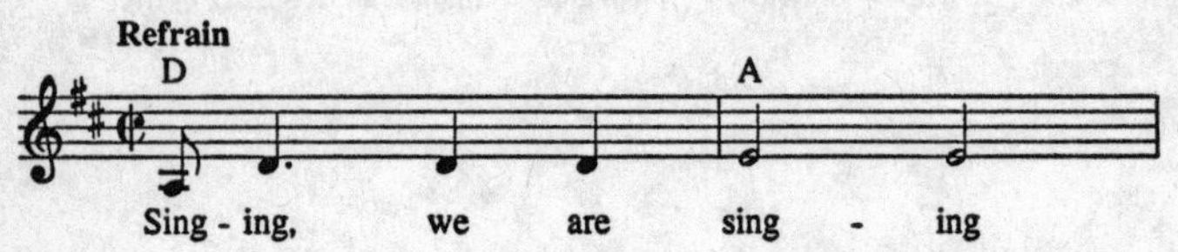
D
A
Sing - ing, we are sing - ing

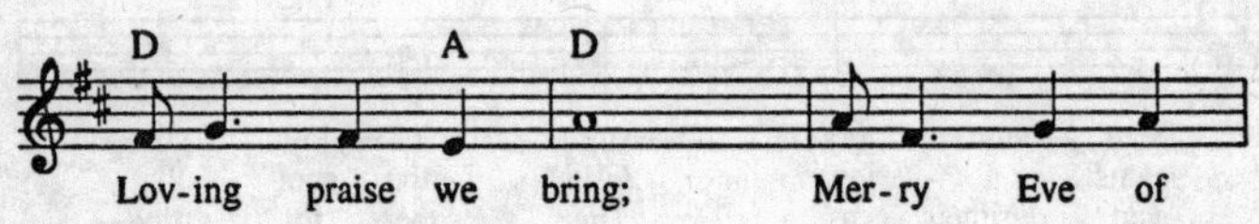
D
A
D
Lov-ing praise we bring; Mer-ry Eve of

G
A7
D/A
A7
D
Christ - mas, Mer-ry Eve of Christ - mas,

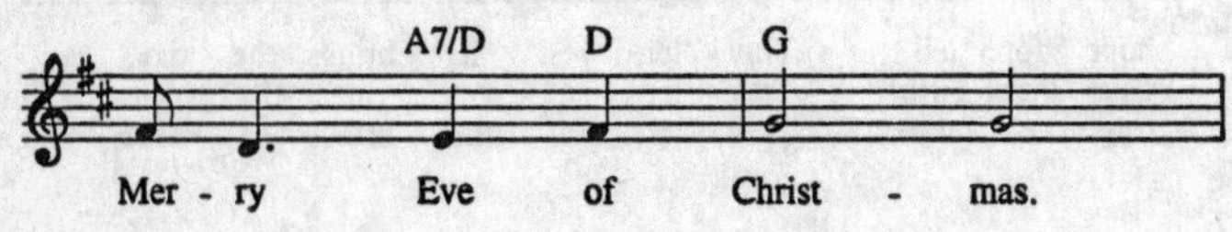
A7/D
D
G
Mer - ry Eve of Christ - mas.

D/A
A
D/A
A
D
Fine
To Thee, In - fant King.

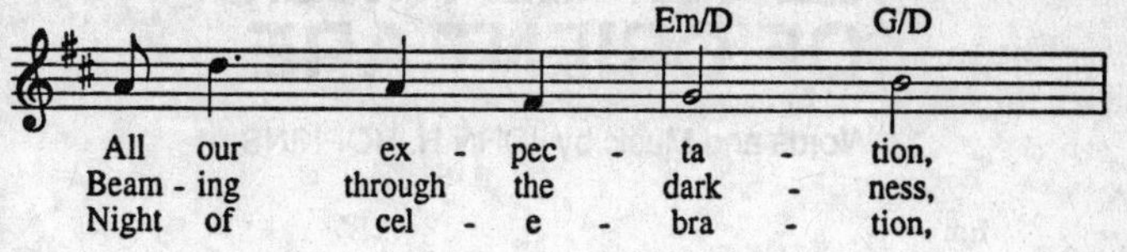
Em/D G/D
All our ex - pec - ta - tion,
Beam - ing through the dark - ness,
Night of cel - e - bra - tion,

Em/A A7 D
All our char - i - ty,
Flood - ing rays so bright,
Night of Je - sus' birth,

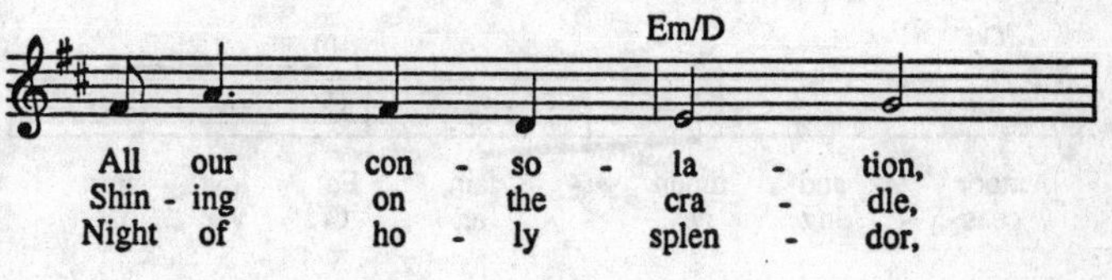
Em/D
All our con - so - la - tion,
Shin - ing on the cra - dle,
Night of ho - ly splen - dor,

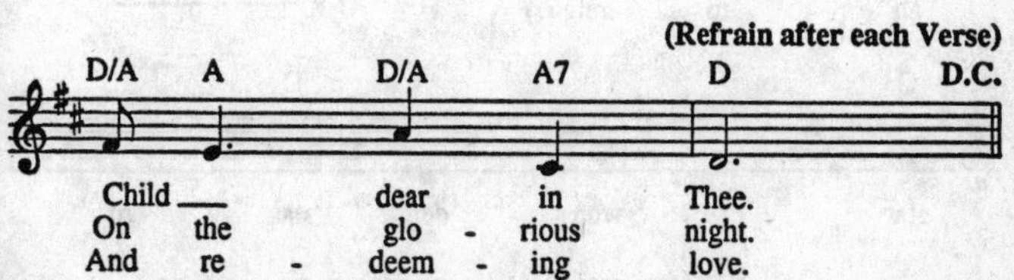
(Refrain after each Verse)
D/A A D/A A7 D D.C.
Child dear in Thee.
On the glo - rious night.
And re - deem - ing love.

# WE THREE KINGS OF ORIENT ARE

Words and Music by JOHN H. HOPKINS

Em
B7
1. We three kings of O - ri - ent
2. Born a King on Beth - le - hem
3.-5. (See additional verses)
Em
B7
are; Bear - ing gifts we tra - verse a -
plain, Gold I bring to crown him a -
Em
D
far, Field and foun - tain,
gain, King for - ev - er,
G
Am
moor and moun - tain, Fol - low - ing
ceas - ing nev - er, O - ver us
B7
Em
Refrain
D7
yon - der star.
all to reign.
O
G
C
star of won - der, star of

G
night,
Star
with
roy
-
al

C
G
Em
D
G
beau
-
ty
bright,
West
-
ward
lead
-
ing,

C
G
D
G
still
pro
-
ceed
-
ing,
Guide
us

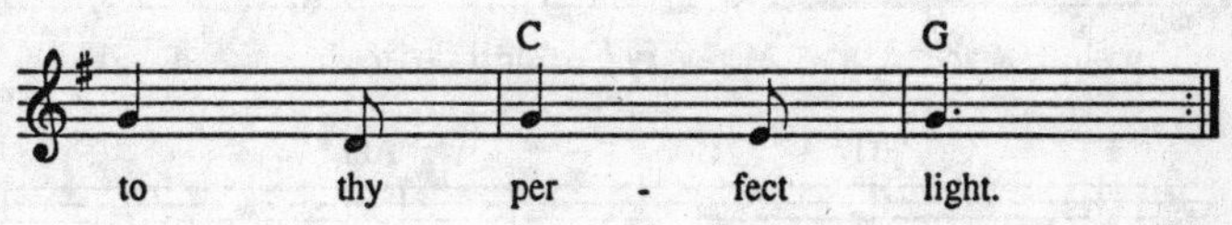
C
G
to
thy
per
-
fect
light.

*Additional Verses*

3. Frankincense to offer have I;
Incense owns a Deity nigh;
Prayer and praising, all men raising,
Worship Him, God most high.
*(Refrain)*

4. Myrhh is mine: its bitter perfume
Breathes a life of gathering gloom:
Sorrowing, sighing, bleeding, dying;
Sealed in the stone-cold tomb.
*(Refrain)*

5. Glorious now, behold Him arise,
King and God, and Sacrifice!
Heav'n sings alleluya,
Alleluya the earth replies:
*(Refrain)*

# WE WISH YOU A MERRY CHRISTMAS

Traditional English Folksong

C
F
We wish you a Mer - ry Christ - mas, we
D7
G7
wish you a Mer - ry Christ - mas, we
E7
Am
wish you a Mer - ry Christ - mas, And a
F
G7
C
Am
Hap - py New Year! Good ti - dings to
Em
D7
G
you, wher - ev - er you are; Good
C
G
ti - dings for Christ - mas, And a
D7
G7
C
Hap - py New Year!

# WHENCE ART THOU, MY MAIDEN?

Translation by WILLIAM McLENNAN, 1866
Traditional French-Canadian Melody

Bb F7 Bb C9
"Whence art thou, my maid - en, whence art
"What saw'st thou, my maid - en, what saw'st
"Noth - ing more, my maid - en, noth - ing
"Noth - ing more, my maid - en, noth - ing
"Noth - ing more, my maid - en, noth - ing
F Cm7 Bb
thou?" "I come from the sta - ble
thou? "There with - in a man - ger, a
more? "There I saw the vir - gin,
more? "I saw ass and ox - en,
more? "There were three bright an - gels,
Cm F7
where, this ver - y night, I, a shep - herd
ti - ny Child I saw, Ly - ing soft - ly
her sweet Ba - by hold, And the fa - ther
kneel - ing meek and mild, Soft - ly their
come down from the sky, Sing - ing forth great
Gm Bb/D Eb F7 Bb
maid - en, saw a marv' - lous sight."
sleep - ing, on a bed of straw."
Jo - seph, trem - bling with the cold."
breath - ing, warmed the ho - ly Child."
prais - es, to our God on high."

# WELSH CAROL

Words by PASTOR K.E. ROBERTS
Traditional Welsh Carol

Am E7/B Am E
A - wake were they on - ly, those
May light new en - fold us, O
Am Dm E Am E
shep-herds so lone - ly, On guard in that si -
Lord, for be - hold us Like shep-herds, from tu -
Am/E E Am E/G♯ Am E7/B
lence pro - found, When co - lor had fad -
mult with - drawn, Nor heav - ing, nor see -
Am E Am Dm E7
ed, when night - time had shad - ed, Their
ing, all oth - er care flee - ing, We
Am Am/E E Am/E E Am G G7
sens - es from sight and from sound. Lo,
wait the in - eff - a - ble dawn. O

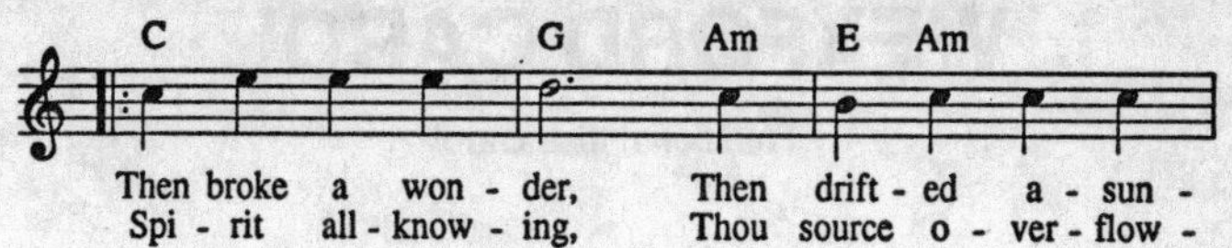
C G Am E Am
Then broke a won - der, Then drift - ed a - sun -
Spi - rit all - know - ing, Thou source o - ver - flow -

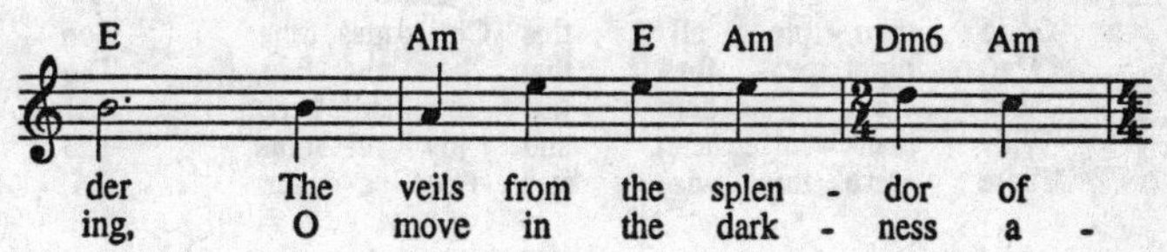
E Am E Am Dm6 Am
der The veils from the splen - dor of
ing, O move in the dark - ness a -

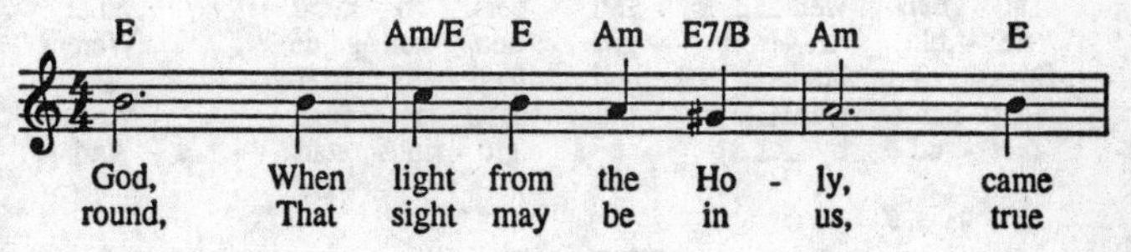
E Am/E E Am E7/B Am E
God, When light from the Ho - ly, came
round, That sight may be in us, true

Am Dm6 Dm E7 Am Am/E E
down to the low - ly, And heav'n to the earth
hear - ing to win us, Glad tid - ings where Christ

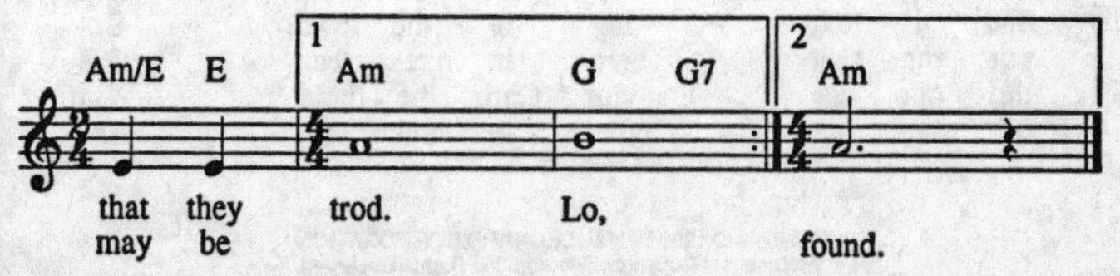
Am/E E 1 Am G G7 2 Am
that they trod. Lo,
may be found.

# WEXFORD CAROL

Traditional Irish Carol

G
D7/G
G
Good peo - ple all this Christ-mas time, Con -
The night be - fore that hap - py tide, The
Near Beth - le - hem did shep-herds keep, Their
With thank - ful heart and joy - ful mind, The
There were three wise men from a - far Di -
D7
Em
D/F#
G6
F
C/E
Dm
D
si - der well and bear in mind, What
no - ble Vir - gin and her guide, Were
flocks of lambs and feed - ing sheep; To
shep - herds went the babe to find, And
rect - ed by a glo - rious star, And
G
D7/G
G
our good God for us has done, In
long time seek - ing up and down, To
whom God's an - gels did ap - pear, Which
as God's an - gel had fore - told, They
on they wan - dered night and day, Un -
C/G
D/F#
Em
D/F#
C/E
C
G
C/G
send - ing his be - lov - ed Son. With
find a lodg - ing in the town. But
put the shep - herds in great fear. 'Pre -
did our Sa - vior Christ be - hold. With -
til they came where Je - sus lay. And

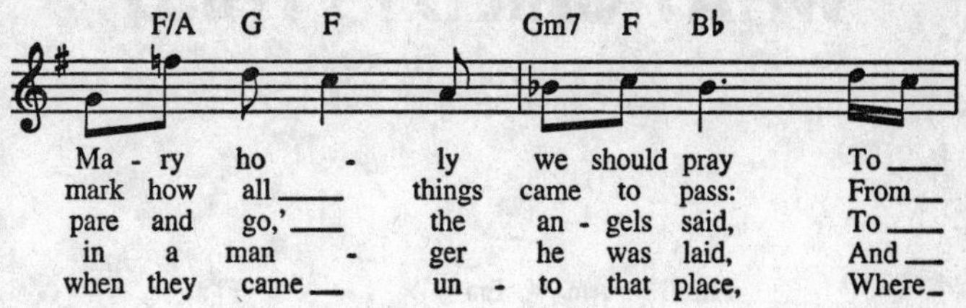
F/A G F Gm7 F B♭
Ma - ry ho - ly we should pray To
mark how all things came to pass: From
pare and go,' the an - gels said, To
in a man - ger he was laid, And
when they came un - to that place, Where

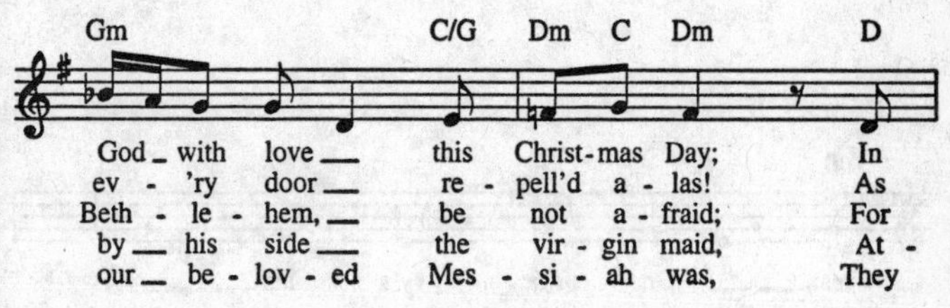
Gm C/G Dm C Dm D
God with love this Christ-mas Day; In
ev - 'ry door re - pell'd a - las! As
Beth - le - hem, be not a - fraid; For
by his side the vir - gin maid, At -
our be - lov - ed Mes - si - ah was, They

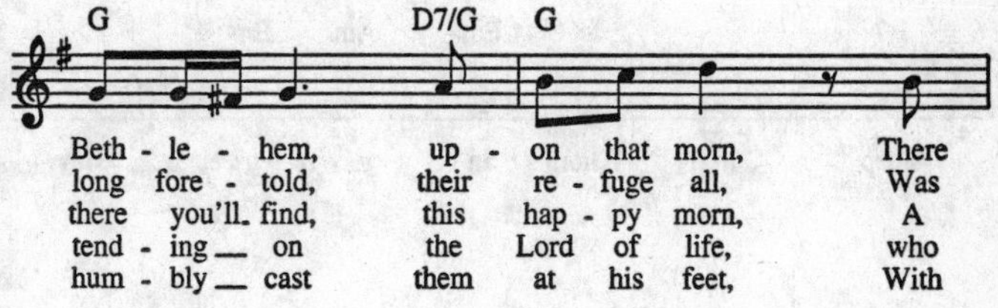
G D7/G G
Beth - le - hem, up - on that morn, There
long fore - told, their re - fuge all, Was
there you'll find, this hap - py morn, A
tend - ing on the Lord of life, who
hum - bly cast them at his feet, With

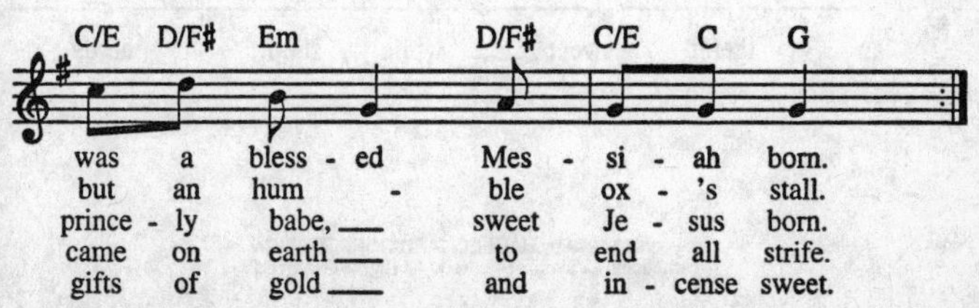
C/E D/F# Em D/F# C/E C G
was a bless - ed Mes - si - ah born.
but an hum - ble ox - 's stall.
prince - ly babe, sweet Je - sus born.
came on earth to end all strife.
gifts of gold and in - cense sweet.

# WHAT CHILD IS THIS?

Words by WILLIAM C. DIX
16th Century English Melody

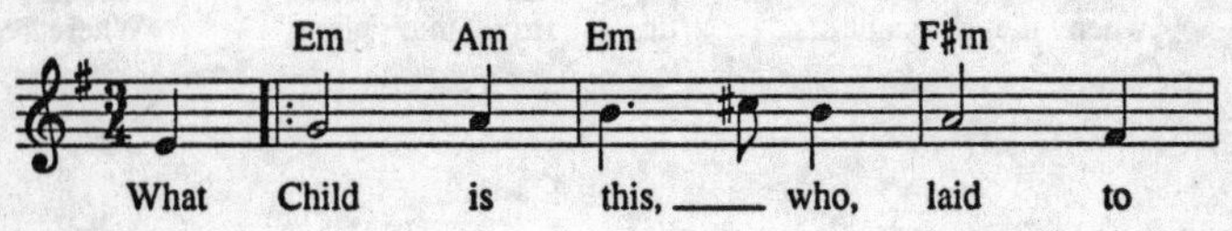
Em Am Em F#m
What Child is this, who, laid to

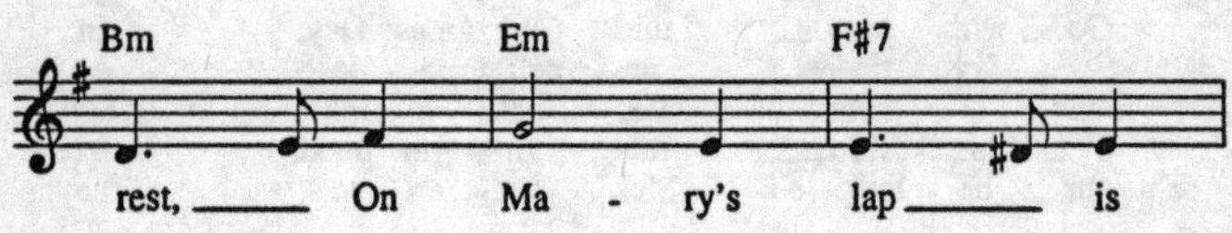
Bm Em F#7
rest, On Ma - ry's lap is

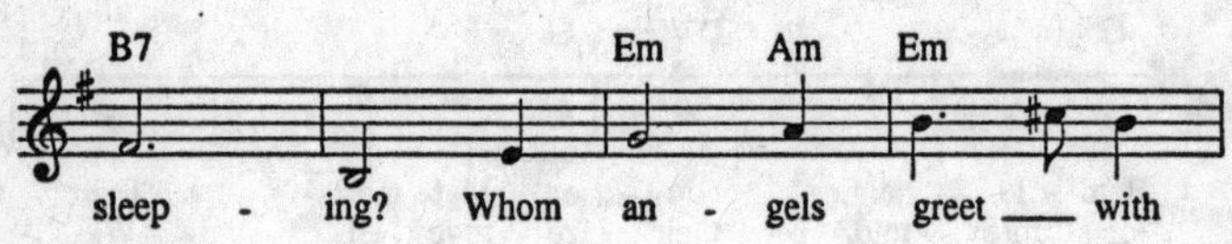
B7 Em Am Em
sleep - ing? Whom an - gels greet with

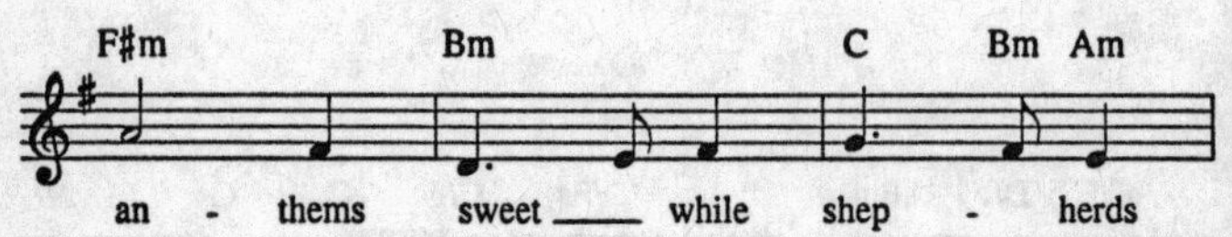
F#m Bm C Bm Am
an - thems sweet while shep - herds

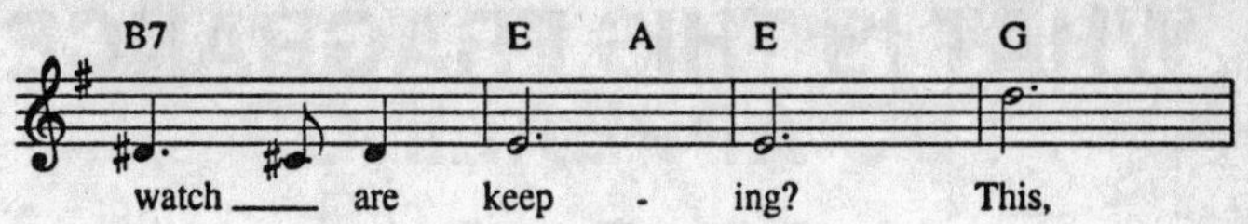
B7
E
A
E
G
watch ___ are keep - ing? This,

F#m
Bm
this ___ is Christ the King, ___ Whom

Em
F#7
B
shep - herds guard ___ and an - gels

B7
G
F#m
sing: Haste haste ___ to bring him

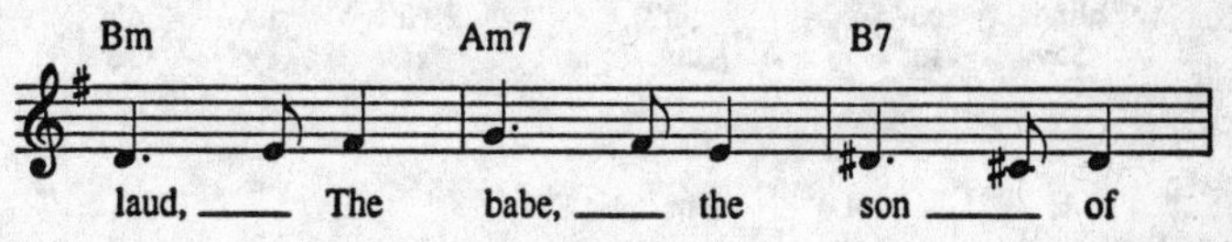
Bm
Am7
B7
laud, ___ The babe, ___ the son ___ of

1
Am
Em
2
E
Ma - ry. What Ma - ry.

# WHAT IS THIS FRAGRANCE SO APPEALING?

Traditional French Carol

D
A/C#
Bm7
D/A
What is this fra - grance so ap -
What is this star with bril - liance
In Beth - le - hem, a sim - ple
G
D
Gmaj7
peal - ing, Shep - herds, that fills the
shin - ing deep in the dark that
man - ger, is born to you a
D/A
A7
D
Bm
wind - chilled air? Love - li - er
blinds our sight? Nev - er did
Sav - ior King. Hur - ry to
E
A
Bm
E7
A
per - fume ne'er came steal - ing
morn - ing's sun come dawn - ing
kneel be - side His man - ger

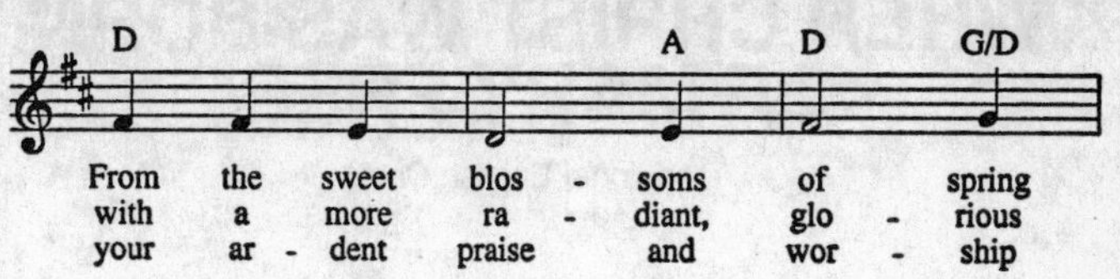
D
A
D
G/D
From the sweet blos - soms of spring
with a more ra - diant, glo - rious
your ar - dent praise and wor - ship

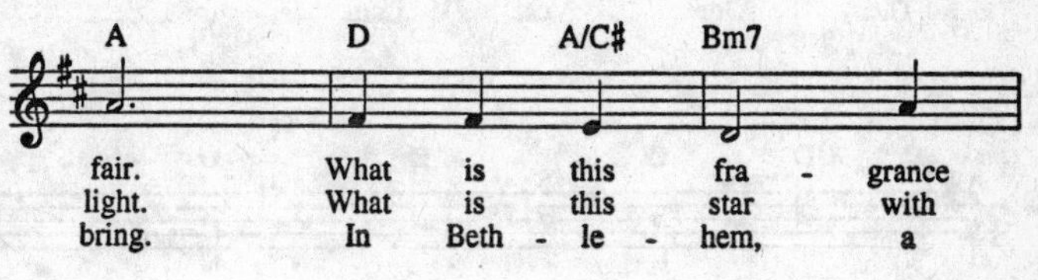
A
D
A/C#
Bm7
fair. What is this fra - grance
light. What is this star with
bring. In Beth - le - hem, a

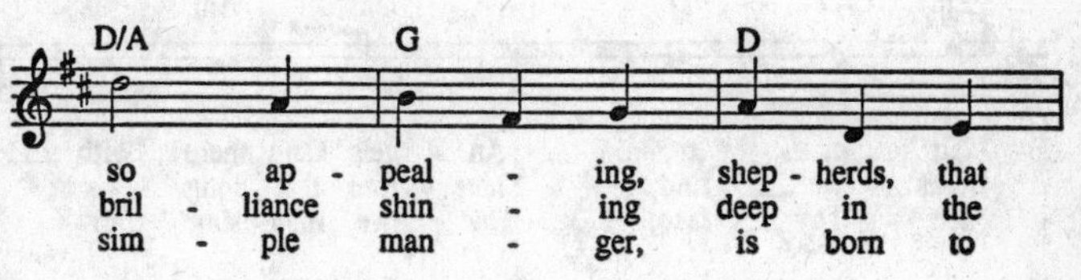
D/A
G
D
so ap - peal - ing, shep - herds, that
bril - liance shin - ing deep in the
sim - ple man - ger, is born to

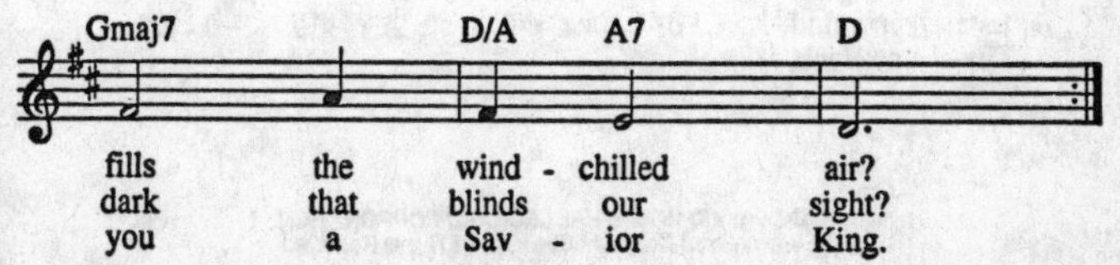
Gmaj7
D/A
A7
D
fills the wind - chilled air?
dark that blinds our sight?
you a Sav - ior King.

# WHEN CHRIST WAS BORN OF MARY FREE

Traditional English Carol

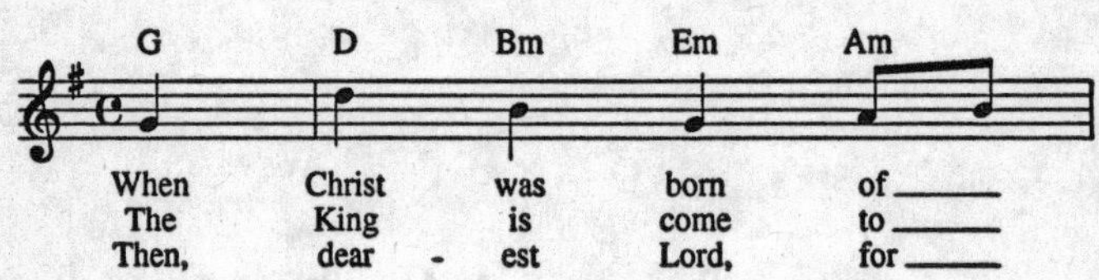
G D Bm Em Am
When Christ was born of
The King is come to
Then, dear - est Lord, for

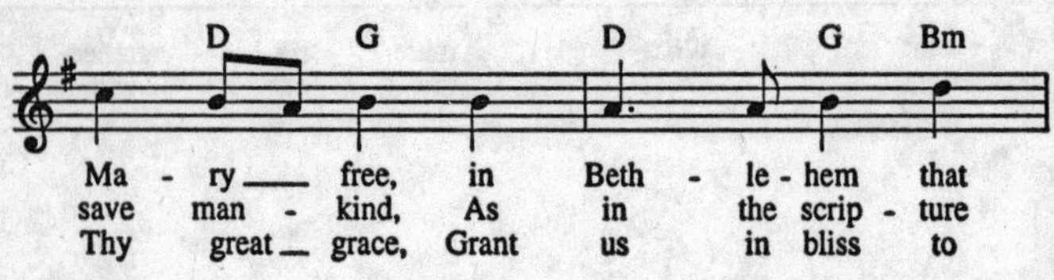
D G D G Bm
Ma - ry free, in Beth - le - hem that
save man - kind, As in the scrip - ture
Thy great grace, Grant us in bliss to

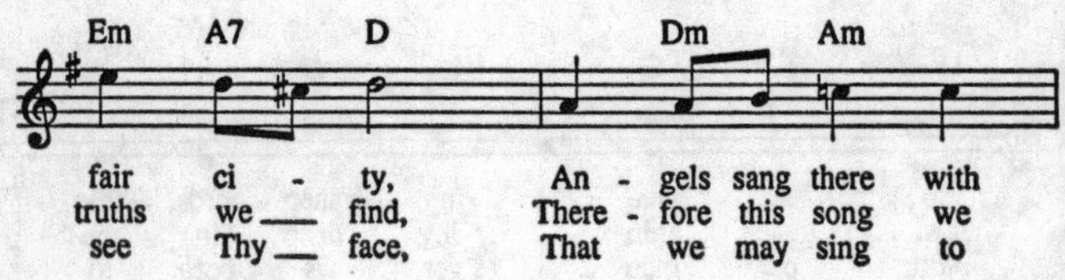
Em A7 D Dm Am
fair ci - ty, An - gels sang there with
truths we find, There - fore this song we
see Thy face, That we may sing to

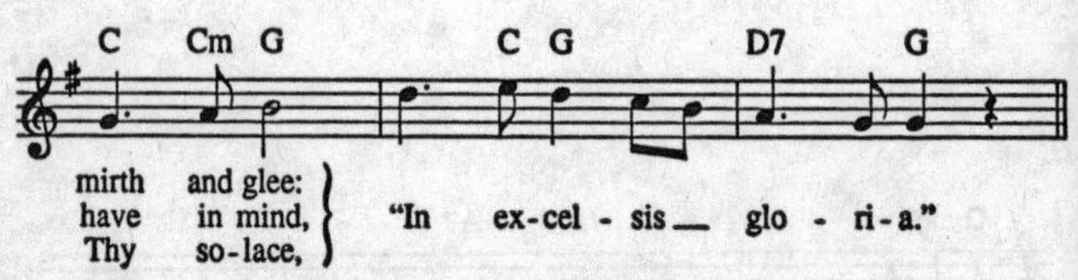
C Cm G C G D7 G
mirth and glee:
have in mind,
Thy so-lace,
"In ex-cel - sis glo - ri-a."

C G
In ex - cel - sis glo - ri - a,

D Am7 G D G
In ex - cel - sis glo - ri - a,

Em C G Am D
In ex - cel - sis glo - ri - a,

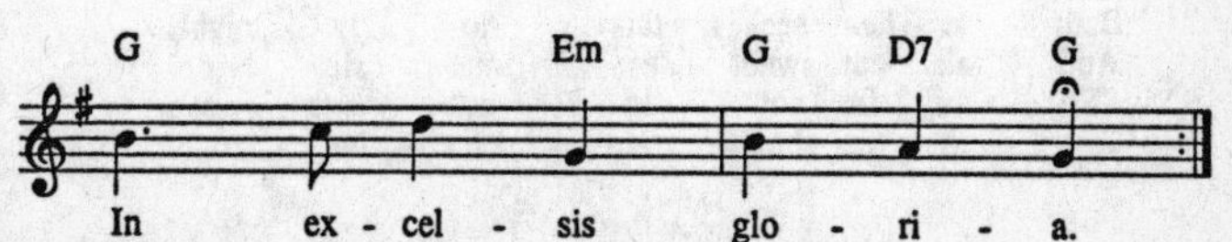
G Em G D7 G
In ex - cel - sis glo - ri - a.

# WHENCE COMES THIS RUSH OF WINGS

Traditional French Carol

Gm F B♭ F
Whence comes this rush of wings a - far,
"Tell us, ye birds, why come ye here,
Hark how the green finch bears his part,
An - gels and shep - herds, birds of the sky,
Gm F Gm Dm A7 Dm
Fol - low - ing straight the No - el star?
In - to this sta - ble poor and drear?"
Phil - o - mel, too, with ten - der heart
Come where the Son of God doth lie.
Gm F B♭ F
Birds from the woods in won - drous flight,
"Hast - 'ning we seek the new - born King,
Chants from her leaf - y dark re - treat,
Christ on ___ earth with man doth dwell,
B♭ F/C B♭/D Cm Gm/D D7 Gm
Beth - le - hem seek this ho - ly night.
And all our sweet - est mu - sic bring.
"Re mi fa sol" in ac - cents sweet.
Join in the shout, "No - el, No - el."

# WINDS THROUGH THE OLIVE TREES

19th Century American Carol

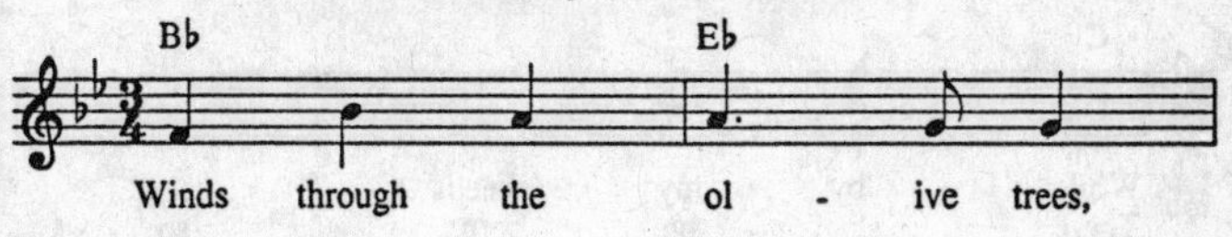
B♭
E♭
Winds through the ol - ive trees,

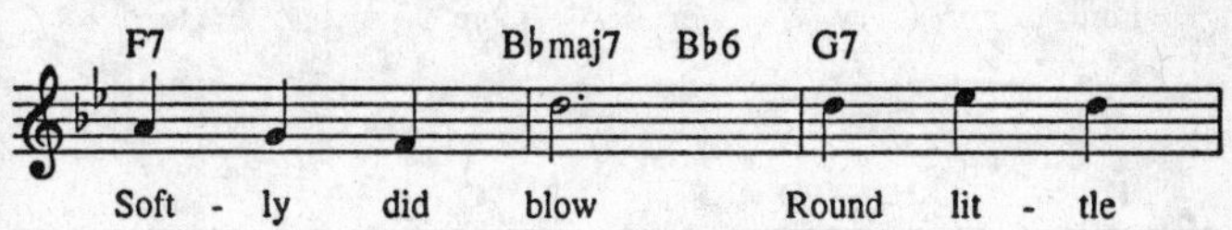
F7
B♭maj7 B♭6
G7
Soft - ly did blow
Round lit - tle

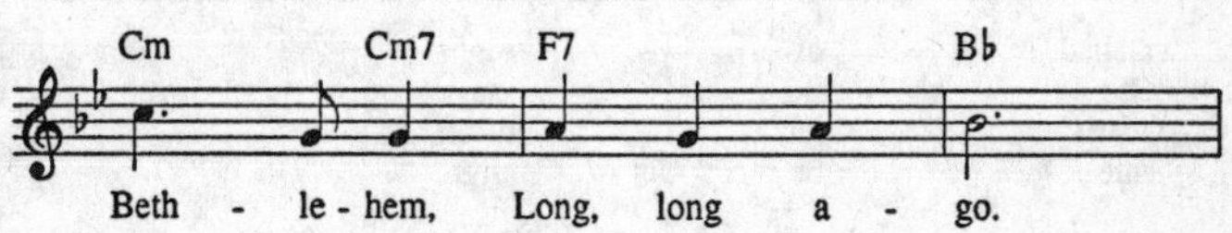
Cm
Cm7
F7
B♭
Beth - le - hem, Long, long a - go.

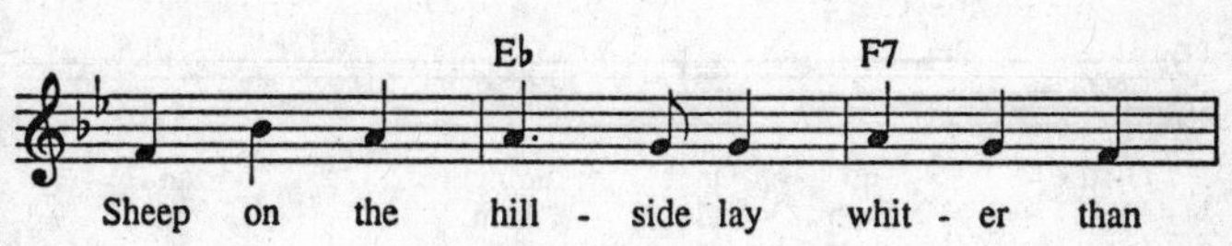
E♭
F7
Sheep on the hill - side lay whit - er than

B♭maj7 B♭6
G7
Cm
Cm7
snow, Shep - herds were watch - ing them,

F7
B♭
Long, long a - go.

# WHILE BY MY SHEEP

Traditional German Carol

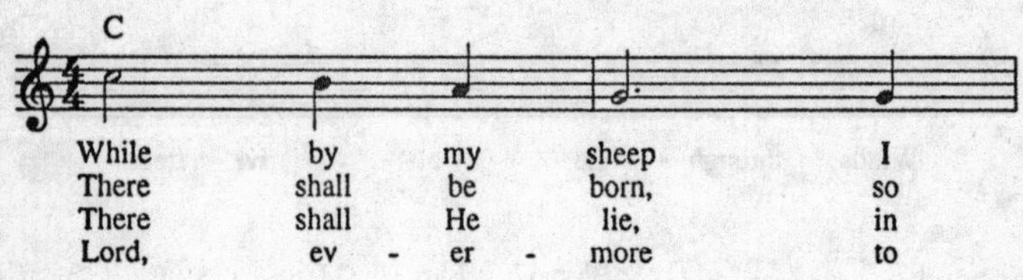
C
While by my sheep I
There shall be born, so
There shall He lie, in
Lord, ev - er - more to

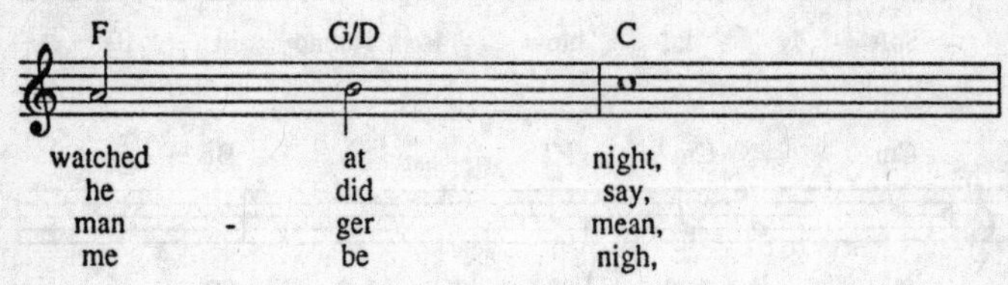
F G/D C
watched at night,
he did say,
man - ger mean,
me be nigh,

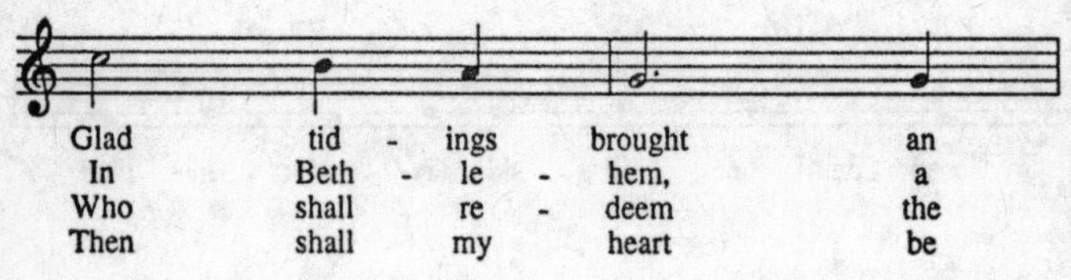
Glad tid - ings brought an
In Beth - le - hem, a
Who shall re - deem the
Then shall my heart be

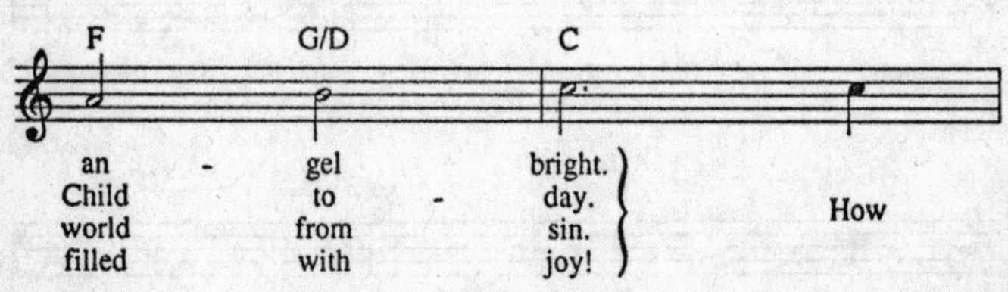
F G/D C
an - gel bright.
Child to - day.
world from sin.
filled with joy!
How

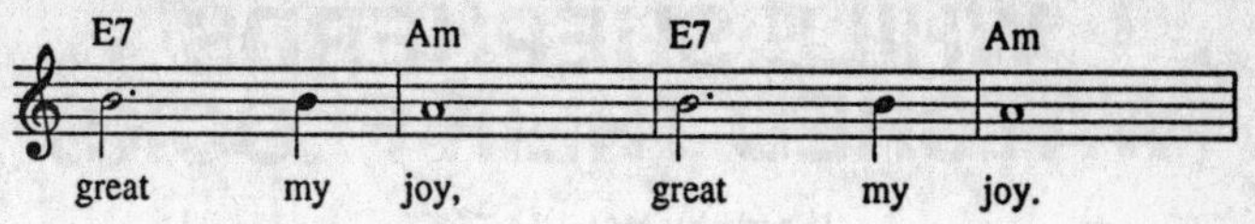
E7
Am
E7
Am
great my joy, great my joy.

G
C
Am
G
C
Joy, joy, joy, Joy, joy, joy!

Dm
E7
F
Dm6
E
Am
Praise to the Lord in Heav'n on high.

C
Dm
E7
F
Dm6
E
Am
Praise to the Lord in Heav'n on high.

# WHILE SHEPHERDS WATCHED THEIR FLOCKS

Words by NAHUM TATE
Music by GEORGE F. HANDEL

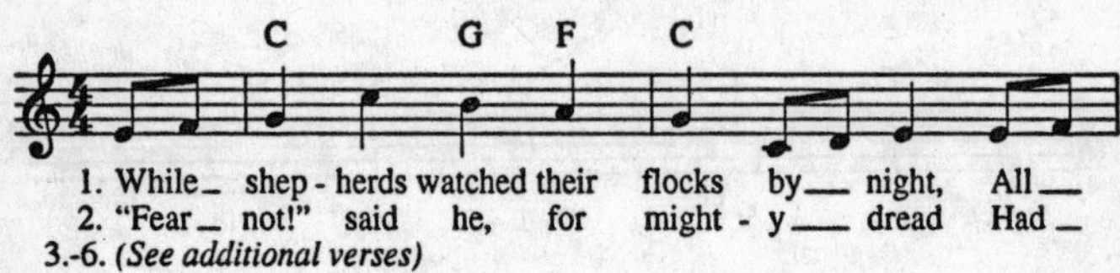
C G F C
1. While shep - herds watched their flocks by night, All
2. "Fear not!" said he, for might - y dread Had
3.-6. (See additional verses)

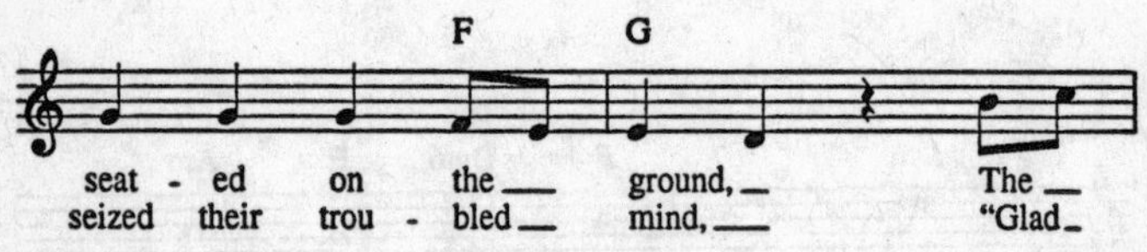
F G
seat - ed on the ground, The
seized their trou - bled mind, "Glad

C7 Dm G C
an - gel of the Lord came down, And
ti - dings of great joy I bring, To

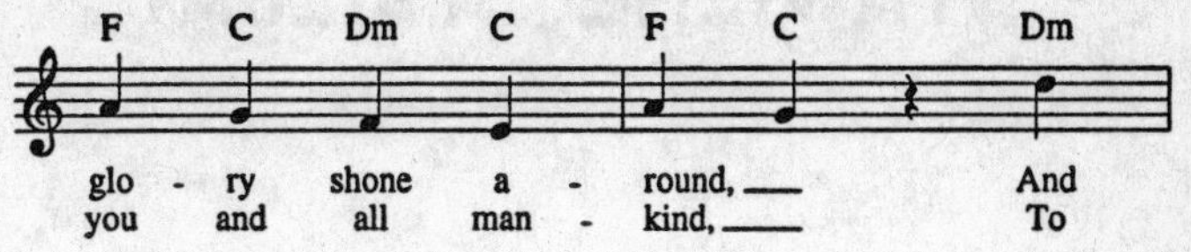
F C Dm C F C Dm
glo - ry shone a - round, And
you and all man - kind, To

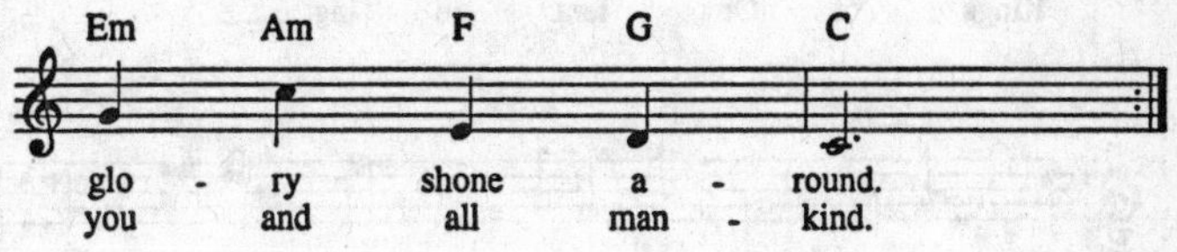
Em Am F G C
glo - ry shone a - round.
you and all man - kind.

*Additional Verses*

3. "To you, in David's town this day,
Is born of David's line,
The Saviour, who is Christ the Lord;
And this shall be the sign,
And this shall be the sign:

4. "The heavenly Babe you there shall find
To human view displayed,
All meanly wrapped in swathing bands,
And in a manger laid,
And in a manger laid."

5. Thus spake the seraph; and forthwith
Appeared a shining throng
Of angels praising God on high,
Who this addressed their song:
Who this addressed their song:

6. "All glory be to God on high,
And to the earth be peace;
Good will henceforth from heaven to men,
Begin and never cease!"
Begin and never cease!"

# YA VIENE LA VIEJA

Traditional Spanish Carol

F
C7/G
F
Come, my dear old wom - an,
Kings of Or - ient rid - ing,
Kings of Or - ient rid - ing,
C7/G
F
Eb
With a lit - tle pres - ent,
That you love so
Cross the san - dy des - ert,
Bring - ing to the
Guid - ed by the star - light,
Bring - ing to the
F
C7/G
dear - ly.
Of - fer it to
Child,
Wine and cook - ies
Child,
Gifts of love to -
F/C
C7
F/C
C7
Je - sus.
sweet.
night.
We're weav - ing a gar - ment of green lem - on
F/C
C7
F/C
C7
F
leaves, For sweet Vir - gin Ma - ry, the Moth - er of God!

# YULETIDE IS HERE AGAIN

Traditional Swedish Dance Carol

Ab
Yule-tide is here a-gain, the yule-tide is here a-gain, Let's

Db Ab/C
cel - e-brate, re - joice 'til Eas - ter.

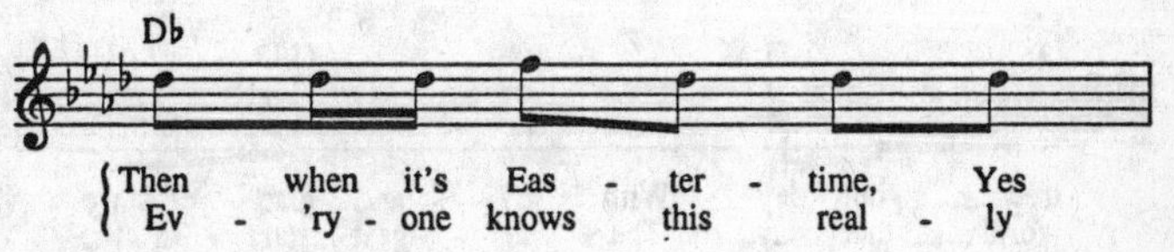
Db
Then when it's Eas - ter - time, Yes
Ev - 'ry - one knows this real - ly

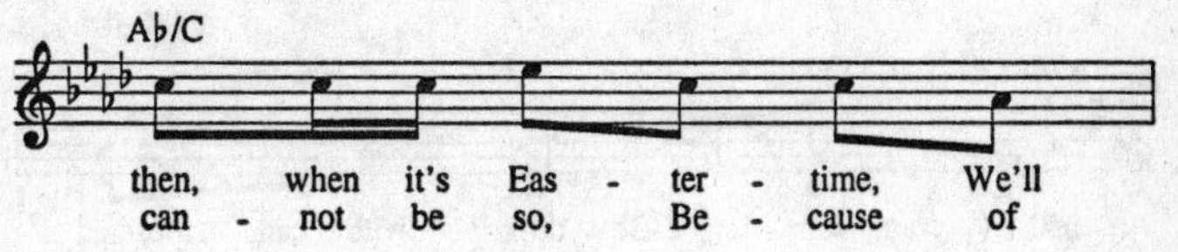
Ab/C
then, when it's Eas - ter - time, We'll
can - not be so, Be - cause of

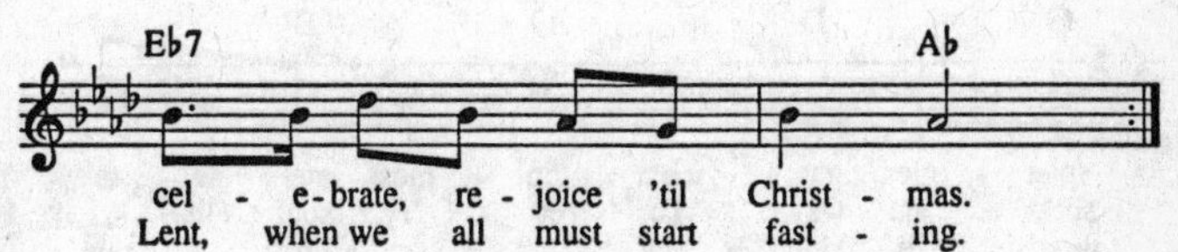
Eb7 Ab
cel - e-brate, re - joice 'til Christ - mas.
Lent, when we all must start fast - ing.

# YOU GREEN AND GLITTERING TREE

Words by JOHAN KROHN
Music by C.E.F. WEYSE

G C/G
You green and glit - ter - ing
When Je - sus came to the
Oft - times at eve - ning a -
D G C G/D
tree ___ good - day! With joy and glad - ness we
world ___ that day, The lar - gest star in the
round ___ the hearth, Our dear - est Moth - er would
A7/E G/D D7 G C/G
hail your com - ing, Be - decked with can - dles and
sky He light - ed; He gave a bea - con to
tell the sto - ry Of Je - sus' love and his
G D A7 D
span - gles gay, Your top - most star is as
show the way, To ev - 'ry soul His sal -
words di - vine, The mem - 'ry fills ___ our

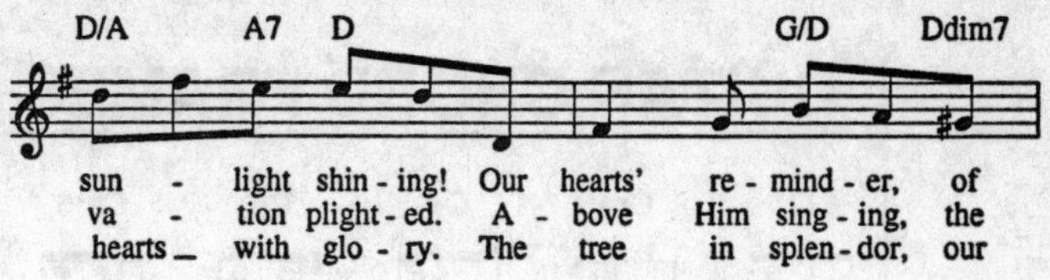
D/A A7 D G/D Ddim7
sun - light shin - ing! Our hearts' re - mind - er, of
va - tion plight - ed. A - bove Him sing - ing, the
hearts with glo - ry. The tree in splen - dor, our

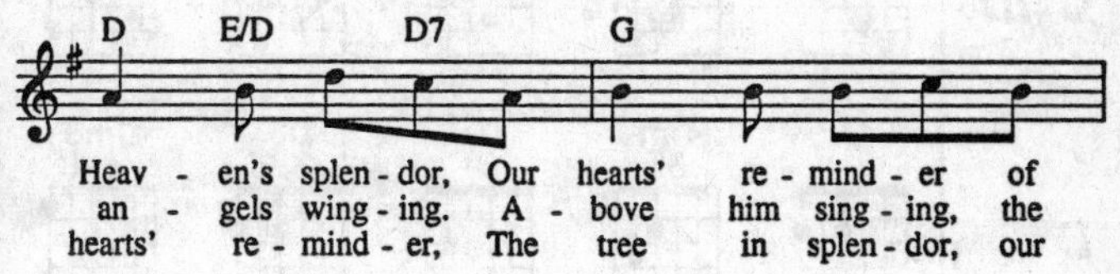
D E/D D7 G
Heav - en's splen - dor, Our hearts' re - mind - er of
an - gels wing - ing. A - bove him sing - ing, the
hearts' re - mind - er, The tree in splen - dor, our

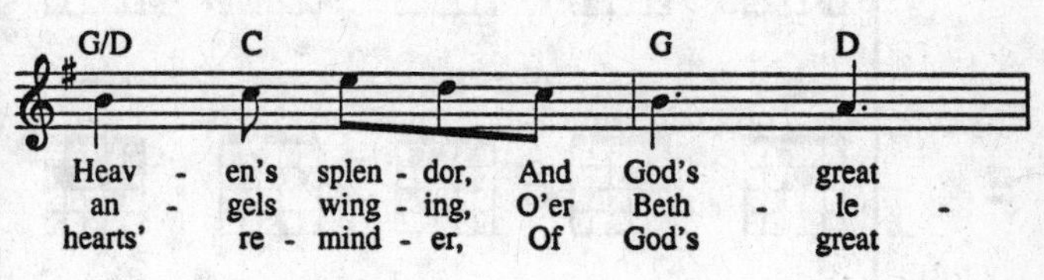
G/D C G D
Heav - en's splen - dor, And God's great
an - gels wing - ing, O'er Beth - le -
hearts' re - mind - er, Of God's great

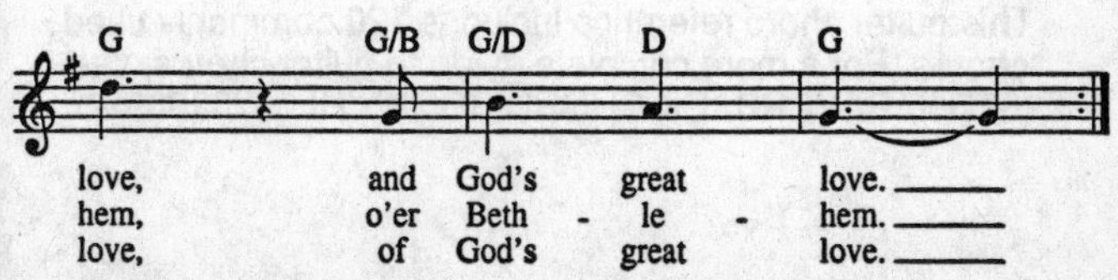
G G/B G/D D G
love, and God's great love.
hem, o'er Beth - le - hem.
love, of God's great love.

# GUITAR CHORD FRAMES

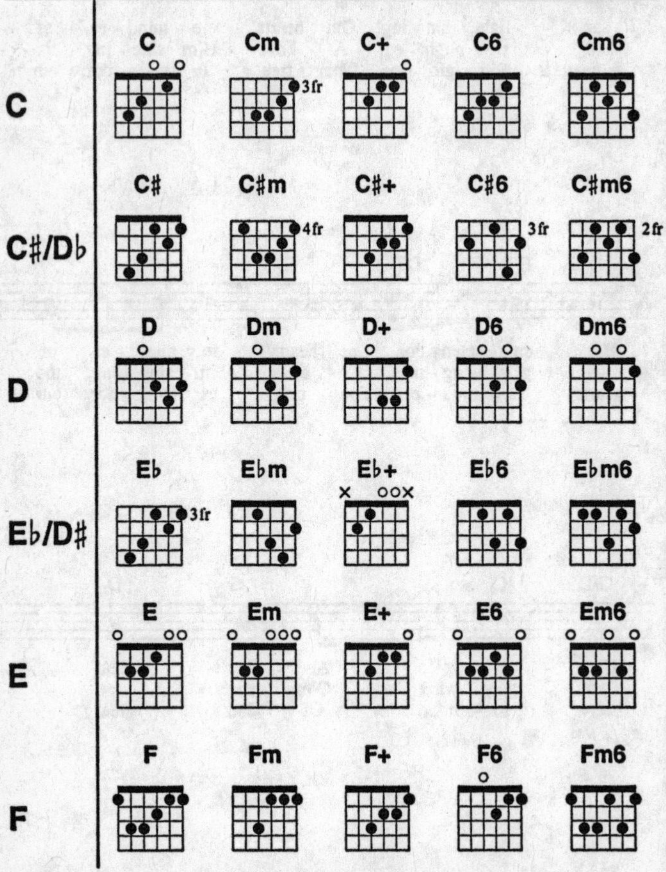

| | | | | | |
|---|---|---|---|---|---|
| **C** | C | Cm (3fr) | C+ | C6 | Cm6 |
| **C♯/D♭** | C♯ | C♯m (4fr) | C♯+ | C♯6 (3fr) | C♯m6 (2fr) |
| **D** | D | Dm | D+ | D6 | Dm6 |
| **E♭/D♯** | E♭ (3fr) | E♭m | E♭+ | E♭6 | E♭m6 |
| **E** | E | Em | E+ | E6 | Em6 |
| **F** | F | Fm | F+ | F6 | Fm6 |

This guitar chord reference includes 120 commonly used chords. For a more complete guide to guitar chords, see "THE PAPERBACK CHORD BOOK" (HL00702009).

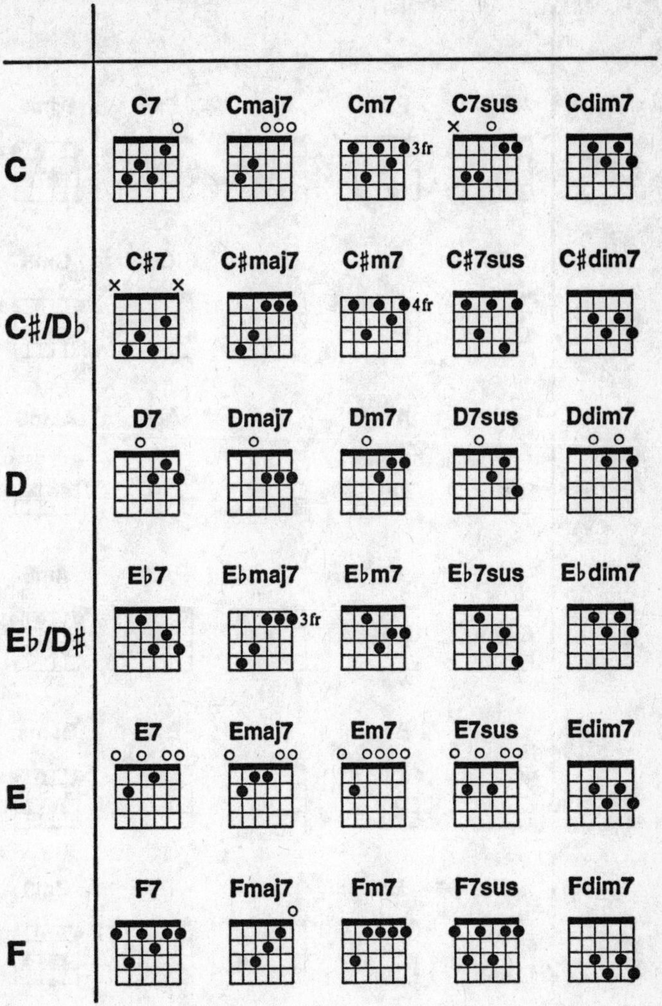

| | | | | | |
|---|---|---|---|---|---|
| C | C7 | Cmaj7 | Cm7 3fr | C7sus | Cdim7 |
| C♯/D♭ | C♯7 | C♯maj7 | C♯m7 4fr | C♯7sus | C♯dim7 |
| D | D7 | Dmaj7 | Dm7 | D7sus | Ddim7 |
| E♭/D♯ | E♭7 | E♭maj7 3fr | E♭m7 | E♭7sus | E♭dim7 |
| E | E7 | Emaj7 | Em7 | E7sus | Edim7 |
| F | F7 | Fmaj7 | Fm7 | F7sus | Fdim7 |

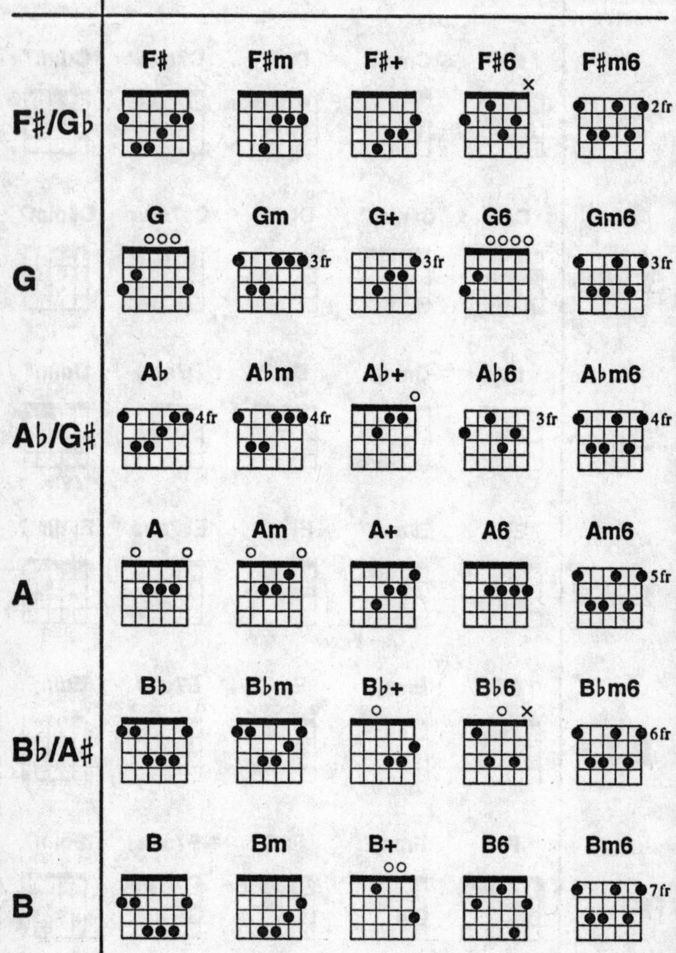
F♯/G♭
F♯
F♯m
F♯+
F♯6
F♯m6
2fr
G
Gm
G+
G6
Gm6
3fr
3fr
3fr
A♭/G♯
A♭
A♭m
A♭+
A♭6
A♭m6
4fr
4fr
3fr
4fr
A
Am
A+
A6
Am6
5fr
B♭/A♯
B♭
B♭m
B♭+
B♭6
B♭m6
6fr
B
Bm
B+
B6
Bm6
7fr

| | | | | | |
|---|---|---|---|---|---|
| **F♯/G♭** | F♯7 | F♯maj7 | F♯m7 | F♯7sus | F♯dim7 |
| **G** | G7 | Gmaj7 | Gm7<br>3fr | G7sus | Gdim7 |
| **A♭/G♯** | A♭7<br>4fr | A♭maj7 | A♭m7<br>4fr | A♭7sus | A♭dim7<br>4fr |
| **A** | A7 | Amaj7 | Am7 | A7sus | Adim7 |
| **B♭/A♯** | B♭7 | B♭maj7 | B♭m7 | B♭7sus | B♭dim7 |
| **B** | B7 | Bmaj7 | Bm7<br>2fr | B7sus<br>4fr | Bdim7 |